D1300753

From Ottomanism to Arabism

C. ERNEST DAWN

From Ottomanism to Arabism

ESSAYS ON THE ORIGINS OF ARAB NATIONALISM

UNIVERSITY OF ILLINOIS PRESS
Urbana Chicago London

Manufactured in the United States of America
Library of Congress Catalog Card No. 72-88953

ISBN 0-252-00202-4

To my parents

FRED HARTMAN DAWN

HETTIE LOU GIBSON DAWN

Preface

ANALYSIS, not comprehensive narration, is the intent of this study. Ideally, historians develop the former from the latter, but the ideal procedure can be employed only after the sources have been identified, located, and put in order. When this condition is not met, fruitful analysis still may be carried out by focusing on those strategic aspects of a major subject for which available sources are adequate, though not necessarily ideal. Such was the origin of this study, which first appeared as a series of articles. Despite the passage of time and the progress of scholarship, the sources for modern Arab history still present serious difficulties. At the same time, the conclusions reached in these articles seem to be fully consistent with subsequent studies which have been able to utilize newly accessible sources. Consequently, these essays are being reissued without any substantial changes. The component studies are presented in the order in which they were written, the order of analytical progression. Thus the origin of the Arab Revolt is dealt with before its chronological antecedents and causal conditions, the origin of Arabism.

The core of this study, the articles which deal with the origin and victory of Arabism, are presented without change except modifications for editorial consistency. The first publication of these essays was as follows (listed here with the numerical designation assigned them in this book):

I. "The Amir of Mecca al-Ḥusayn ibn-ʿAli and the Origin of the Arab Revolt," *Proceedings of the American Philosophical Society*, IV (1960), 11–34.

II. "ʿAbdallāh ibn al-Ḥusein, Lord Kitchener, e l'idea della rivolta araba," trans. V. Vacca, *Oriente Moderno*, XXXVII (1957), 1–12.

III. "Ideological Influences in the Arab Revolt," *The World of Islam*, ed. James Kritzeck and R. Bayly Winder

(London and New York: Macmillan and St. Martin's Press, 1959, Copyright Department of Near Eastern Studies, Princeton University), pp. 233–248.

V. "From Ottomanism to Arabism: The Origin of an Ideology," *Review of Politics,* XXIII (1961), 378–400.

VI. "The Rise of Arabism in Syria," *The Middle East Journal,* XVI (1962), 145–168.

Where appropriate, footnotes have been expanded to take note of publications which have appeared since the first publication of these articles.

The passage of time and the progress of scholarship have generated some additions to the nucleus. The opening of British repositories has produced a number of new studies relating to British-Arab relations during World War I. Some of the old controversies have been rekindled. A survey of this literature led to an assessment of the positions taken on the major issues by the various authors. The result is the fourth essay in this volume, "Hashimite Aims and Policy in the Light of Recent Scholarship on Anglo-Arab Relations during World War I." The central concern of the essays, the change from Ottomanism to Arabism, impinges on other subjects which have been much discussed of late, notably nationalism and what is usually called "modernization." These ramifications have already been explored in two articles:

"The Rise and Progress of Middle Eastern Nationalism," *Social Education,* XXV (1961), 20–24.

"Arab Islām in the Modern Age," *The Middle East Journal,* XIX (1965), 435–446.

The essential parts of these two articles, which remain after the elimination of repetitions and other material made unnecessary by the change in context, form the nucleus of the concluding essay, but the reflections have been extended to themes not taken up in the earlier articles.

I gratefully acknowledge the kindness of the original publishers or copyright holders of the articles for enabling their republication here.

The usual explanations regarding the rendering of Islamic

proper names is in order. No problem arises from such familiar cities as Mecca, Medina, Damascus, or Aleppo, or from eminent personages like Mohammed, the Islamic prophet. Lesser-known persons and places are entirely different. Except for scholars, almost every person who romanizes Islamic names produces a unique spelling. Furthermore, these lesser-known names occur so infrequently that it is unlikely that any romanization will become standard. Accordingly, the only means of providing the necessary consistency is to transliterate from the Arabic script. Under this procedure, Arabic places and persons present no difficulty. Because of the replacement of the Arabic script with the Latin in Turkey, Turkish names are another matter. Here the modern Turkish is used for persons whose eminence has familiarized the romanized versions of their names. The names of lesser-known persons are transliterated from the Arabic. The reader's attention should be called to one more practice in connection with Arab personal names. When giving the name in full, with patronymic, the article "al" is always used, but when the personal name alone is given, the article "al" is omitted, in keeping with the practice of modern spoken Arabic. Thus, "al-Ḥusayn ibn-ʿAli," but "Ḥusayn."

My debts are too numerous to mention. I must, however, voice my gratitude to those who gave me access to the vital sources: the Research Board and the Library of the University of Illinois for providing funds for the purchase of uncommon materials and for the efficiency of the Library's Acquisition Department in obtaining them. I have also had the benefit of acute comment and advice from Professor L. Carl Brown, to whom I express my gratitude.

C. Ernest Dawn

Contents

ONE

The Amir of Mecca al-Ḥusayn ibn-ʿAli and the Origin of the Arab Revolt

One of the dominant characteristics of the twentieth century, according to prevailing opinion, has been the rapid adoption by the traditional civilizations of the non-European world of the peculiarly European ideological and institutional complex known as nationalism. The growth of nationalism outside Europe is sometimes attributed to the appeal of the idea itself, perhaps more often to the usefulness of the idea to an emergent class, once the middle class but more frequently now the "masses," searching for weapons with which to join battle with the old order.

Developments within the Arab world have not escaped interpretation in accordance with the prevailing interest in nationalism. An event of the greatest influence in directing non-Arab attention to the problem of the Arabs was the revolt which was raised in June, 1916, by the Amir of Mecca al-Ḥusayn ibn-ʿAli. The Arabs themselves called this movement "the Arab Revolt," and most students, Arab and non-Arab alike, have viewed it as the culmination of an Arab Awakening which had long since been developing among the Arab peoples. Arab Awakening and Arab Revolt alike, it was agreed, were produced by the growth of national sentiment or by the underlying social forces of class change and conflict which are said to masquerade under the guise of nationalism.[1]

Since there had been a well-publicized nationalist movement among the Arabs during the decade which preceded 1916, little attention was paid to the pre-war policies of the Hashimites,

1. Richard Coke, *The Arab's Place in the Sun* (London: Thornton Butterworth, 1929), pp. 188–192; Hans Kohn, *A History of Nationalism in the East*, trans. Margaret M. Green (New York: Harcourt, Brace and Company, 1929), pp. 266–267, 278; and above all, George Antonius, *The Arab Awakening* (Philadelphia: Lippincott, 1937), pp. 126–132 and *passim.*

as the Amir Ḥusayn and his son styled themselves after the proclamation of the Revolt, despite the fact that the Revolt, in its origin and in its execution, was primarily their work. The Arabs in those regions where the pre-war nationalists were strongest, Syria and Iraq, never rose against the Turks, and their only contribution to the Hashimite Arab Army consisted of Arab Ottoman officers and men who were taken prisoner by (or, more rarely, who deserted to) the British or Arab forces. The initial stage of the insurrection was carried out entirely with Hijazi forces, and the non-Hijazi increments were gained only as the Revolt made progress and were proportional to that progress. Thus nationalism may be regarded as significant to the Arab Revolt only to the extent that the Hashimites may be regarded as nationalists.

The origin and political position of the Hashimite rebellion has been made problematical by recent research which shows that in 1916 the Hashimites were at best recent converts to Arabism. The only solution to the new question which has as yet been advanced is that Ḥusayn was led to revolt by a consuming ambition for the universal caliphate over all the Moslems of the world.[2] Yet the new explanation, like the earlier, is contradictory to the apologias and documents provided by the two principal instigators of the revolt, the Amir Ḥusayn and his son ʿAbdullāh.[3] Neither depicted himself as a romantic revolutionary; both appeared as staunch adherents of the old order who from choice and preference remained faithful to

2. Elie Kedourie, *England and the Middle East: The Destruction of the Ottoman Empire, 1914–1921* (London: Bowes and Bowes, 1956), pp. 48–56. This thesis was first suggested by Sylvia G. Haim, "'The Arab Awakening,' a Source for the Historian?" *Die Welt des Islams*, n.s., II (1953), 247.

3. See the proclamation issued by Ḥusayn on June 26, 1916. Two texts, each represented by its editor as authentic, have been published. One, longer and more verbose, is in Amīn Saʿīd, *al-Thawrah al-ʿarabīyah al-kubra* [*The Great Arab Revolt*], 3 vols. (Cairo: ʿIsa al-Bābi al-Ḥalabi, [1934?]), I, 149–157; the second is in *Revue du Monde Musulman* (hereafter cited as *RMM*), XLVI (1921), 4–10, 20–21. See also the interview with Ḥusayn in Dec., 1920, reprinted by Georg Kampffmeyer in *Mitteilungen des Seminars für Orientalische Sprachen zu Berlin*, XXVI–XXVII (1924), 84–86. ʿAbdullāh ibn-al-Ḥusayn, *Mudhakkarāti* [*My Memoirs*], 1st ed. (Jerusalem: Maṭbaʿah Bayt al-Muqaddas, 1945); I have not been able to obtain the second edition.

the Ottoman Empire and the bond of Islam until finally, much against their will, they were compelled to rebel by the irreligious policy of the Young Turks. In order to determine the origin of the Arab Revolt and its precise relationship with the Arab nationalist movement, a thorough examination of the evidence is therefore necessary.

I

The Sharif and Amir of Mecca [4] was one of the most privileged and respected grandees of the Ottoman Empire. Since the middle of the tenth century Mecca and the Hijaz had been autonomous under the rule of the Amir of Mecca, who was always one of the numerous *sharīfs,* or descendants of Mohammed, native to the Hijaz. By the Ottoman period Mecca and Medina had become of great importance to the powerful Moslem sultans such as the Moghuls, the Mamluks, and the Ottomans, who sought to bolster their positions by patronizing Islam in order to validate their assumption of the honorifics and prerogatives of the caliphate; the protection of the two Holy Cities was one of the notable means of doing this.[5] Moreover, the Ottomans venerated Mohammed and his descendants, the sharifs, to an extent without precedent, and consequently the sharifs throughout the Ottoman Empire enjoyed an increase in their already great privileges and prestige.[6] So important was Islam to the Ottoman sultans that the annual pilgrimage to Mecca and Medina was given a special official organization,[7] and the

4. Literally, "the Sharif of Mecca and its Amir"; this is the style almost invariably applied in Arabic sources.

5. On the history of the sharifate-amirate, see A. J. Wensinck, "Mecca," *Encyclopaedia of Islâm,* 1st ed., and Gerald De Gaury, *Rulers of Mecca* (New York: Roy, [1954?]). On the later meaning of the caliphate and the importance of the Holy Cities, see Sir Thomas W. Arnold, *The Caliphate* (Oxford: Clarendon Press, 1924), pp. 89–183, and H. A. R. Gibb, "Some Considerations on the Sunni Theory of the Caliphate," *Archives d'Histoire du Droit Oriental,* III (1948), 401–410.

6. Jean Sauvaget, *Alep* (Paris: Geuthner, 1941), p. 196.

7. Jean Sauveget, "Esquisse d'un histoire de la ville de Damas," *Revue des Études Islamiques,* 1934, pp. 468–470.

religious and educational foundations of Mecca and Medina were greatly increased by the sultans who proudly bore the title, "Protector of the Two Holy Cities."

The Amirs of Mecca, honored and powerful though they were, could never assert complete independence. Although the Ottomans lacked the capability of subjugating the Hijaz to direct rule, they could on occasion employ irresistible pressure or force. The sharifs were also divided into several rival clans, so that the foreign overlords could always employ a rival sharif to depose any reigning Amir whose conduct might be in any way unsatisfactory. From 1840 on, the political life of the Hijaz revolved around the rivalries of the two leading princely clans (the Dhawu-Zayd and the Dhawu-ʿAwn) on the one hand, and the attempts of the Ottomans to establish direct rule by Turkish officials on the other. A long, see-saw struggle marked by the use of violence and deceit ensued. During this conflict several Ottoman governors were recalled, and many noble sharifs of both clans were taken into luxurious exile in Turkey. By the time of the Young Turk Revolution of 1908, the Dhawu-ʿAwn were represented in Constantinople by al-Ḥusayn ibn-ʿAli, who, with his three sons ʿAli, ʿAbdullāh, and Fayṣal, had been brought to Constantinople in 1894 because of a disagreement with his uncle, the then reigning Amir of Mecca.[8] The outstanding personality of the Dhawu-Zayd was ʿAli Ḥaydar, who had spent his entire life in Constantinople.[9]

When the Amirate of Mecca became vacant in the summer of 1908, the rivalry between the two Meccan clans for the office became entangled with the rivalry between the victorious Committee of Union and Progress and the "Old Turks." ʿAli Ḥaydar, who had long been at outs with Sultan ʿAbd al-Ḥamīd, sought obtain the appointment.[10] According to ʿAbdullāh, the Young Turks tried to name ʿAli Ḥaydar to the position.[11] But

8. ʿAbdullāh, pp. 13, 15–17, 26.

9. George Stitt, *A Prince of Arabia* (London: George Allen and Unwin, 1948), pp. 37–91.

10. *Ibid.*, pp. 86–94, 103.

11. ʿAbdullāh, p. 18. There is no clear evidence from any other source that at the time ʿAli Ḥaydar was supported by the Unionists, although there are

the Grand Vizier, Kāmil Pasha, and the Sultan were working to limit the influence of the Committee; for this purpose they appointed Ḥusayn Amir of Mecca. The Unionists were enraged by the appointment.[12] ʿAli Ḥaydar was amazed.[13] Before leaving for Mecca Ḥusayn had an audience with the Sultan in which ʿAbd al-Ḥamīd expressed his distrust of the Unionists who had tried to prevent his appointing Ḥusayn to the Amirate. Ḥusayn assured him that, if needed, the Arab countries and above all the Hijaz would come to the aid of the Sultan, but ʿAbd al-Ḥamīd said that the time for action had not yet come. When Kāmil Pasha came to the ship to see Ḥusayn off, he brought with him a memorandum from the Sultan assuring Ḥusayn that he was to carry out his duties in accordance with the traditional law and ties binding the Amirate to the Sultanate, and that this was the first point of contest between the Sultan and the Unionists.[14]

Ḥusayn's policy as Amir followed the general lines of ʿAbd al-Ḥamīd's memorandum. He stressed his loyalty to the Ottoman Sultan and the religious sentiment which bound the Hijaz to the Empire and provided the basis for the prestige and authority of the Amir of Mecca. On the other hand, he resisted the efforts of the Unionist government and its adherents in the

indications that he was: he "hated" ʿAbd al-Ḥamīd, he welcomed the revolution, and he had many friends in the Committee (but it is not clear that he was friendly with them before the revolution, although he did know Mahmud Shevket "from the time that he was a young colonel"); Stitt, pp. 115–116, 137. Two passages in the memoirs of ʿAli Ḥaydar's daughter seem to confirm ʿAbdullāh's account, but they are vague and may refer to a later period; Musbah Ḥaydar, *Arabesque* (London: Hutchinson, 1945), pp. 59, 80.

12. ʿAbdullāh, pp. 19–20. The statement by Shakīb Arslān that ʿAbd al-Ḥamīd unwillingly appointed Ḥusayn at the insistence of the Unionists seems to be contradictory to ʿAli Ḥaydar's diary; Shakīb Arslān, notes and additions to *Ḥāḍir al-ʿālam al-islāmi,* by Lothrop Stoddard, trans. ʿAjjāj Nuwayhiḍ (Cairo: al-Maṭbaʿah al-Salafīyah, 1343H/1925), II, 397. Arslān is unreliable when a bias of his is involved, as in his claim that Jemal was the Turkish leader most strongly attached to Turanianism and Enver the one least attached (*ibid.,* 146, n. 1), and he is clearly hostile to Ḥusayn.

13. Stitt, p. 103.

14. ʿAbdullāh, pp. 27–28. A conflict between Kāmil and the Unionists did develop very early; see Ismail Kemal, *Memoirs,* ed. Sommerville Story (London: Constable and Company, 1920), pp. 321–325. At a later period, at least, some of the Sultan's supporters were also supporters of Kāmil in this conflict; see Stitt, pp. 134, 140–141.

Hijaz to encroach on the special position of the Amir. Ḥusayn was greeted in Jidda by a delegation of the local Party of Union and Progress with the words, "We have come to welcome the constitutional Amir whose rule we hope will leave off the ancient administrative principles. . . . And we greet in him the Amir who knows the spirit of the age and the desired reforms, under the constitution which is the lamp of security." Ḥusayn took the opportunity to state his policy in his reply, "Verily I have stepped into the place of my predecessors and my fathers on the conditions with which Sultan Selim I conferred it upon abu-Numayy, and verily these are the lands of God in which nothing will ever stand except the Sharīʿah of God. . . . The constitution of the lands of God is the Sharīʿah of God and the Sunnah of His Prophet." [15]

Loyalty to the Sultan under the ancient traditions was of considerable value to Ḥusayn in increasing his authority in the Hijaz and in maintaining the prestige of his office. Because the Amir's position depended primarily upon guaranteeing the security of the pilgrimage, it was especially important for the Amir to control the tribes, who were the principal disturbers of the pilgrimage and in addition provided a source of revenue through payment of the tithe to the Amir. During the pilgrimage season of December, 1908–January, 1909, the tribes interfered with the pilgrimage to so great an extent that the Amir publicly expressed his regrets to the Egyptian pilgrims. During the pilgrimage season and after, the tribesmen around Medina made several attacks on the railroad but were driven off by Ottoman troops, which soon took the initiative and pacified the district.[16] Two tribes located along the eastern frontier of the Hijaz had been attacking the pilgrims and the lands of other tribes; they continued their lawless ways and neglected paying the tithe to the Amir. In the summer of 1909 Ḥusayn sent raiding parties against the two recalcitrant tribes and forced them to submit. He was then able to announce that

15. ʿAbdullāh, pp. 34–35.
16. *RMM*, VII (1909), 471–473, and IX (1909), 477–478.

because of his efforts the pilgrimage could enjoy uninterrupted passage.[17]

Ḥusayn also disputed the overlordship of another border tribe, the ʿUtaybah, with a rival Arabian potentate, ʿAbd al-ʿAzīz ibn-ʿAbd-al-Raḥmān Āl-Suʿūd, the Amir of Najd. Although the Vali refused to provide troops, in the summer of 1910 Ḥusayn as representative of the Sultan led an expedition of all the amirs and sharifs owing allegiance to him into Najd and captured the Amir Saʿd, brother of ʿAbd al-ʿAzīz, who was collecting the tithe from the ʿUtaybah. An agreement was signed by ʿAbd al-ʿAzīz in which he affirmed his sincere attachment to the Turkish state and to the sharifs.[18]

Although Ḥusayn found it to his advantage to be the representative of the Sublime Porte in dealing with the tribesmen and with rival amirs, he resisted the efforts of the Unionists to weaken his influence in the Hijaz. As early as January, 1909, Unionist officials attempted to take over Ḥusayn's principal function, that of guaranteeing the security of the pilgrimage. At the close of the pilgrimage the Amir of the Syrian pilgrimage, ʿAbd al-Raḥmān Bey al-Yūsuf, a Damascene Unionist, announced in Mecca that the pilgrimage party would return by sea, alleging that the road was not safe and that he feared attack by the tribes. Ḥusayn could not consent to this action, since he believed that the aims of al-Yūsuf were "to show thus the incompetency of the new Amir" and to derogate from him his chief responsibility, that of establishing security in the Hijaz, and thus to cause him to lose all influence among the tribes. The Amir, therefore, did not allow the party to return by sea, but sent it by land to Damascus under the leadership of his brother; al-Yūsuf returned alone by sea.[19] Ottoman function-

17. *RMM,* IX (1909), 503; ʿAbdullāh, pp. 44–45.

18. ʿAbdullāh, p. 47, where the name is incorrectly given as Saʿīd; Ḥāfiẓ Wahbah, *Jazīrah al-ʿarab fi-al-qarn al-ʿishrīn* [*The Arabian Peninsula in the Twentieth Century*], 2nd ed. (Cairo: Maṭbaʿah li-Jannah al-Taʾlīf wa al-Tarjamah wa al-Nashr, 1946), pp. 200, 312–314, based on Suʿūdi sources; *RMM,* XII (1910), 675–676.

19. ʿAbdullāh, pp. 40–42; Saʿīd, I, 104–105.

aries in the Hijaz, who were members of the Committee of Union and Progress, organized local committees and frequently leveled the charge of reaction against Ḥusayn. The local committees unsuccessfully challenged the Amir in the elections for the first Ottoman Parliament, when ʿAbdullāh and Shaykh Ḥasan al-Shayba, an adherent of the Amir, were elected deputies from Mecca. Their election was protested by telegrams to the Parliament from the Unionists of Mecca on the grounds that ʿAbdullāh was not of age and that Ḥasan could not read or write in either Arabic or Turkish, but nevertheless the Chamber seated them. After the arrival of the first Vali, Fu'ād Pasha, in late spring, 1909, the conflict between Ḥusayn and the Unionists became especially bitter. The Amir, through his influence at Constantinople, succeeded in having four Unionist officials removed and tried by court martial. The conflict reached its peak when the Vali charged, on the basis of a woman's rumor, that Ḥusayn's kinsman and Deputy at al-Ṭā'if was plotting rebellion against the government. As a result of the Amir's protest the government recalled the Vali and the Commander of the Gendarmerie. Later in the year Ḥusayn became dissatisfied with the behavior of the acting Vali, who was a Unionist, and had him removed.[20] Thereafter the Unionists were without influence in the Hijaz. In 1911, some months before the elections for the Ottoman Parliament of 1912, the Unionists clubs in Mecca and Jidda "died a natural death," and in the elections ʿAbdullāh was returned as deputy from Mecca and his younger brother Fayṣal was elected from Jidda.[21] At the beginning of 1911 the Amir not only retained all the traditional prerogatives of his office but had reduced the position of the Ottoman Vali to insignificance. So great was Ḥusayn's prestige and authority that foreign consuls in Jidda

20. ʿAbdullāh, pp. 35, 44–47, 51–53, 56; Saʿīd, I, 104; *RMM*, X (1910), 570–571.

21. Memorandum enclosed in a dispatch dated Mar. 18, 1914, from Sir Louis Mallet to Sir Edward Grey, Great Britain, Foreign Office, *British Documents on the Origins of the War*, ed. G. P. Gooch and Harold Temperly, X, pt. 2 (London: H.M.S.O., 1938), 829.

took matters to him that legally were within the jurisdiction of the Vali.[22]

Even though Ḥusayn had used Turkish soldiers against the Arab tribesmen, he was able to count on their support in opposing the extension of strong Ottoman rule to the Hijaz, because Unionist policy was contrary to Hijazi interests and opinion. In 1909 the Vali, Fu'ād Pasha, attempted to apply the Ottoman prohibition of slavery, but the tribes threatened to cut the road from Mecca to Jidda and forced the Vali to renounce his plans.[23] The Hijaz Railroad was of prime importance for the execution of Unionist policy in the Hijaz and of equal importance in creating Hijazi opposition to the government. From the beginning the Amir of Mecca and his supporters had opposed the construction of the railroad. In April, 1908, as the line was being completed to Medina, the reigning Amir revolted in protest, but the revolt was suppressed and the railroad was opened to traffic on September 1.[24] The Young Turks from the start made public their intention to extend the line from Medina through Mecca to Jidda, and the budget for 1911 included a provision for building the Jidda-Mecca line.[25] In the summer of 1910 the government revealed to Ḥusayn and the tribesmen the use it expected to make of improved communications. While Ḥusayn was away on the expedition against the ʿUtaybah, the Muḥāfiẓ of Medina, ʿAli Riḍa Pasha al-Rikābi, gave a grand reception and announced to the Amir's deputy that thereafter he had no functions. The deputy informed ʿAbdullāh, who was in Mecca in charge of the Amirate. The sharifs and heads of the tribes were disturbed by the action and telegraphed to ʿAbdullāh protesting the separation of Medina from the Amirate. ʿAbdullāh sent a wire to the Sublime Porte inquiring concerning the responsibilities of the Amirate

22. H. Kazem Zadeh, "Relation d'un pèlerinage à la Mecque en 1910–1911," *RMM*, XIX (1912), 179–182.

23. *RMM*, XII (1910), 305.

24. Gertrude Bell, *Syria, the Desert and the Sown* (London: W. Heinemann, 1907), p. 136; *RMM*, VI (1908), 262, 264.

25. *RMM*, IX (1909), 169–170, and XV (1911), 378.

with reference to the pilgrimage caravans, whether it was to Madā'in Ṣāliḥ as in the past or to some other place between the Holy Cities. The Porte replied, "the connection of Medina to the center of the Sultanate by telegraph and railroad insures speed in communication so that the Muḥāfaẓah of Medina is considered as an independent Maḥāfaẓah, bound directly to the Ministry of the Interior, not to the Vilayet. The responsibilities and rights of the noble Amirate remain as they were, from Mecca to Madā'in Ṣāliḥ." [26] Although this action meant no immediate loss of power or privilege by the Amirate, the reference to the telegraph and railroad as insuring secure communication between the capital and Medina and justifying closer control over Medina by Constantinople must have had an ominous sound to Ḥusayn.

Despite his difficulties with the Unionists from 1908 to 1911, Ḥusayn showed himself to be a loyal subject of the Sultan when in 1911 the revolt against the Turks of Sayyid al-Idrīsi in ʿAsīr presented to Ḥusayn an opportunity to choose between the two conflicting ideologies of Arabism and Ottomanism. In the Arab press discussions about the conflict between the Turkish and Arab nations, already very popular, greatly increased in number, and most Arab papers were very hostile to the Ottoman cabinet.[27] Ḥusayn had already been made aware that Arabism was an ideology that could be useful to him. When the Syrian pilgrimage party returned to Damascus in January, 1909, ʿAbdullāh accompanied it. While ʿAbdullāh was a guest of the Damascene notable ʿAṭa Pasha al-Bakri, he learned of the feeling of Arabism that was then beginning to manifest itself among the men, and especially the young men, of Damascus.[28] As a deputy in the Ottoman Parliament, ʿAbdullāh often came into contact with the chiefs of the Arab nationalist movement, some of whom begged him to persuade Ḥusayn to lead the movement.[29] In 1911 the Arab deputies in the Ottoman

26. ʿAbdullāh, pp. 47–48.
27. *RMM,* XIII (1911), 356, 361–362.
28. ʿAbdullāh, pp. 40–42. See below, p. 56.
29. Fayṣal ibn-al-Ḥusayn, quoted in Mrs. Steuart Erskine, *King Faysal of Iraq* (London: Hutchinson, 1933), pp. 40–41.

Parliament sent to Ḥusayn through ʿAbdullāh a letter dated February 12, requesting him to lead the Arabs in throwing off the Turkish yoke. The letter included a declaration signed by thirty-five Arab deputies which stated,

> Nous . . . confions à Hussaïn pacha le gouvernement de La Mecque, et nous lui reconnaissons à lui seul la suprématie religieuse sur tous les pays Arabes, en notre propre nom et au nom des pays que nous représentons. Nous sommes prêts, s'il y a lieu, à rendre la présent déclaration publique. . . .[30]

However, Ḥusayn did not respond to the Arab call. When the Turkish government requested his aid in suppressing al-Idrīsi, Ḥusayn responded affirmatively. He first assisted the Turks in settling their difficulties with the Imam Yaḥya of the Yaman by writing to the Imam and also by requesting the Sultan of Laḥij to use his influence with Yaḥya to bring about a peaceful settlement.[31] Ḥusayn then led from the Hijaz a force of Turkish troops and Arab irregulars to relieve the Turks besieged in Abha.[32]

Despite Ḥusayn's loyalty to the Ottoman Caliphate, the campaign in ʿAsīr led to the first really serious crisis in the relations between Ḥusayn and the government. Since the Hijazi force was not successful in the battle of Qawz aba-al-ʿĪr, bad blood developed between the Arabs and the Turks. Moreover, the Turkish Commander and Mutaṣarrif of ʿAsīr, Sulayman Pasha, who had refused to accept Ḥusayn's advice, also insisted that, until he received instructions from the Porte, he should command the regular Turkish troops which Ḥusayn had brought from the Hijaz. "Upon this, and when he [Ḥusayn] saw with his eyes the pattern in the killing of Arabs, and the oppressive acts committed by the Ottoman Army and its commanders, he left Abha and returned to the Hijaz with the

30. K. T. Khairallah, *Les Régions arabes libérées* (Paris: Leroux, 1919), pp. 32–33. The authenticity of the document is not confirmed, but its contents are consistent with statements by Fayṣal (above, n. 29) and Wahbah (below, n. 42).

31. Harold F. Jacob, *Kings of Arabia* (London: Mills and Boon, 1923), p. 118.

32. ʿAbdullāh, pp. 58–59.

Hashimite forces." [33] Ḥusayn's disaffection with the Turks was compounded as soon as he reached the Hijaz. When the Hashimite force, which had returned by land, neared al-Ṭā'if, Ḥusayn was met by the First Secretary of the Vilayet, representing the Vali, and the Mīr-al-Alay Aḥmad Bey, representing the Commandant. The Secretary informed Ḥusayn that the Sharif Nāṣir ibn-Muḥsin had been spreading tales about the rout of the Ottoman forces, and had said that Ḥusayn had been killed. When the party arrived at al-Ṭā'if, it was met by the Vali, Ḥāzim Bey, and a party including the Sharif Nāṣir. When Ḥusayn saw Nāṣir he ordered that he be removed.

The Vali said, "He came with me."

Ḥusayn replied, "And if he came with you?"

The Vali said, "I am the representative of the Sultan and this action is disrespectful of the Sultan himself."

Ḥusayn replied, "Have you left any part of the Sultan undefiled? I am the representative of the Sultan here, not you."

The Amir turned and questioned the Qadi of Mecca and the Commandant Munīr Pasha, then inspected the troops and rode to the Amirate building.[34]

Ḥusayn's forwardness exhausted the patience of the Unionist cabinet, but the international difficulties of Turkey insured Ḥusayn's triumph. Three days after the return to al-Ṭā'if, Ḥusayn was ordered by the Grand Vizier to apologize for the Nāṣir affair. The Amir replied that Nāṣir had spread rumors which could only have had the purpose of creating a revolt. The Porte was not satisfied with Ḥusayn's reply, but the Amir would not retreat from his position. Ramaḍān (in 1911, August 26–September 24) came and passed without mending the complete break between the Amirate and the Vilayet.[35] In the meantime the cabinet had considered deposing Ḥusayn; the Minister of the Interior, Ḥājji ʿĀdil Bey, proposed to replace Ḥusayn with ʿAli Ḥaydar, but Mahmud Shevket, the Minister

33. *Ibid.*, pp. 58–67 (quotation on p. 67). In 1912, the British consul at Jidda was told that the government had ordered Ḥusayn to withdraw the Arab forces from ʿAsīr; *Brit. Doc.*, X, pt. 2, 829.

34. ʿAbdullāh, pp. 67–68.

35. *Ibid.*, pp. 68–69.

of War, "deprecated" the suggestion.[36] On the night of the ʿĪd (September 25 in 1911), ʿUthmān Bey, Commander of the Gendarmerie, visited Ḥusayn's eldest son, ʿAli, and told him that the Vali had been ordered to visit the Amir and apologize. At this point the Italian attack on Tripoli occurred and Saʿīd Pasha became Grand Vizier. Ḥusayn telegraphed the new Grand Vizier to review the correspondence between the Amirate and the Grand Vizierate. Ḥāzim Bey was immediately transferred, and the Commandant Munīr Pasha was appointed Vali.[37]

Although ʿAbdullāh characterized the campaign in ʿAsīr as "the most important event in the Amirate of the lamented [Ḥusayn] with respect to the change of mind which set him to giving up his sincere attachment to his Turkish Ottomanism," there was no immediate outward change in the relationship of Ḥusayn with the government.[38] The strained relations of late 1911 certainly created strong suspicions of Ḥusayn in the minds of the Young Turks and a series of rumors about the intentions of Ḥusayn. In 1912 rumor circulated in Constantinople that the government was planning to remove the Amir of Mecca and that the latter was planning revolt. A meeting between ʿAbdullāh and Lord Kitchener in Cairo in 1912 (or 1913) created speculation in the Constantinople press. High Turkish officials were certain that the Sharif had approached the British for assistance.[39] Such reports seem to have been based on nothing more than rumors and suspicions, however. Ḥusayn took no action against the Turks in 1912 and 1913, and indeed he had no cause to do so. The Vali Munīr Pasha was not a member of the Committee of Union and Progress, and his relations with the Amir were cordial from the beginning of his appointment.[40]

36. Stitt, p. 137; the incident is dated only as "a year or two before sometime between July 11, 1912, and Jan. 23, 1913.

37. ʿAbdullāh, pp. 69–70, 77.

38. *Ibid.*, p. 58. This seems to be the basis for the translation of G. Khuri, *Memoirs of King Abdullah of Transjordan*, ed. Philip P. Graves (New York: Philosophical Library, 1950), p. 83: "It was after his return from Asir that my father began laying the foundations of the Arab revolt."

39. Wahbah, pp. 147, 152; ʿAbdullāh, pp. 73–74 (on ʿAbdullāh's meeting with Kitchener, see below); Arslān, II, 397.

40. ʿAbdullāh, p. 77.

Before long the will of Ḥusayn was supreme in the Hijaz, and the power of the Vali had "sunk to nothing." In the second half of 1912, the practice of extorting from the pilgrims was resumed. Three Indian pilgrims were murdered in the Medina district, it was said by some at the instigation of Ḥusayn, who in this way "was deliberately seeking to create disturbances in the Medina district so as to convince the government of the necessity of bringing it also under his authority." [41]

The Arab nationalists, who before the ʿAsīr campaign had begged Ḥusayn to assume the leadership of the movement, appear not only to have turned away from him but even to have become hostile to him, even though the campaign strained relations between Ḥusayn and the Ottoman government.[42] In the spring of 1912, the leaders of the most important Arab nationalist societies began secret negotiations with some of the independent amirs of Arabia for the purpose of instigating a general Arab rising. The Shaykh of Kuwayt, the Amirs of Muscat and Muḥammarah, Ibn-Suʿūd, and Sayyid al-Idrīsi all were approached at the outset, but the available evidence coming directly from nationalist sources is completely silent regarding any negotiations with Ḥusayn or his sons. The nationalists seem to have put Ḥusayn in the same category as the Turks, because as late as April 24, 1913, one of the Arab revolutionaries was of the opinion that al-Idrīsi should be induced to march on Mecca, in conjunction with a general Arab rising in Iraq and Syria.[43] Even as late as November or early December, 1913, when accounts of Arab nationalist activities among the Arabian chieftains began to appear in the Arabic press of Iraq and to

41. *Brit. Doc.*, X, pt. 2, 829.

42. Cf. the words of Wahbah, pp. 199–200: "When the Sharif Ḥusayn was appointed to the Amirate of Mecca . . . we thought that there would be a new epoch for the Arab lands . . . but he showed rather that he was a tool in the hands of the Turks for striking the Arabs, then he and his sons proceeded with the attack which the Turks launched to strike al-Idrīsi in ʿAsīr; and all this was in order to prove to the Turks his complete loyalty." See below, pp. 57–58.

43. Turkey, Fourth Army, *La Vérité sur la question syrienne* (Stamboul: Tanine, 1916), pp. 102–103, and the letter of Fuʾād al-Khaṭīb, dated April 24, 1913, reproduced as Facsimile No. 31, from which an extract is quoted in translation on p. 103.

reach Constantinople, Ḥusayn was not reported as one of those who was to participate in a projected congress of Arabian potentates.[44] In fact, according to one account, after the rumors of the impending congress reached Constantinople, the government counted on Ḥusayn to act as a moderator on behalf of the government with the chieftains.[45] The press reports apparently did not include Ḥusayn among the alleged participants until a few weeks later, the end of December, 1913, or the beginning of 1914.[46] Although Ḥusayn may have been approached by the nationalists at this time, in the latter part of February, 1914, he still was not claimed as an adherent by the Arab officers who sought to impress Sir Louis Mallet with the strength of their movement in Iraq and Arabia.[47] From 1912 until the beginning of 1914, then, Ḥusayn was generally regarded by Arabs and Turks alike as a supporter of the Ottoman state, and not as an Arab nationalist.[48]

After the end of the Balkan wars the Turks intensified the policy of centralization. By attempting to reassert and to strengthen their control over the Hijaz, they created a crisis which caused the Hashimites to consider seriously the idea

44. *Die Welt des Islams,* II (1914), 53–54; *Brit Doc.,* X, pt. 2, 827; Eugene Jung, *La Révolte arabe* (Paris: Libraire Colbert, Ch. Bohrer, 1925), I, 76–77.

45. Jung, I, 77; if this unidentified "correspondence" could be identified as coming from an Arab nationalist source, as so much of Jung's material did, it would be bona fide evidence that Arab nationalists still regarded Ḥusayn as pro-Turk. However, the occurrence of "l'émir Ibn Esséoud; l'émir Abdul-Aziz, cheikh du Nedjed," suggests a European, or at least a non-Arab, source.

46. *Welt Is.,* II (1914), 60–61, 313–314; *Brit. Doc.,* X, pt. 2, 827.

47. *Brit. Doc.,* X, pt. 2, 828, 833. Stephen H. Longrigg, *Iraq, 1900 to 1950* (London and New York: Oxford University Press, 1953), p. 47, accepts the report that Ḥusayn was included in the negotiations, but he adds that the congress never met because of the opposition of the government and the "hesitations" of the amirs. The basis for including Ḥusayn among those who were to take part may have been the reports of his reconciliation with Ibn-Suʿūd that appeared simultaneously with but separately from the earliest reports of the congress; *Welt Is.,* II (1914), 53; *The Near East,* VI (1914), 283. The reports published in the spring of 1914 about a congress of Arabian amirs, including Ḥusayn, which was to be held in Ḥāʾil, were probably without foundation; Jung, I, 96; Franz Stuhlmann, *Der Kampf um Arabien zwischen der Turkei und England* (Hamburg: George Westermann, 1916), pp. 55–56.

48. Cf. "X," "Les Courants politiques dans le milieu arabe," *RMM,* XIX (1913), 279–280; *Brit. Doc.,* X, pt. 2, 828–829.

of revolution and which perhaps turned the eyes of Arab nationalists once more toward Mecca. Toward the end of 1913, Wahīb Bey, who was well known for his belief that the Arab movement could best be disposed of by forcible suppression, was appointed Vali and Commander of Troops. In the Hijaz this appointment was interpreted as a change of policy, because relations with the previous governor had been good. In February, 1914, Wahīb arrived in the Hijaz, provided with military reinforcements comprised of seven battalions of infantry and one of artillery, and with instructions to apply the Law of the Vilayets and to extend the railroad from Medina to Mecca. Since both measures included in Wahīb's instructions were strongly opposed by the people of the Hijaz, it was not long before the bedouin cut the roads between Mecca and Medina and between the coast and the interior, and the cities thus were brought to the verge of famine. Ḥusayn went to see the Vali, and a crowd gathered around the government building. The Amir declared:

> You see the desire of the people of the Hijaz to cling to its ancient rights and to the conditions by which Sultan Selim I was confirmed in the caliphate. I had desired that there be no consideration of this, while orders from the State to apply the Law of the Vilayets to this land and to strip it of its privileges were in your hands. Then we saw these orders, no indication of which had reached me from the Sublime Porte. If the aim is the execution of a change in the Amirate, then I will remain here until a ship upon which I shall travel from Jidda comes, lest something happen the responsibilities for which will be attributed to me.

Meanwhile, the crowd outside was shouting, denouncing any change in the privileges of the Hijaz, demanding that the railroad not be extended to Mecca, and calling to Ḥusayn, "Blood always." Ḥusayn then sent a telegram to Constantinople urging that the status quo be maintained. He then left the building amidst cries of "Blood always." That evening the Defterdar and the Commander of the Gendarmerie took their forces out toward Jidda, but, since they fell into the hands of the tribes,

Jidda was cut off completely from Mecca, and the people from the *wadis* of the countryside were prevented from taking their produce to Mecca.[49]

Unionist attempts to remove Ḥusayn were frustrated by the vigor of the bedouin opposition to the government's policy and by Ḥusayn's influence with "Old Turk" statesmen. Wahīb advised the government that Ḥusayn ought to be deposed and that at least two divisions should be sent for this purpose. The government did not adopt Wahīb's recommendation, because to do so might provoke great disorder.[50] In Constantinople the opposition of the bedouin to the new policy was thought to be adamant and independent of Ḥusayn's instigation.[51] The Grand Vizier, Saʿīd Ḥalīm, who was a personal friend of Ḥusayn, intervened with the promise to send the Amir a warning. When this failed to dissuade Ḥusayn, the Minister of the Interior, Talât, initiated steps to send a division from Smyrna to the Hijaz to depose the Amir. But it came to the attention of the Grand Vizier, who again successfully intervened on the ground that such an act would have had an adverse effect upon obtaining a desired loan from France.[52] The crisis was settled in favor of the Amir of Mecca, and Ḥusayn received an answer to his telegram from the Grand Vizier, assuring him that no restriction of the rights of the Amirate or of the privileges of the Hijaz was contemplated and that for the present the government would not persist in extending the railroad to Mecca. After this wire was read in the mosque, the situation returned to normal.[53]

The gravity of the crisis led both sides to desire immediate discussions of the problem. ʿAbdullāh, who before the arrival of Wahīb had left the Hijaz for Constantinople in order to attend the coming session of the Ottoman Parliament, spent the period of the crisis in Egypt, where he was made aware

49. ʿAbdullāh, pp. 77, 79–80 (quotation on p. 79); Saʿīd, I, 54–55, 125–126. Cf. Kitchener to Grey, Feb. 14, 1914, *Brit. Doc.*, X, pt. 2, 827.

50. Ahmad Djemal (Jemal), *Memories of a Turkish Statesman, 1913–1919* (New York: G. H. Doran Co., 1922), pp. 227–228.

51. *Near East*, VII (1914), 171.

52. Stitt, pp. 142–144.

53. ʿAbdullāh, p. 80; Saʿīd, I, 126.

of the seriousness of the situation. Both Ḥusayn and the government kept urging ʿAbdullāh to proceed to the capital immediately, but he remained in Egypt until after the crisis was settled.[54]

In Constantinople, ʿAbdullāh attempted to win the cabinet to his father's policy. Talât opened a conversation with the Amir, which had been arranged by the Grand Vizier, with the statement that the crisis in the Hijaz had been settled, and then inquired, "What happened?" ʿAbdullāh replied that the government wished to end the special position of the Hijaz and make it an Ottoman vilayet, but the Sharif was determined to maintain everything as it was. ʿAbdullāh then argued that Ḥusayn's policy was in the best interest of the Ottoman State:

> He [Ḥusayn] thinks that the end which the government seeks is the establishment of peace and security of communications and the security of the pilgrims. You, with your desire for these things, wish to place the Hijaz under the Law of the Vilayets; if you set the Sharifate to serving the government in the Hijaz, and upon the basis of the true Islamic brotherhood between the Islamic world and the State of the Caliphate, you would learn that Mecca is the beating heart of this policy, and that the Sharif is the mover of this heart and its arteries, and that the advantage to the government from the support of the Hijaz is greater by far than what you seek by the application of the Law of the Vilayets in it.

To Talât's question as to why Ḥusayn opposed the construction of the railroad from Medina to Mecca, the Amir replied that the cabinet had forgotten ʿAbd al-Ḥamīd's aims. The latter, said ʿAbdullāh, undertook the construction of the Hijaz line as "great propaganda for his person," and to indicate to Russia that Turkey regarded England as the enemy, not Russia. He continued:

> And that which concerns the Sharif today must also concern you. Is it not the construction of an Islamic policy whose center is the Hijaz, and the one to whom it is entrusted is the Sharif?

54. ʿAbdullāh, pp. 71, 77–80; cf. Mallet to Grey, Mar. 18, 1914, *Brit. Doc.*, X, pt. 2, 828.

> And the completion of this line disturbs the employment which is the natural right of those who live today by the practice of transport by camel and the instruction of the pilgrims in the circumambulations and the way to visit al-Muṣṭafa. . . . That is what the Sharif was unable to make you understand and what you were unable to understand.

ʿAbdullāh left Talât, who requested the Amir to meet with him the next day, and met with Enver, the Minister of War, whose attitude was very conciliatory.[55]

The government answered ʿAbdullāh's objection to the construction of the railroad with a compromise offer. When the Amir and Talât met again on the following day, the latter was angry. The government did not mind changing valis every month, if necessary, but the completion of the railroad from Medina to Mecca, from Jidda to Mecca, and from Yanbūʿ to Medina was a necessity. ʿAbdullāh was authorized to return with terms which the government was willing to grant in return for the construction of the railroad. The Sharif was to have complete control over one-third of the revenues of the railroad; in addition, the force necessary for the execution of the project was to be commanded by the Amir, and he was to have a quarter of a million guineas to spend among the tribes. Finally, the Amirate was to be Ḥusayn's for life and then hereditary in his family.[56]

In the meantime, certain events were leading ʿAbdullāh to consider the possibility that the British might enable his father to resist the Turks. British interest in the conditions of the pilgrimage had been made clear to ʿAbdullāh as early as the spring of either 1912 or 1913, when Lord Kitchener, the British Agent in Egypt, called on the Amir, who was then in Cairo as the guest of the Khedive. Kitchener expressed the pleasure of his government with the improvement in the conditions of the pilgrimage which had taken place since Ḥusayn became Amir of Mecca, since these conditions affected Britain's Indian subjects. A year or two later, early in February, 1914, during the

55. ʿAbdullāh, pp. 81–88 (quotation on p. 84).
56. *Ibid.*, pp. 88–89.

height of the crisis in the Hijaz, Kitchener seems to have called again on ʿAbdullāh, who then, it seems, returned the visit. According to ʿAbdullāh the British Agent began the conversation with the statement that he had knowledge that the Turks had strengthened their forces in the Hijaz and intended to introduce fundamental changes there. In the course of the discussion, Kitchener asked ʿAbdullāh what his father would do in case the Turks should try to remove him. ʿAbdullāh replied by asking whether Great Britain would aid Ḥusayn if he resisted the Turks. Kitchener's reply was that Britain could not interfere in the internal affairs of Turkey, with which Great Britain had friendly relations. ʿAbdullāh then proceeded to Constantinople and discussed the question of the Hijaz with the Grand Vizier, Talât, and Enver. In April, during his return trip to the Hijaz, ʿAbdullāh again stopped in Cairo and communicated with Kitchener, who sent Ronald Storrs, the Oriental Secretary, to see him. In the course of a lengthy conversation ʿAbdullāh asked Storrs whether Great Britain might not send a dozen or a half-dozen machine guns to Ḥusayn for use against the Turks. Storrs replied that his government could not supply arms for use against a friendly power, and that Great Britain's only interest in the Hijaz was the safety of the Indian and Egyptian pilgrims.[57]

Although both Kitchener and Storrs had stated that Great Britain could not intervene in Turkish affairs, Kitchener's initiative in opening discussions of Hashimite-Turkish relations on two different occasions and the repeated expressions of concern for the safety of the pilgrims seem to have convinced ʿAbdullāh that Great Britain was interested enough in the Hijaz to support Ḥusayn against the Turks. ʿAbdullāh's conviction was not unreasonable, since at that time practically all Arab politicians believed that the British government had territorial ambitions in Arabia and favored the establishment of an independent Arab state. Nor could Kitchener's legalistic disclaimer of intervention sound convincing to ʿAbdullāh, who (as he reminded

57. See below, pp. 58–68, for a full discussion of the sources for this and the following two paragraphs.

the British Agent in February) remembered British intervention in Kuwayt and witnessed successful British intervention on behalf of the Arab officer ʿAzīz ʿAli al-Miṣri during the period February 12–April 12, 1914.

ʿAbdullāh's knowledge of the Arab nationalist movement also helped convince him that a revolt could be successful. On the other hand, the crisis of early 1914 seems to have impelled ʿAbdullāh to join the nationalist movement. The nationalists had confided in ʿAbdullāh since 1909, and ʿAbdullāh's pride in the Arabs as the founders of Islam and his concept of the Islamic brotherhood were ridiculed and rejected by the Turkish nationalists whom the Amir met in Constantinople. But ʿAbdullāh had difficulty in giving up his attachment to the Ottoman Empire as the expression of Moslem unity. The campaign against al-Idrīsi caused disaffection with Ḥusayn in nationalist circles, but the actions of Wahīb seem to have brought ʿAbdullāh and the nationalists together. It was probably in the first half of 1914 that Muḥammad Rashīd Riḍa met with ʿAbdullāh in Cairo and administered to him the oath of membership in the Society of the Arab League.

In April, 1914, ʿAbdullāh returned to the Hijaz to present to his father the government's offer and, in addition, his own plans and arguments for a revolutionary solution. Ḥusayn responded to his son's description of the government's offer with the words, "Are they bribing me?" [58] Although the cabinet was willing to give up its attempts to apply the provincial law in the Hijaz, its insistence on extending the railroad worried ʿAbdullāh because, as he had explained to Storrs, the extension of the railroad would have destroyed the means of livelihood of the bedouin, and (as he might have added but did not) because it would have aided greatly any future Turkish efforts to subdue the Amir of Mecca by military means. A series of family councils was held to discuss the problem. ʿAbdullāh argued that the Hijaz, with the aid of the Arab units in the Ottoman forces in Syria and Iraq and with British diplomatic support, could obtain independence from the Turks and then

58. ʿAbdullāh, p. 90.

work for the formation of a large, independent Arab state. Specifically, ʿAbdullāh proposed to seize the pilgrims during the great feast so that the foreign governments interested (England, France, Italy, and Holland) would make representations to the Porte for their release. When the Porte failed to secure the release of the pilgrims, the Powers would be forced to negotiate directly with Ḥusayn, who would be happy to release the pilgrims in return for a "promise [from the Powers] of immunity from Turkey in the future." Fayṣal and ʿAli, Ḥusayn's other sons, opposed the scheme on the ground that Turkey was too strong, but the plan was finally adopted, provisionally, with action being set for some time in 1915, apparently as a measure of last resort in case accommodation with the Turks should prove impossible.[59]

At the same time Ḥusayn also delayed and made compromise proposals to the Turks. After ʿAbdullāh informed him of Talât's proposals, the Amir of Mecca wired the government his reply:

> My son . . . has transmitted to me the high proposals and decisions from the Grand Vizier in the matter of the extension of the Hijaz Railroad to Mecca. There is nothing which requires that consideration be given to what my share will be, while I enjoy the prosperity of the Caliphate. At the first opportunity, I shall send by my son . . . my impressions regarding possible means of attaining this high goal without affecting the means of livelihood of the tribes and of the population of the Islamic holy lands.

But Ḥusayn sent ʿAbdullāh on an expedition against the Dawāsir rather than sending him immediately back to Constantinople. As a result, the government sent a series of telegrams to the Hijaz requesting that ʿAbdullāh be sent to the capital at once. When ʿAbdullāh returned from the expedition, he proceeded to Constantinople, where he arrived on July 1,

59. Information given to Lawrence by Fayṣal in Dec., 1916, and by ʿAbdullāh in April, 1917. T. E. Lawrence, *Secret Despatches from Arabia*, ed. A. W. Lawrence (London: Golden Cockerel Press, n.d.), pp. 52, 96 (quotation, from ʿAbdullāh, on p. 96); cf. Erskine, p. 41.

1914, two days after the assassination at Sarajevo. The day after his arrival ʿAbdullāh delivered his father's reply to the office of the Grand Vizier. Ḥusayn began with a protestation of loyalty to the Sultan, but he added, "If the completion of the road and the assurance of the loyalty of the tribes and their livelihood is what His Majesty and the government wish, then there are means [of achieving these goals] which do not require a quarter of the expenditures which ʿAbdullāh described. . . ." The Amir of Mecca requested the formation of a committee under his presidency which would meet with the Grand Vizier and the Shaykh al-Islam or some minister and draw up and agree to certain projects the execution of which was prerequisite to the construction of the railroad. "Under any conditions," concluded the Amir, "it will be necessary to station a full division along the right of way and at the water works and the villages between the two cities. After that, work may begin." Upon receiving the note, the Grand Vizier told ʿAbdullāh that they would meet with Talât in two days' time. But when the meeting took place, Talât replied to ʿAbdullāh's questions about the Hijaz with, "Is this the time for thinking about the building of railroads. . . . We wish you to travel immediately to the Hijaz to raise volunteers, for it is possible that the State will be forced to enter the war." [60]

During the period from 1908 to July, 1914, Ḥusayn followed a policy of strengthening the powers of the Amirate of Mecca and of aggrandizing its territories. In support of this policy Ḥusayn used Islam as a political ideology and proposed to cooperate with the Ottoman government in carrying out an active Pan-Islamic program. The Amir of Mecca indeed went so far as to use Arab forces in support of Turkish troops against the Arabs of ʿAsīr. However, the Unionist policy of centralization ran counter to Ḥusayn's aspirations, and conflict between the Amir and the Sublime Porte was the inevitable result. The Unionist policy also conflicted with the interests of the Hijazi bedouin, and even though Ḥusayn's strong hand might have been irksome to the tribesmen, the latter could only support

60. ʿAbdullāh, pp. 90–93 (quotations on pp. 90–91, 92, and 93).

Ḥusayn against the Turks. Although the Unionists believed it necessary to remove Ḥusayn from the Amirate, their external problems and Ḥusayn's influence with and value to the "Old Turks," with whom the Committee could never dispense entirely, prevented the deposition of the Amir. By July, 1914, therefore, relations between the Amir of Mecca and the Unionist government were so strained that one of the Amir's sons had come to favor a revolutionary solution, but the two opposing forces still rested in an uneasy balance, and both sides were still willing at least to talk of compromise.

II

The coming of war in 1914 and the subsequent Ottoman involvement put aside the questions of the application of the provincial law in the Hijaz and the extension of the railroad and created a new dilemma for Ḥusayn and his sons. On the Hashimite side, since the war changed the conditions upon which the tentatively planned revolt had been predicated, the provisional plan was dropped.[61] On the other hand, the Ottoman government began to press Ḥusayn to support the Empire's war effort. ʿAbdullāh was quick to see that the government, by stationing Turkish regulars in the Arab area while sending Arab volunteers to more distant fronts, could use Hijazi participation in the war as a means of weakening the Hashimite position. In a conversation in July with Enver, who had repeated Talât's request to return to the Hijaz and raise volunteers, ʿAbdullāh asked where the Hijazis would be used. When the Minister of War said that the Arabs would be used with regular troops in the Caucasus and Europe, while regular Turkish forces manned the Egyptian front, the Amir declared that the volunteers must be employed on the Egyptian front. Ḥusayn saw other dangers. When ʿAbdullāh returned from Constantinople and informed his father of the talks in Constantinople, the latter wrote a letter to the Sultan in which he advised against entering the war. As

61. Lawrence, pp. 52, 96.

a result of the Empire's being cut off from her source of supply in Germany, the Ottoman forces might be left without equipment. In addition (and this consideration must have carried much more weight with Ḥusayn than did the first), Basra, the Yaman, and the Hijaz would be placed in an especially critical position because they were extremely vulnerable to the pressure of British sea power.[62]

The policy adopted by the Sharif of Mecca mixed delay with requests for military and economic arrangements designed to reduce the perils of the situation. In August the Amir wrote the Grand Vizier that if the Empire should enter the war it would be necessary to provision at once the Yaman, ʿAsīr, and the Hijaz with three years' stores of supplies, arms, and equipment for both regular troops and volunteers. In addition, a five years' supply of provisions should be stockpiled in the same three provinces. After Turkey entered the war, Ḥusayn wired the government requesting the sending of money to the Yaman, ʿAsīr, and the Hijaz. The Amir received neither supplies nor money and repeated requests received the same treatment.[63] The implementation of the Sharif's proposals would have lessened the dangers of participation in the war on the side of the Turks, inasmuch as the provision of military supplies and money to the Hijaz for the raising of volunteers would have given a military force to the Sharif rather than to the Turks, and the supply of foodstuffs would have diminished the pressure of a British blockade. Meanwhile, to the letters from Jemal Pasha, an ardent Pan-Islamist who had taken command in Syria in December, 1914, requesting the proclamation of the Holy War and the sending of volunteers, Ḥusayn returned assurances of loyalty and devotion to the Caliphate and of religious enthusiasms for the Holy War, which were, however, "expressed somewhat vaguely." As Jemal's entreaties continued during and after the first Turkish campaign against the Suez Canal, Ḥusayn finally promised to send a force from the Hijaz

62. ʿAbdullāh, pp. 93–94, 98–99. See also the press interview with Ḥusayn in Dec., 1920, *Mit. Sem. Or. Sp.*, XXVI–XXVII (1924), 85.

63. ʿAbdullāh, pp. 99–100, 104.

to assist the second expedition, which was planned for the winter of 1915.[64]

Ḥusayn, meanwhile, had been approached by British authorities. About October 17, 1914, ʿAbdullāh received a letter from Storrs containing a message from Kitchener inquiring whether Ḥusayn would support Turkey or Great Britain in case Turkey should enter the war on the side of Germany. ʿAbdullāh's reply on behalf of his father, which reached Cairo on October 30, was friendly and, though cautious, indicated that the Amir would not willingly and of his own accord support the Turks. At the beginning of November, immediately after Turkey's entry into the war, Storrs sent another letter to ʿAbdullāh containing a message from Kitchener. The message stated that if the Sharif and the "Arab Nation" aided Great Britain in the war, Britain would recognize and support the independence of the Amirate and of the Arabs and would guarantee Arabia against intervention and the Arabs against external aggression. Britain, moreover, expressed approval of the assumption of the caliphate by an Arab. The Sharif's reply, which reached Cairo on December 10, was that he would not adopt a policy hostile to Great Britain, but that because of his position in Islam he could not break immediately with Turkey.[65] During the first half of 1915 contacts between the British authorities in Egypt and the Amir of Mecca continued, principally through the intermediary of Sir Reginald Wingate, the Governor-General of the Sudan. Throughout the entire period Ḥusayn expressed no change in his position, but in April Wingate informed him that His Majesty's Government "would make it an essential condition in the peace terms that the Arabian Peninsula and its Muhammadan

64. Djemal, pp. 201–202, 211–212.

65. Sir Ronald Storrs, *Memoirs* (New York: G. P. Putnam's Sons, 1937), p. 166; Great Britain, Committee of Imperial Defence, Historical Section, *History of the Great War Based on Official Documents. Military Operations, Egypt and Palestine, from the Outbreak of War with Germany to June, 1917,* compiled by Lieut.-General Sir George MacMun and Capt. Cyril Falls, I (London: H.M.S.O., 1928), 213–214; Great Britain, Foreign Office, *Correspondence between Sir Henry McMahon . . . and the Sherif Hussein of Mecca, July 1915–March 1916,* Cmd. 5957 (House of Commons Sessional Papers, 1938–1939, vol. 27), p. 4 (McMahon to Ḥusayn, Aug. 30, 1915); ʿAbdullāh, pp. 101–102, and Saʿīd, I, 127–128, are confused; Kedourie, pp. 49, 52.

Holy Places should remain in the hands of an independent sovereign state. It was impossible to define at the moment how much territory should be included in this state." [66]

In January, 1915, the secret nationalist societies *al-Fatāt* and *al-ʿAhd* approached the Amir of Mecca. As a result of the friendship between the Hashimites and the Bakris of Damascus, established on the occasion of the pilgrimage of 1909, Ḥusayn had used his influence to get the young Bakri men assigned to his bodyguard whenever they were called to military service. As a result of the general conscriptions of August, 1914, Aḥmad Fawzi Bey al-Bakri was called to service and assigned to Mecca, where he arrived in the summer of 1914.[67] Fawzi, whose older brother Nasīb was a member of *al-Fatāt*, was selected by the nationalist leaders to reveal the existence of the societies and their plans to Ḥusayn. Fawzi arrived in Mecca in January, 1915, told Ḥusayn of the nationalist plans, and proposed that Ḥusayn assume the leadership of the Arab revolt. It would take the form of a mutiny by the Arab troops stationed in Syria, whose officers were members of *al-ʿAhd*.[68]

In January, 1915, an accident revealed to Ḥusayn how far the Young Turks had been prepared to go in order to unseat him. At Jemal's request, Ḥusayn had ordered an Arab force under the command of ʿAli to accompany the Turkish force which Wahīb was moving north to join in the attack on the Suez Canal. When Wahīb set out in January, ʿAli accompanied him from Mecca to Medina, but in the latter place ʿAli declared that Ḥusayn had ordered him to leave Wahīb here, and then "began to interfere with the functions of the Commandant. . . ." [69] ʿAli had withdrawn from Wahīb's train because on the way to Medina a case had fallen from the baggage of a well-known Hijazi supporter of the Committee of Union and Progress and had been discovered by one of ʿAli's men, who immediately

66. *Hist. Gt. War*, I, 214–215; Storrs, p. 166 (quotation).

67. Saʿīd, I, 105. Compare the slightly different account of Fawzi's appointment in Antonius, p. 149.

68. Report by Lawrence dated Jan. 8, 1917, *Sec. Desp.*, p. 69; Saʿīd, I, 105; Antonius, pp. 149–150.

69. Djemal, pp. 152–153.

took it to the Amir. The case contained correspondence between Wahīb and Constantinople which dealt with plans to depose Ḥusayn and his family and to end the special position of the Hijaz. Only the outbreak of war had interfered with the execution of these plans. Therefore ʿAli stopped at Medina and then went to Mecca, where he showed the documents to his father.[70] This unexpectedly discovered proof of Unionist intentions, coming when it did, placed Ḥusayn in a quandary. He personally was still inclined toward seeking a solution within the Ottoman Empire. Fayṣal was therefore charged with presenting the documents to the Grand Vizier and seeking redress for the plot. At the same time, Fayṣal was to make contacts with the nationalists in Syria, surveying the situation in order to estimate the extent to which a revolution was likely and what preparations had been made for such a revolution.[71]

Fayṣal arrived in Damascus on March 26, 1915, and became a guest of ʿAṭa Pasha al-Bakri. During the four weeks which Fayṣal spent in Damascus as a guest of the Bakris, he received the leaders of *al-Fatāt* and *al-ʿAhd* and discussed the political situation with them.[72] Fayṣal found the situation in Syria confused. Many persons begged Fayṣal to accept the leadership of the revolt which would begin soon, and three of the regular divisions in Syria (all Arab divisions) were ready to revolt. But public opinion was divided, and in military circles the opinion that Germany would soon win the war prevailed. Fayṣal took the position that he was charged only with surveying the situation and that he could not accept the responsibility for a revolt unless he were assured of the support of "some powerful organization or of one of the Great Powers." [73]

In Constantinople Fayṣal, who remained in the capital about a month after his arival on April 23, received only limited satisfaction for his family's grievance and concluded that conditions

70. Saʿīd, I, 105–106.

71. Erskine, p. 40.

72. Antonius, pp. 152–153, 156. Saʿīd's assertion that Fayṣal did not meet with the Arab leaders on this visit is incorrect; Saʿīd, I, 105–107. The dates for Fayṣal's itinerary given by Jemal and followed by Saʿīd cannot be correct.

73. Lawrence, p. 69; Erskine, p. 42.

favored revolution. Fayṣal presented the evidence of Wahīb's intrigues to the Sultan, the Grand Vizier, Talât, and Enver, who disapproved Wahīb's actions, ordered his transfer, and promised an official inquiry and court martial.[74] However, the ministers told Fayṣal that if Ḥusayn declared the Holy War, "the task of redressing the situation in the Hijaz in his favour would be simplified and he could then count on receiving the fullest satisfaction." [75] Fayṣal assured the Sultan and the ministers of his family's complete loyalty and promised to lead a Hijazi force in the planned second attack on the canal.[76] Since the British attack on the Dardanelles had reached full force, Fayṣal believed that conditions were favorable to an Arab revolt.[77] Fayṣal also met with several notables in Constantinople, among whom were two generals who advised him to return to the Hijaz and warn his father about joining the Unionists, "who were dragging the Empire to ruin," and who gave it as their opinion that it was Ḥusayn's duty to save the Empire by joining the Allies. Fayṣal then decided to join the revolutionists.[78]

During Fayṣal's stay in Constantinople the leaders of *al-Fatāt* and of *al-ʿAhd* had drawn up a protocol for presentation to the British through Ḥusayn. The Damascus Protocol included Great Britain's recognition of the independence of the Arab countries east of Egypt except for Aden, with somewhat generously drawn frontiers, and the abolition of all capitulatory privileges; in return, "the future independent Arab state" would conclude a defensive alliance with and grant economic preference to Great Britain.[79] When Fayṣal returned to Damascus on

74. Saʿīd, I, 106; Erskine, p. 42; Lawrence, p. 96. Djemal, p. 166, seems to indicate that Wahīb had been transferred before Fayṣal's trip to Constantinople.

75. Antonius, p. 157.

76. Djemal, p. 213. Saʿīd, I, 106, quoting the memoirs of ʿAli Fuʾād, Chief of Staff of the Ottoman Fourth Army. Although this entire passage from ʿAli Fuʾād's memoirs is quoted in connection with Fayṣal's conversations in Constantinople, the conversation with Enver could not have taken place at that time and the memorandum presented to the Grand Vizier is identical with Ḥusayn's correspondence with the Grand Vizier one year later.

77. Lawrence, p. 69.

78. Erskine, pp. 42–43.

79. Antonius, p. 157.

May 23, 1915, he found that some of the Arab divisions upon which the revolt was to have been based had been transferred and that the advocates of revolt were in an urgent mood. He was importuned to return to Mecca and persuade his father to accept the leadership of the revolt and to negotiate with the British on the basis of the Damascus Protocol. Fayṣal was doubtful that the British would accept the Arab terms, but he agreed to present the proposition to Ḥusayn and then to return to Syria, where the rising was to be proclaimed; whereupon nine of the nationalist leaders signed a manifesto agreeing to recognize Ḥusayn as King of the Arabs and promised a rebellion in Syria if Ḥusayn obtained agreement with Britain on the basis of the Damascus Protocol.[80]

Courtesy demanded that Fayṣal pay a visit to Jemal Pasha, who was then on a tour of inspection in the South. But, since time was pressing, Fayṣal visited Jemal in Jerusalem rather than waiting for his return to Damascus. Upon the urging of Jemal, who received Fayṣal with great honor, Fayṣal agreed that Ḥusayn should send under his command a volunteer force of 1,500 camelry. In an address to the headquarters staff, Fayṣal swore by the soul of the Prophet that he would come back with his forces "to fight the foes of the Faith to the death." Fayṣal then returned to Damascus, where he caught the train for Medina.[81]

On June 20 Fayṣal arrived in Mecca, reported to his father, and declared himself to be a convert to revolution.[82] Ḥusayn then went on to his summer residence at al-Ṭā'if, where his sons soon joined him for a discussion of policy. Fayṣal, although now an advocate of revolt, argued that the time was not ripe and urged his father to delay the revolt until the British had been properly approached and until Turkey had either suffered crippling losses or an Allied landing had been made at Alexan-

80. Erskine, p. 44; Saʿīd, I, 107, 108–109. Antonius, pp. 157–159, is slightly different, the chief difference being the statement that six nationalist leaders took an oath binding themselves to recognize Ḥusayn as spokesman for the Arabs.

81. Djemal, p. 213; Erskine, p. 43; Antonius, p. 159.

82. Antonius, p. 159; Saʿīd, I, 109.

dretta. ʿAbdullāh told Ḥusayn that Fayṣal was afraid and argued for proclaiming the revolt. ʿAbdullāh seems to have carried the day with this argument: "The war could have only one consequence for the Arabs: they would remain in the noose of [tyrannical] government whether the Turks and Germany or the French and British won; it was necessary to proclaim the Arab movement and [thus] escape through war the necessary consequence of submission to alien rule." The upshot was that at al-Ṭā'if the Hashimites decided to undertake the leadership of a general rising by the Arabs and to begin negotiations with the British; the date of the rising was placed in June, 1916.[83]

The Hashimites having decided to undertake the revolt, Ḥusayn initiated negotiations with Great Britain by sending an unsigned and undated letter to Sir Henry McMahon, British High Commissioner at Cairo, which was sent with a letter dated July 14, 1915, from ʿAbdullāh to Storrs. In the exchange of letters which followed during the second half of 1915, Ḥusayn sought to obtain British recognition of an Arab state within the frontiers specified by the Damascus Protocol, while McMahon sought to exclude certain areas in which Great Britain and France had special interests. By the end of 1915 agreement had been reached on all points except certain vaguely defined territories in Syria wherein French interests were involved. In a letter dated January 1, 1916, Ḥusayn stated to McMahon that the Vilayets of Aleppo and Beirut could not be excluded by the Arab kingdom, but that in order not to damage the alliance between Britain and France he would postpone his demands until the end of the war.[84] Ḥusayn's negotiations with the British, then, were not entirely satisfactory in achieving acceptance of Arab territorial demands.

Even in January, 1916, Ḥusayn apparently had not decided

83. ʿAbdullāh, p. 104 (quotation); Saʿīd, I, 110, 128; Lawrence, pp. 52, 62. See below, p. 54.

84. See the official texts of the Ḥusayn-McMahon correspondence contained in Cmd. 5957, pp. 3–14; these have been collated with the translation of Antonius and with an unofficial Arabic version by Ettore Rossi, *Documenti sull' origine e gli sviluppi della questione araba, 1875–1944* (Rome: Istituto per l'Oriente, 1944), pp. 18–40. To these should be added the apparently official Arabic texts of some of the letters in Wahbah, pp. 153–160.

definitely upon a course of action. Jemal had been continuing to telegraph demands that Fayṣal return to Damascus with the promised contingent. Ḥusayn was not entirely satisfied with the British reply, and the situation in Syria was not favorable to an Arab rising. It was decided, therefore, to have Fayṣal return to Syria in order to allay Turkish suspicions.[85] Fayṣal, accompanied by an escort of about fifty men, returned to Damascus, where he stayed at Jemal's headquarters for the purpose of helping in sending the equipment for the volunteers to Mecca.[86] At the same time Fayṣal surveyed the situation and reported his conclusions and recommendations to Ḥusayn. The arrest of nationalists and the transferral of Arab military units had left only a few Arab leaders of the second rank upon whom a revolt could be based. Fayṣal decided therefore to await the arrival in Syria of new forces raised in such Arab districts as Aleppo and Mosul, which were expected to number 100,000 men. If the majority of these should be Arab, he would begin the movement with them; if they should be Turkish, he would wait until these troops were engaged in an attack on the Canal, when he would begin the revolt. Ḥusayn then decided to send ʿAli to Medina with forces sufficient to support Fayṣal in Syria by occupying the railroad or by carrying out any other movement that seemed opportune.[87]

The weakening of the Arab position in Syria, as reported by Fayṣal, perhaps led Ḥusayn to come to some sort of agreement with the British. Ḥusayn's letter to McMahon of January 1 had persisted in maintaining the Arab claim to the vilayets of Aleppo and Beirut, in their entirety, even though Ḥusayn expressed a willingness to defer the matter until the end of the war. McMahon gave Ḥusayn no comfort when he replied on January 25 by noting with satisfaction Ḥusayn's desire to avoid any action with respect to Syria which might damage the Anglo-French alliance; he added that Britain was determined that nothing should be permitted to interfere with this alliance,

85. Erskine, p. 45.
86. *Ibid.*, p. 45; Djemal, p. 214.
87. Ḥusayn to McMahon, Feb. 18, 1916, Cmd. 5957, pp. 15–16; Erskine, p. 45.

which would be even stronger at the conclusion of the war. Ḥusayn, in a reply dated February 18, expressed his delight with McMahon's letter, which had filled him "with the utmost pleasure and satisfaction at the attainment of the required understanding and the intimacy desired."[88] Thus an ambiguous agreement was reached between the Sharif of Mecca, on behalf of the Arabs, and the British government.

Agreement having been reached on political matters, subsequent negotiations were devoted entirely to making arrangements through which British material assistance to the Arabs could be made available. Ḥusayn's letter of February 18 reported to McMahon the Hashimite plans and specified in detail the money and supplies required and the way in which these were to be sent to the Hijaz. On March 10 McMahon wrote to Ḥusayn accepting his requests and setting forth the arrangements made to deliver them to the Sharif.[89] Then the delivery of the money and supplies began by way of Port Sudan, on the African shore of the Red Sea opposite Jidda. The Hashimites planned to begin the revolt on June 16, but McMahon urged the Amir to delay the rising until it was possible to equip the Arab forces adequately.[90]

While Ḥusayn was arriving at a definite understanding with the British government, he was also carrying out negotiations with Turkish authorities. The Ottoman government undertook to send money and arms for the purpose of raising, equipping, and training the volunteers, and by the beginning of April the Turks had sent some fifty or sixty thousand Turkish pounds in gold to Ḥusayn.[91] In the meantime, in his conversations with Jemal, Fayṣal had been suggesting that, in return for Ḥusayn's raising and leading the volunteers, the government should recall the Vali of the Hijaz and assign his powers and duties to Ḥusayn. But Jemal persisted in requesting the immediate dispatch of the volunteers to the front and would give no assurance beyond the statement (which must have been more fright-

88. Cmd. 5957, pp. 14–15.
89. *Ibid.*, pp. 15–18.
90. *Hist. Gt. War*, I, 220; Storrs, p. 171.
91. Djemal, p. 222.

ening than reassuring to the Hashimites) that if any of Ḥusayn's rights should be encroached upon, he would give the Amir all the aid in his power, even if in doing so he "came into conflict with other people, however highly placed." [92] At the same time a show of loyalty was maintained by Ḥusayn and his sons. At the beginning of March Enver visited Syria and, accompanied by Fayṣal and Jemal, went on to Medina, where he arrived on March 8. Enver made a fiery speech to the pilgrims, and the visit was climaxed by the presentation of a sword of honor by Fayṣal on behalf of his father to Enver. Enver then returned to Damascus without visiting Mecca, and Fayṣal returned soon thereafter.[93] A little later (in the second half of March) ʿAli, who was assigned to the command of the volunteers, moved to Medina, where a large camp was formed outside the city as a garrison and training area for the volunteers.[94]

After the middle of March—i.e., after a definite understanding with Great Britain had been reached and after it had become clear that Jemal would not support Ḥusayn's aspirations —Ḥusayn ceased to temporize with the Turks and began to take positive action. Soon after his return to Damascus Jemal was informed by Baṣri Pasha, the Governor of Medina, that ʿAli was interfering in the government of Medina and assuming rights that did not belong to him. Jemal informed Baṣri that ʿAli was still a youth and that he should request him to desist from such actions; at the same time Jemal communicated to Ḥusayn a request that he restrain ʿAli.[95] The Turks had been continuing to press the Hashimites to declare the Holy War and to send the volunteers to Sinai, and Enver had repeated these urgings during his visit. An official request that the volunteers be sent at once to the front, which was sent to Ḥusayn by Enver after his return to Constantinople, led Ḥusayn to reveal his demands. Ḥusayn's reply, sent evidently about the begin-

92. Alois Musil, *Zur Zeitgeschichte von Arabien* (Leipzig: S. Hirzel, and Vienna: Manz, 1918), p. 28; Djemal, pp. 168, 215–216 (quotation); ʿAbdullāh, pp. 104–105.

93. Djemal, pp. 168, 214, 220–221; ʿAbdullāh, p. 105; Musil, pp. 28–29.

94. Djemal, p. 222; Musil, p. 29.

95. Djemal, p. 215; Saʿīd, I, 112.

ning of April, stated that Arab aspirations would have to be satisfied before the volunteers could be sent and the Holy War proclaimed. Arab demands consisted of the grant of a general amnesty to the Arab political prisoners and of decentralized regimes in Syria and Iraq and the recognition of the Amirate of Mecca as hereditary in the house of Ḥusayn, with a confirmation of its traditional status and privileges. When these demands were met, Ḥusayn would send the volunteers to Fayṣal in Damascus, and he would also send another of his sons to the Iraqi front, "after he had put an end to any unfriendly chieftaincy to the east of the Hijaz." Unless these demands were met, Ḥusayn could do nothing for the Empire except pray for victory.[96]

Ḥusayn's proposition prompted the Turkish authorities to deliver a near ultimatum to the Sharif. The Grand Vizier and Enver replied to Ḥusayn, denying his demands out of hand, emphasizing that the political prisoners would receive their just deserts, and closed with a warning that Ḥusayn would not see his son Fayṣal again until he had sent the volunteers to the front.[97] The Hashimites also received a strong warning from Jemal, to whom Enver had sent a copy of Ḥusayn's telegram. Jemal sent for Fayṣal, showed him the telegram, and, after reviewing the matter of ʿAli's behavior in Medina, warned Fayṣal that Ḥusayn had many enemies in Constantinople. Fayṣal excused Ḥusayn by saying that he did not know Turkish very well and that the message had been written by a clerk with only an imperfect understanding of Arabic. Fayṣal closed with the oath, "God forbid that my father should ever contemplate such a notion." To Ḥusayn Jemal then telegraphed a message in which he said that it was impossible to pardon traitors, and that the time was not opportune for bringing up the matter of a hereditary Amirate. The message warned Ḥusayn by asking that even if the government granted his demands in order to keep him quiet, "If the war came to a victorious conclusion, who could

96. ʿAbdullāh, p. 105; Saʿīd, I, 110–111; Djemal, pp. 215, 225.

97. ʿAbdullāh, p. 106; Saʿīd, I, 111, which adds, "I advise you to call your son ʿAli from Medina to Mecca at once. . . ."

prevent the Government from dealing with you with the greatest severity when it is over?" [98]

Ḥusayn did not give in to the Turkish threats. He remained firm and seems to have induced the Grand Vizier to take a more moderate stand. To the Grand Vizier and the Minister of War the Amir replied that he could only repeat his previous advice and that Fayṣal was a guest of the state; moreover, he said, the volunteers would not leave Arabia until Fayṣal came to lead them.[99] Ḥusayn also replied to Jemal, recommending a general amnesty and complaining about the actions of the Governor of Medina; he stated that he could not allow the Governor to encroach on the legal rights of the Amir of Mecca.[100] Two days after the Sharif's wire to the Grand Vizier was sent, the latter sent a conciliatory message to Ḥusayn, stating that, if Ḥusayn sent the volunteers to Damascus, the government would instruct Jemal to consult with Fayṣal in the matter of the political prisoners. To Constantinople the Amir replied that the volunteers would not arrive until Fayṣal came to lead them, to which the Grand Vizier replied immediately that Fayṣal would leave for Medina to fetch the volunteers to Damascus and requested that Ḥusayn recall ʿAli from Medina because of the latter's difficulties with the Governor. Ḥusayn replied at once, "With the arrival of the Sharif Fayṣal Bey, the Sharif ʿAli Bey will leave Medina." [101]

However, Jemal and Enver were led by Ḥusayn's stand to adopt a definitely menacing attitude toward the Hashimites. Jemal reacted violently to Ḥusayn's reply to his warning; although he did not communicate with Ḥusayn, he did warn Fayṣal about the actions of his father and of his brother ʿAli and requested Fayṣal to write to ʿAli to come to Damascus with the volunteers at once and to stop arrogating to himself the powers of the Governor of Medina. Fayṣal again protested the

98. Djemal, pp. 215–217.

99. ʿAbdullāh, p. 106; Saʿīd, I, 111. The texts are somewhat different.

100. Djemal, p. 221; see also the Arabic translation of the same passage in Saʿīd, I, 113.

101. ʿAbdullāh, pp. 106–170. Saʿīd, I, 111, does not mention more than two exchanges of correspondence between Ḥusayn and Constantinople.

loyalty of himself and of his family to the Empire.[102] Jemal's warning was followed by a more material threat. Toward the end of April a new Turkish force, some 3,500 strong, arrived in Medina en route to the Yaman.[103] The Turks meanwhile had sent to Medina the rifles necessary for the equipment of the 1,500 volunteers, but Ḥusayn's message to Jemal caused the latter to decide against sending the arms on to Mecca and to inform Ḥusayn that because of transport difficulties it would be necessary to send the volunteers to Medina, where arms would be supplied them.[104] Finally, around May 12, Enver sent a threatening wire to Ḥusayn, which made it clear that the government was not willing to make any concession to Ḥusayn and to the Arabs:

> Every official must remain within the limits of his post and not exceed them and interfere in matters of the State, otherwise I will be compelled to take the necesary measures in situations such as this. It is necessary to send the volunteers without hesitation and to recall ʿAli from Medina.[105]

Even though Ḥusayn was perhaps still reluctant to undertake the revolt, as conditions were unfavorable, the unqualified rejection of his proposals by Enver and Jemal left him no alternative. All the while Fayṣal had been in secret correspondence with his father concerning conditions in Syria and Arab plans. Because of the replacement of Arab military units in Syria with Turkish units and the arrest and execution of the Syrian nationalists, it was obvious that the rising could not depend principally on Syria, as had been originally planned, but must be based entirely on the Hijaz.[106] As Turkish actions became more threatening in the first half of May, it was decided that the break would have to be made soon. About the middle of May

102. Djemal, pp. 220–221.
103. *Hist Gt. War*, I, 228–230; Djemal, p. 223; Saʿīd, I, 115.
104. Djemal, p. 222.
105. Saʿīd, I, 116–117, calls this the last wire from Enver to Ḥusayn. Djemal, p. 225, relates that about three weeks before June 2, Enver wired Ḥusayn that ʿAli would have to act "very differently" toward the governor of Medina.
106. Erskine, p. 45; Saʿīd, I, 114.

Fayṣal visited Jemal, told him that Ḥusayn had ordered ʿAli to lead the volunteers to join the army in Sinai, and asked Jemal's permission to go to Medina to accompany the troops to Jerusalem. Although he was somewhat suspicious, Jemal gave his permission, so Fayṣal left Damascus by rail for Medina about the middle of May.[107]

The actions taken by Jemal Pasha because of his suspicions of the Hashimites led them to hasten preparations for the revolt. At the time of Fayṣal's departure from Damascus, Jemal instructed the Governor of Medina to hold in Medina the special forces destined for the Yaman and to arm them with the rifles sent originally for the equipment of the Arab volunteers. A short while later, Jemal sent Fakhri Pasha, Deputy Commander of the Fourth Army, to Medina with instructions to be wary of Fayṣal and ʿAli, and to arrange with the Governor, Baṣri Pasha, plans for the defense of the city.[108] Fakhri arrived in Medina shortly after Fayṣal and assumed command. Although the Hashimites had not completed preparations for the revolt, they were certain that the Yamani expeditionary force had in fact been sent to suppress the Amirate of Mecca. Ḥusayn therefore ordered Fayṣal to set out for Mecca in order that the revolt might begin; Fayṣal replied with a request for postponement until August, but Ḥusayn responded with a reiteration of the necessity for haste.[109] ʿAbdullāh sent a message to McMahon, which was telegraphed from Port Sudan to Cairo on May 23, requesting that Storrs come at once to the Arabian coast to meet him; the wire closed, "Movement will begin as soon as Faisal arrives at Mecca." However, before June 5, when Storrs reached the Arabian coast, the Hashimite plans were changed and the date of the rising was again pushed forward, from June 16 to June 10. The revolt was to begin simultaneously at Medina by ʿAli and Fayṣal, who were not to return to Mecca, at Mecca by Ḥusayn, at al-Ṭāʾif by ʿAbdullāh, and at Jidda by the Sharif Muḥsin, the Amir of the Ḥarb.[110] On June 2

107. Djemal, p. 222; Saʿīd, I, 115.
108. Djemal, p. 223.
109. Saʿīd, I, 115–116.
110. Storrs, pp. 169, 171.

ʿAli and Fayṣal, by the use of guileful stratagems, succeeded in slipping away from Medina with the volunteers and began to raise the tribes of the district.[111] At the same time ʿAbdullāh was at al-Ṭāʾif covertly preparing the tribes for the rebellion, under the suspicious eyes of the Turkish governor and his troops.[112]

After the Hashimites had completed their hasty preparations and had ascertained that there was no possibility of an agreement with the Turks, the Arab Revolt was begun. On the morning of June 2 Fayṣal, before leaving Medina, had written a letter to Fakhri in which he said that because of the hostility of the government, he and ʿAli were returning to Mecca; Fayṣal sent this letter to Fakhri together with two enciphered telegrams from Ḥusayn to Jemal and to the Grand Vizier. In these telegrams Ḥusayn informed the Ottoman authorities that he could not participate in the expedition against the canal until the conditions that he had earlier laid down were met.[113] On June 9, 1916, Fayṣal and ʿAli, having received no reply from the Turks, cut the railroad near Medina. On the following morning, June 10, 1916, Arab forces attacked the Turks in the cities of the Hijaz. In Mecca, the Amir Ḥusayn proclaimed the beginning of the Arab Revolt.[114]

The conditions created by World War I were decisive in leading Ḥusayn to revolt. The conflict between Ḥusayn and the Unionists probably could only have been settled by force, yet even in July, 1914, Ḥusayn still preferred compromise with the government to the use of force. The extremely cautious policy followed by Ḥusayn from the latter part of 1914 up to June, 1916, indicates that Ḥusayn was most reluctant to revolt under any conditions. The entry of the Ottoman Empire in the war, however, made some decision necessary. To have entered the

111. Djemal, p. 224; Saʿīd, I, 116–117, 145.

112. ʿAbdullāh, pp. 111–114; Saʿīd, I, 146.

113. Djemal, pp. 224–225. Jemal also mentions an apologetic wire from Fayṣal, but he does not include it among those sent by Fakhri.

114. ʿAbdullāh, pp. 107–108, 114–116; Saʿīd, I, 117, 145–147. According to ʿAbdullāh, before cutting the railroad on June 9 Fayṣal sent a final wire to Jemal in which he stated that unless the conditions previously laid down by Ḥusayn were met, the Arabs and Turks would be in a state of war.

war at once in accordance with the plans outlined by Enver would have meant weakening the Hashimite position vis-à-vis the Turks and, at the same time, the subjection of the Hijaz to British pressure and even occupation. To have resisted the Turks at once might have resulted in the subjugation of the Hijaz by Turkish troops, although it seems doubtful that the Turks had the necessary troops to spare. A policy of complete inaction was dangerous, both because of the real pressures and threats from the British and the Turks, and because of the probability that, even if Ḥusayn succeeded in remaining inactive until the end of the war, the victors, whoever they might be, would be able to do as they wished in the Hijaz. Ḥusayn was enabled to take a strong position toward the Ottoman government by the arrangements with the Arabs societies and with the British. His discovery of Turkish plans to depose him impelled him to take action. But even so, Ḥusayn used his increased strength in an unsuccessful effort to come to an understanding with the Ottoman government.

III

Ḥusayn rose against his government only when that government refused, in the spring of 1916, to guarantee his Amirate in the Hijaz. The Sharif's negotiations with the British undoubtedly raised prospects of something far greater than an autonomous Amirate of Mecca, but it seems unwarranted to argue, as Elie Kedourie (*England and the Middle East,* pp. 52–57) has done, that the Sharif revolted as a result of an ambition for the universal caliphate which was aroused by Kitchener's message. For Ḥusayn, whatever he may have thought his new prospects were, was still willing to settle with the Ottomans for as little as the achievement of his pre-war aims, i.e., the guarantee of a hereditary autonomous amirate in Arabia. The caliphate, moreover, was not the only prospect raised by Ḥusayn's negotiations. The Arab nationalists approached Ḥusayn contemporaneously with Kitchener, and from them the Sharif received no hint of any office other than Arab kingship, or perhaps "spokesmanship." The problem remains, then, of defining the Sharif's conception of his new prospects.

Kitchener's "hint of the caliphate" was not received by a man who lacked opinions concerning the nature and worth of the office. At that time Ḥusayn's views were those of standard Sunnite Islam. The caliphate, in the sense of the sole legitimate monarchy which embraced all the Moslems of the world (i.e., the "classical" or the "universal" caliphate), had become extinct at a very early time. It was succeeded by a series of temporal sovereignties which, if they enforced the holy law, were deserving of the appellation "caliphate" (Arabic *khilāfah*). These temporal sovereignties, or caliphates, were by no means to be thought of as the sole legitimate state of all Moslems, and their monarchs were not to be regarded as "caliphs" (Arabic *khalīfah*); in fact, there might be more than one such caliphate in existence at any one time. Such a caliphate was the Ottoman state.[115]

Ḥusayn's attitude toward the caliphate question as it operated in Ottoman and European imperialist politics in modern times was completely in keeping with his orthodoxy. Any idea of resurrecting the universal caliphate was, as he told Lawrence on July 28, 1917, "not only grammatically absurd but blasphemous." Accordingly, "he could neither acknowledge another's Khalifate, assume one himself, or admit the existence of the theory." Although Ḥusayn regarded any pretension to the universal caliphate by a Moslem leader as an absurdity to most Moslems and therefore useless for dealing with them, he realized that European imperialists who did not correctly comprehend the meaning of the term "caliphate" attributed considerable importance to it. Accordingly, he thought, a Moslem ruler could use the caliphate to advantage in his relations with Europeans. "The idea of a Moslem Khalifate was, said the Sherif,

115. This theory is reflected in the proclamations which Ḥusayn issued in order to justify his actions: see below, pp. 81–83. See also Lawrence, pp. 116–119. The general lack of knowledge concerning the caliphate among Europeans at the time is reflected in the fact that Lawrence (p. 117) calls Ḥusayn's view of the caliphate the "simple Shia one."

suggested to Abdul Hamid by the British, and exploited by him as a stick to beat us [the British] with." [116]

Kitchener's suggestion of an Arab caliphate created an opportunity for Ḥusayn. He took advantage of it when he replied to the British government, in the person of Sir Henry McMahon, on July 14, 1915. The Sharif was primarily concerned with obtaining a British promise of independence for the Arabs within the frontiers demanded by the Arab nationalists, which he very carefully defined. At the end of this request, he added the words, "England to approve of the proclamation of an Arab Khalifate of Islam." [117] The inclusion of this demand probably was intended to induce England to give a formal commitment, already informally given by Kitchener, which would be a useful weapon in the Sharif's further negotiations with the English, even though it would be of no import in his relations with Moslems.

It is reasonably clear that Ḥusayn attached no great intrinsic value to the caliphate which Kitchener had conjured up. McMahon in his reply on August 30, after quoting Kitchener's remarks about the caliphate, reasserted once more his government's willingness to see the caliphate return to the hands of an Arab. On the other hand, Sir Henry thought it premature to discuss limits and boundaries.[118] This was not what Ḥusayn had had in mind. He devoted two-thirds of his reply, sent on September 9, to protesting McMahon's unwillingness to discuss frontiers. He reiterated again and again the idea that the boundaries which he had demanded were those inhabited by the Arabs and those which his people considered necessary for their existence. Into one such statement, the Amir inserted a reference to the caliphate:

> For the aim, honorable Minister, in truth is the establishment of a basis which guarantees the essential sources of life in the future.

116. *Ibid.*, p. 117.

117. Cmd. 5957, p. 3. The Arabic text probably reads "an Arab caliphate over the Moslems"; see the unofficial Arabic text in Saʿīd, I, 131, and cf. Rossi, p. 21.

118. Cmd. 5957, pp. 4–5.

Besides this, the Arabs have not demanded—in those boundaries—regions inhabited by a foreign people. Nay, [anything else] would signify no more than meaningless words and titles.

As to the caliphate, may God approve of it and men be pleased with it.[119]

To McMahon's approval of an Arab caliphate and refusal to discuss boundaries, the Sharif replies that the Arabs desire the boundaries necessary to their existence and inhabited by Arabs rather than "meaningless words and titles." Obviously, he sets no great store by the caliphate promised by McMahon, which he all but puts in the category of "meaningless words and titles." In the Amir's opinion the caliphate might be left to God and the Moslems, but allies for war should reach agreement on limits and boundaries.

So far as is known, Ḥusayn was to bring up the caliphate in his negotiations with the British on only one more occasion. In November, 1916, the Amir took the title, "the king of the Arab country." The British were displeased and made strong protests. Ḥusayn then claimed that, as the British government had wished to bestow the caliphate upon him, it had no reason for objecting to his assumption of the lesser title. Such was the argument which on December 25, 1916, he instructed his agent in Cairo to present to the British:

First, present my compliments to any of his Majesty's agents who may discuss our new title and remind him of their investment of me with the title of "Arab caliphate" at the beginning of our negotiations concerning the rising and how you communicated to us in Ramaḍān their wish to bestow upon us the title "Sultan of the Arabs". . . . [Point out to them] the significance of these things now for our title, which we restricted to "the Arab country," as a result of their authorization and ap-

119. Official English translation in *ibid.*, pp. 5–7. The quotation is from the unofficial Arabic text in Saʿīd, I, 134, and Rossi, p. 25. The rendering of this passage in the official English translation (Cmd. 5957, p. 6) is obviously a mistranslation. A careful comparison of the unofficial Arabic text with the official English text and with the suggested changes of the Anglo-Arab committee on the Ḥusayn-McMahon correspondence shows that the unofficial Arabic text must be very close to the official Arabic, which is inaccessible.

proval for us of the titles "Arab caliphate" and "Sultan of the Arabs," which inherently are more extensive in authority. . . .[120]

Ḥusayn had already used the argument with Storrs during a conversation in Jidda on December 12, 1916. When Storrs strongly protested Ḥusayn's assumption of kingship, the latter replied "that as he had already been officially addressed by the Residency as Khalifa (*a title to which he did not aspire*) he had considered that, the greater including the less, it was superfluous to apprise us of his resolution." [121]

Ḥusayn thus showed no great concern with the caliphate during his negotiations with the British. Did he, however, attempt to obtain the caliphate from the Turks? Certainly not in the course of his protracted negotiations with the Turks in 1915–1916. On the other hand, toward the end of the war further negotiations between the Turks and Ḥusayn took place, not directly, but through Fayṣal, and a passage in a letter from Franz von Papen to the German ambassador in Constantinople, Count Bernstorff, dated May 24, 1918, mentions the caliphate:

> Djemal Pasha, my Army Commander, like Tassim Bey, is convinced that an understanding could be reached even without a settlement of the Caliphate question. It would be enough to provide the Sherif with an autonomous position in Mecca and Medina.[122]

This passage obviously could mean that in the course of negotiations Ḥusayn had demanded the caliphate from the Turks. Yet when Papen wrote on May 24, neither he nor the Turks seem to have received any hint of Ḥusayn's terms. On July 18 Papen again wrote to Bernstorff, "We can at any rate report good progress in our affair, as negotiations have actually been proposed by our opponents. It will now be possible to discover what their demands will be. . . ." [123] Papen's letter on May 24

120. Saʿīd, I, 296; cf. Kedourie, p. 55.

121. Storrs, p. 200 (itailcs added).

122. Count Bernstorff, *The Memoirs of Count Bernstorff*, trans. Eric Sutton (London and Toronto: William Heinemann Ltd., 1936), p. 179. Cf. Kedourie, p. 56.

123. Bernstorff, p. 181. For the Arab account and documents, see Saʿīd, I, 311–314, which indicates that the negotiations, arranged with Fayṣal at the instance of Jemal, did not begin until late July or August.

is best explained by the fact that Jemal and the Germans wished to conciliate the Arabs, but the Turkish government was opposed; this letter most likely reflects no more than an exchange of views among German and Turkish officials regarding possible terms to be offered to Ḥusayn, not comments on any proposal by Ḥusayn. The Germans and the Unionist Turks, understanding orthodox Sunnite thought very imperfectly, like the British officials, thought the caliphate to be a great stake in the struggle; their views must not be ascribed to Ḥusayn. It is significant that on May 24 Papen wrote that Jemal believed that Ḥusayn would be satisfied "with an autonomous position in Mecca and Medina" and "without a settlement of the Caliphate question." Jemal had good grounds for this belief, for as has been seen, this was exactly what Ḥusayn had sought from the Turks in the long negotiations whose failure led to the Arab Revolt.

The examination of all the cases in which the caliphate was, or might have been, a part of Ḥusayn's negotiations has shown that the Sharif made no use of the question except as a bargaining point. In contrast, he attempted again and again to obtain British recognition and support for himself as the head of an Arab kingdom.

Ḥusayn sought, in his own way, to gain a British commitment to recognize Arab sovereignty in the territories which the Arab nationalists had demanded. At the close of his correspondence with McMahon he had accepted the exclusion of Turkish Cilicia, but he had refused to renounce the Arab claim to the other territories in question, even though he was willing to postpone discussion of French demands until the end of the war. He reasserted his and the Arab claims with full vigor in a memorandum which he sent the British on August 28, 1918. According to Ḥusayn, the British had agreed to the establishment of an independent Arab state within the frontiers which he had demanded in his first letter to McMahon, saving only Cilicia.[124]

124. For the memorandum, see Wahbah, pp. 318–320, 161; Great Britain, Foreign Office, *Documents on British Foreign Policy*, ed. E. L. Woodward

Ḥusayn's insistence on Arab independence was not insistence on the exclusion of foreign influence. He had accepted McMahon's provision that Basra and Baghdad should be subject to special arrangements which guaranteed British interests. He decided to postpone discussion of French claims until the end of the war, and in pursuance of this decision he reprimanded his agent in Cairo for agitating against the French. At the same time, however, in May, 1917, when the British and French informed him of at least the general terms of the Sykes-Picot agreement, he made his goal clear. The Sharif was willing to concede the French a special position in certain territories in northwestern Syria, provided the French, in turn, recognized the territories as being part of a sovereign Arab state.[125]

The Sharif thus sought to obtain British, and then French, recognition of Arab independence in the territories claimed by the nationalist societies as Arab. At the same time he tried to win British recognition and support of his kingship over this independent country. He took the first step in November, 1916, by proclaiming himself "king of the Arab country."[126] Even though the title was ambiguous, perhaps deliberately, and might have signified no more than "king of Arabia," the British

and Rohan Butler, 1st ser., I (London: H.M.S.O., 1952), 414, 418–419; Amīn Riḥāni (Ameen Rihani), *Mulūk al-ʿarab* [*The Kings of the Arabs*], 2nd ed. (Beirut: Yūsuf Ṣādir, 1929), I, 60–61 (Englished as *Around the Coasts of Arabia* [London: Constable and Co., 1930], pp. 111–112; the English version of the document is neither complete nor exact). Kampffmeyer in *Mit. Sem. Or. Sp.*, XXVI–XXVII (1920), 128–130.

125. For Ḥusayn's attitude toward and negotiations concerning French claims after the beginning of the revolt, see Kedourie, pp. 39–40, 97, 112, and compare his use of this material. I agree with Kedourie's conclusion to the problem which he set for himself, i.e., that the Sykes-Picot agreement was not contrary to McMahon's commitments to Ḥusayn and that its terms were not kept secret from the Sharif, or from other interested Arabs. I cannot consider adequate Kedourie's treatment of Ḥusayn's attitude, i.e., that he made no "protest" of the agreement. This only partially describes Ḥusayn's activities; it ignores the fact that Ḥusayn, when negotiating with McMahon, had protested and never accepted the exclusion of the territories, and passes over the fact that when Sykes and Picot informed him of the agreement, he took advantage of the occasion to try to obtain French recognition of Arab sovereignty in the territories.

126. Text of proclamation, *RMM*, XLVII (1921), 24–27.

were disturbed by it.[127] A controversy ensued, the English protesting, the Sharif insisting on, the new title. In the end, agreement was reached on the title, "king of the Hijaz."[128] Even though Ḥusayn replaced his grander title with the simpler one, he retained his wider ambition. Time and again he expressed to British representatives the view which was succinctly summarized by one of them, Commander D. G. Hogarth: "It is obvious that the King regards Arab Unity as synonymous with his own Kingship. . . ."[129]

Ḥusayn's change of ambition can hardly have been due to conversion to the theory of Arabism. As he had paid no attention to the Arab nationalists before the coming of the war, so he paid little attention to their theories after he rose against his sovereign. His proclamations to the Moslems and to his countrymen were devoid of Arab nationalist ideas. He even rejected the attempt of a true Arab nationalist ideologue to rewrite his first proclamation. The revolt was justified on the basis of traditional Moslem political theories. When he assumed his kingship, he did use the terms "national" and "patriotic" duties, but they were given legal validity by traditional Moslem arguments, and their territorial application was left undefined.

There was more in Ḥusayn's change of goal, however, than mere expansion of ambition. In a sense his new policy was a continuation of his old. A fundamental aim of each was the assurance of the Amir of Mecca's supremacy over his immediate Arab neighbors. This goal, indeed, appears to have been the

127. The country was designated by *al-bilād al-ʿarabīyah,* which might be, as it usually has been, translated as "the Arab countries," but by 1916 *bilād* had generally come to mean "a country." Morphologically, the word is a plural of *balad/baladah,* "town, district, region," but even in classical literature it had the meaning of "a country": E. W. Lane, *An Arabic-English Lexicon,* I, (London, 1863), s.v. "balada: baladun." For pre-1916 examples of its use as "a country," see Muḥammad ʿAbduh, *al-Islām wa al-naṣrānīyah maʿ al-ʿilm wa al-madanīyah,* ed. Muḥammad Rashīd Riḍa, 7th ed. (Cairo: al-Manār, 1367H/1947–1948), pp. 134, 210. The phrase is very close to *bilād al-ʿarab,* "the land of the Arabs," which was used in McMahon's first letter to Ḥusayn as a translation of "Arabia" (for the Arabic text, see Wahbah, p. 154).

128. Storrs, pp. 192, 199–200; Saʿīd, I, 293–308.

129. Cf. Kedourie, p. 56, n. 2.

one uppermost in the Sharif's mind after his break with the Ottomans. He could agree to British, and even French, privilege within the Arab state. He could even leave in abeyance the French claim to exclude part of Syria from the Arab state. He could not, however, desist from his efforts to gain hegemony over his Arab neighbors, and so, at the very time he was ordering his agent in Cairo to stop agitating the Syrian question, he himself was busy raising the question of sovereignty in Arabia.

The Sharif was obsessed with the need to acquire strong support against his Arab neighbors. He was concerned about al-Idrīsi, but most of his attention was directed to the great threat, as he saw it, of ʿAbd al-ʿAzīz ibn-Suʿūd and the fanatical Wahhabis.[130] His assumption of the title "king of the Arab country" was an attempt to gain British recognition of his sovereignty over his rivals. Although he gave in to the British in the matter of his title, soon thereafter (on March 4, 1917) he made a formal protest against England's conclusion of treaties with al-Idrīsi and Ibn-Suʿūd. Such action, said the Sharif, was contrary to Britain's understanding with him and also would hinder the realization of the "high purpose" for the sake of which he had launched his movement.[131]

What Ḥusayn desired above all was British assistance in bringing and keeping his rival amirs under his suzerainty. When he summarized his claims on the British in August, 1918, he was not satisfied with asserting that England had recognized the independence of the Arab territories. Instead, he began his summary of British commitments with, "(1) Great Britain undertakes the formation of an Arab government which is independent in every meaning of the term . . ." in these territories. The Sharif then continued,

> This government undertakes to respect the treaties and agreements which Great Britain has concluded with any Arab within these boundaries, so that it will occupy its place in respecting

130. Ḥusayn and his sons expressed their concern with al-Idrīsi and their obsession with Ibn-Suʿūd to British officials from the beginning to the end of 1917; see Lawrence, pp. 61, 67, 96–97, 115–116, 124–126, 145–147, 153–154.

131. Cf. Kedourie, pp. 55–56.

> and protecting the rights of those agreements with them, whether they be an amir or an individual.
>
> (2) Great Britain undertakes to preserve and protect this government from any intervention in any form in its internal affairs, and [to protect] the security of its land and sea frontiers from any aggression, so that in the event that an internal rising occurs as a result of some enemy intrigue, or of the envy of some of the amirs, the aforementioned government will assist materially and morally to defeat that rising until it is defeated. This aid in the case of internal risings and revolts is to be for a limited time, i.e., until the afore-mentioned Arab government had completed its material organization.[132]

Ḥusayn's policy during the revolt was a natural extension of his previous one. His primary goal throughout was to secure his position in the Hijaz and to extend his authority over his neighbors, or at least to keep them in check. Before the war the Sharif had been able to use Ottoman material resources and legal claims in furtherance of this aim. However, his revolt made it necessary for him to find a substitute for the Ottoman government. The British could supply the material resources, but they could not supply the legal claims. Ḥusayn therefore had to adopt the goal of the nationalist societies and to seek kingship over the Arab nation in order to acquire a defensible claim to supremacy over his dangerous neighbors.

IV

Hashimite policy was determined by the political realities which confronted the Amir of Mecca. Leaving aside the question of Ḥusayn's ambitions—and he, like his contemporary peers, probably was bent on self-aggrandizement—his position as Amir of Mecca was threatened by many forces. The Unionists, with their determination to create a centralized government, were the most obvious threat to Ḥusayn's desire to maintain his traditional authority and to make it hereditary in his

132. Wahbah, p. 161. The Sharif's concern with the rival amirs is also indicated by the "project of Arab union" which he drew up on 18 Ṣafar 1337H/Nov. 23, 1918; Wahbah, pp. 196, 316.

family. There were also Ḥusayn's rival relatives, the other ambitious sharifs, such as ʿAli Ḥaydar, always ready to seize the opportunity which a misstep by the Amir might create. In themselves, they were not so important, perhaps; but they could intrigue at Constantinople, and they could plot with the tribesmen of the Hijaz. The latter, always resentful of any authority, could be kept subject to the Amir's law and order only by constant vigilance and superior force. Extending to the tribal country along the limits of the Hijaz was the influence of Ḥusayn's rival potentates, al-Idrīsi and Ibn-Suʿūd, whose political power, reinforced by crusading religious zeal, posed a clear danger to Ḥusayn.

In the face of such formidable opponents in Arabia, Ottomanism was an advantageous policy for the Amir of Mecca. In respect of the tribesmen and the rival amirs, Ottoman interests coincided with Ḥusayn's. As the Ottoman government regarded the protection of the pilgrimage and of the holy cities as a great source of prestige, the restraint of the tribes, who were the principal threats to the security of the pilgrimage, took precedence over the restraint of the Amir of Mecca. Ḥusayn, for his part, could only view with sympathy the Ottoman ambition to extend the Sultan's suzerainty to Ibn-Suʿūd and al-Idrīsi. The Ottoman government was therefore a valuable source of material assistance to Ḥusayn's endeavors to keep his rivals in check, and even when Ottoman troops and money were not provided the Amir could enjoy the legal sanction of acting as the Sultan's loyal vassal.

Ḥusayn's Ottomanism was meaningful to him only so long as the Sultan's government permitted him to exercise a degree of authority and autonomy. The Amir was allowed to exercise the required degree of authority because of the internal conditions and foreign problems of the Ottoman Empire. Young Turk policy aimed at eradicating autonomous administrations like the Amirate of Mecca, but Young Turk capabilities were not equal to the task they had set for themselves. Their centralizing tendencies and foreign entanglements led the Ottoman government to disperse its military strength too thinly over a wide area. Their policy redoubled their troubles in the Hijaz, since such modernizing measures as the extension of the railway and the prohibition of slavery created solid tribal support for the Amir by endangering tribal interests in a way in which his heavy hand never did. Thus, while Young Turk policy threatened Ḥusayn, the threat remained a distant one, a potentiality rather than an actuality, unlike the more pressing danger in Arabia.

The ability of the Unionists to execute their designs against the will of the Amir of Mecca was also limited by the political situation within the purely Turkish element of the Empire. The Young Turks were subtly but effectively opposed by more conservative elements. Ḥusayn therefore was able to rely on the assistance of these "Old Turks" in restraining Unionist action in the Hijaz, and he might even look forward to the displacement of the Unionists by these more congenial conservatives.

Ḥusayn's policy of Ottomanism was consistent. He cooperated with the Ottoman government in controlling his Arabian rivals and with the "Old Turks" against the Young Turks. He defined his policy ideologically as the struggle of traditional Moslem Ottomanism with both Arab factionalism and schism and atheistic Young Turk modernism. There is no reason to doubt Ḥusayn's oft-proclaimed zeal for Islam and for Ottomanism. The ideological position which he professed was in harmony with his political interests; therefore he, like most of his contemporary coreligionists, could be sincerely firm in his conviction that a truly Moslem Ottoman state was the best hope of defending Islam from the political and intellectual encroachments of Christian Europe. His age, it should be remembered, was one of Pan-Islamic revival in which even the ideologues of Arabism justified their doctrines on the ground that an Arab revival was the necessary first condition of Moslem revival.

Ottomanism held a risk for Ḥusayn as long as the Young Turks were the preeminent element within the Turkish state. This risk was increased by the Ottoman demand for Hashimite participation in World War I. The coming of the war accordingly brought the conflict between the Young Turks and Ḥusayn to a new crisis. Nevertheless, an open rupture might well have been avoided, since Turkish preoccupations outside Arabia allowed Ḥusayn to pursue a policy of delay. To judge from his action in the first years of the war, the Amir favored delay, but a new force, the British Empire, extended its influence to the Hijaz. Caught as he was between the British and the Ottomans, Ḥusayn was compelled to decide. Of special weight was the consideration, advanced by ʿAbdullāh, that even if the Hashimites succeeded in remaining neutral, the victors, whoever they might be, would be able to impose their will in the Hijaz. The war also created a new opportunity. For the first time Ḥusayn possessed in the British an ally which might enable him to rid himself of the Unionists and also provide the assistance necessary to control the Hijaz and its neighbors. Under these conditions Arabism, supported by the British and with Ḥusayn as its acknowledged leader, was a practical alternative to Ottomanism.

Spurred by new pressures and lured by new prospects, Ḥusayn brought matters to a head. In choosing between Ottomanism and Arabism political realities, not abstract considerations, were paramount. The military potential of Arabism can have played no significant role in Ḥusayn's decision, since he revolted at a time when nationalist military capability had been reduced to such an extent that the man in closest contact with the nationalists, Fayṣal, was opposed to rebellion. In fact, the Amir appears still to have preferred Ottomanism, since he used his new strength in an effort to reach agreement with the Turks and revolted only when this effort failed. British military reverses in Iraq and on the Dardanelles perhaps influenced him more than did the relative attractions of Arabism and Ottomanism. Certainly in the center of his attention was the problem of his immediate neighbors. His final approach to the Turks and his revolt against them had one objective in common. In his last attempt to reach agreement with the Young Turks, Ḥusayn promised to join in the war against the British after "he had put an end to any unfriendly chieftaincy to the east of the Hijaz." After he revolted, the Amir set about using his new allies as weapons which would enable him to secure predominance over his Arab rivals.

The Arab Revolt was a significant step in the growth of nationalism among the Arabs, the most important such step before 1918, even though Arab nationalism as an independent force was of minor significance to the origin of the Arab Revolt. The Sharif Ḥusayn adopted and put into effect the political program of Arabism, despite his failure to be attracted to its ideology. The origin of the Revolt provides a case study in the spread and growth of Arab nationalism. In this case neither the appeal of the idea of nationalism nor class change and conflict had much influence. Ḥusayn's policy was designed to meet the requirements of conflict, but the conflict in question was one between rival elements within the ruling class of Ottoman and Arabian society. Ottomanism was the adopted policy until the war both compelled and encouraged the Amir to rid Ottomanism of its one serious defect, Unionist centralism, or else to abandon it. Then Arabism was adopted, but Arabism to the Hashimites of Mecca was meaningless unless it served the same purposes which Ottomanism previously had. Ranking high among these goals was the assurance of the Amir of Mecca's position against the threats of all his rivals, Arab as well as Turk.

That stage in the growth of Arab nationalism known as the Arab Revolt was produced by the effect of World War I on the various political forces which met in the Hijaz. The Hashimite conversion to Arabism, then, is an instance of the adoption of a new ideology by one element of the ruling class as an instrument of conflict with its rivals within that class.

TWO

'Abdullāh ibn-al-Ḥusayn, Lord Kitchener, and the Idea of an Arab Revolt

By July, 1914, ʿAbdullāh, the second son of the Sharif Ḥusayn, Amir of Mecca, had come to believe that a complete break with Turkey was necessary and feasible. He argued the matter with his father and brothers in family councils, strongly advancing the view that they must break with the Turks. He further argued that the Arabs of the Hijaz, with the help of the Arab-manned military units of Syria and Iraq and with the diplomatic support of Great Britain and perhaps other interested Powers, could defeat Turkish efforts to control the Hijaz. In particular, he believed that by seizing the pilgrims the Sharif and Amir of Mecca could win the diplomatic assistance of Europe. The interested governments (Holland, France, and especially Great Britain), so ʿAbdullāh's argument ran, would make representations for the release of the imprisoned pilgrims to the Porte, and after the failure of their efforts in Constantinople they would be forced to approach Ḥusayn directly. The latter would be eager to grant the wishes of the Powers in return for "a promise [from the Powers] of immunity from Turkey in the future." Ḥusayn's other sons, Fayṣal and ʿAli, opposed the scheme on the grounds that Turkey was too strong.[1]

No contemporary documentary evidence is available regarding the stages by which, and the time when, ʿAbdullāh

1. Information given to T. E. Lawrence by Fayṣal in December, 1916, and by ʿAbdullāh in April, 1917; T. E. Lawrence, *Secret Despatches from Arabia*, ed. A. W. Lawrence (London: Golden Cockerel Press, n.d.), pp. 52, 96 (quotation, from ʿAbdullāh); and by Fayṣal in the spring of 1933, Mrs. Steuart Erskine, *King Faisal of Iraq* (London: Hutchinson and Co., 1933), pp. 38, 40–41. See also above, pp. 30–31.

developed his views, or the circumstances surrounding this development. It can be said with confidence only that such were his opinions and recommendations by July, 1914, but the fact that the plan depends heavily upon the support of the Arab troops in the Turkish armies in Syria and Iraq and upon the diplomatic support of the Powers, especially England, indicates that ʿAbdullāh had been influenced to an important degree by contact with Arab nationalists and British officials. The fact that Ḥusayn intended to achieve as much independence of Turkish control as possible and worked to achieve it from the day he took office, and the fact that the Turkish government worked to achieve complete integration of the Hijaz into the Turkish provincial system, meant that sooner or later the idea of a break between Ḥusayn and the Turks would occur to the Hashimites. But this question nevertheless remains: In the development of the idea of independence in the mind of ʿAbdullāh, what was the exact role of contacts between ʿAbdullāh and Arab nationalists on the one hand and British officials in Egypt on the other?

Perhaps the most generally accepted answer to the problem is that contact with the Arab nationalists was decisive, that ʿAbdullāh was an Arab nationalist, a member of one of the secret Arab political societies, and that at a relatively early date (long before 1914) he was convinced of the desirability of his family's leading the Arabs to national independence and was actively urging his father to take the lead. Further, motivated by the desire for national independence, and having decided upon breaking with the Turks, the Amir sought out British officials in Egypt for the purpose of sounding out their probable attitude toward an Arab movement against the Ottoman state.[2] But in his memoirs ʿAbdullāh does little more than allude to the Arab nationalists, and he conspicuously does not mention having been a member of an Arab secret society. His emphasis is overwhelmingly upon the loyalty of his family to the Ottoman state, as long as it operated upon its Islamic basis

2. See especially George Antonius, *The Arab Awakening* (Philadelphia: Lippincott, 1939), *passim*, esp. pp. 126–128.

(unlike Antonius, ʿAbdullāh has little but good to say of ʿAbd al-Ḥamīd II), and upon the Hashimite desire to avoid a break with the Ottoman state. He stresses the patience of his family in the face of the continuous encroachment by the Unionist governments on the traditional Islamic constitution of the Empire, including the special position of the Hijaz and of the Sharif and Amir of Mecca. Finally ʿAbdullāh represents Lord Kitchener as having taken the initiative in opening conversations with him and as having indicated Britain's interest in Ḥusayn's continued occupancy of the position of Amir of Mecca, even in the face of Turkish displeasure.[3]

ʿAbdullāh did become a convert to Arabism before July, 1914. He first became aware of the Arab nationalist movement when he accompanied the Syrian pilgrimage on its return to Damascus in 1909 and was the guest of ʿAṭa al-Bakri.[4] In Constantinople as a deputy ʿAbdullāh had frequent contacts with Arab leaders, who pleaded with him to persuade his father to lead the Arabs to national independence.[5] Early in 1911 at least thirty-five Arab deputies in the Ottoman Parliament sent Ḥusayn, apparently by way of ʿAbdullāh, a written appeal to lead the Arabs in rising against the Turks. The Arab deputies also declared their confirmation of Ḥusayn's government of Mecca and his religious supremacy over all the Arab countries.[6] However, ʿAbdullāh was still strongly attached to the Ottoman Empire as the center of the Moslem world, and to Constantinople as the place where the brotherhood of Islam was everywhere exemplified. At the same time, the Turkish nationalism of the Young Turks, whom ʿAbdullāh met in Constantinople, and their disdain for the Arabs ran counter to his concept of the

3. ʿAbdullāh ibn-al-Ḥusayn, *Mudhakkarāti* [*My Memoirs*], 1st ed. (Jerusalem: Maṭbaʿah Bayt al-Muqaddas, 1945), *passim;* the second edition has not been available. The translation by G. Khuri, *Memoirs of King Abdullah of Transjordan*, ed. Philip P. Graves (New York: Philosophical Library, 1950) is incomplete and unreliable; see the reviews, *American Historical Review*, LVI (1951), 980; *The Middle East Journal*, V (1951), 251–252; *The Muslim World*, LII (1952), 76–77.

4. ʿAbdullāh, pp. 40–42.

5. Erskine, pp. 40–41.

6. K. T. Khairallah, *Les Régions arabes libéerés* (Paris: Leroux, 1919), pp. 32–33. See also above, pp. 10–11.

Islamic bond and to his pride in the Arabs as the founders of Islam.[7] ʿAbdullāh resolved the conflict in favor of Arabism when, at some time before the outbreak of war in 1914, during one of his visits to Cairo Muḥammad Rashīd Riḍa met with him and obtained his adherence to one of the Arab secret societies, the Society of the Arab League. This society had been founded after 1910 by Rashīd Riḍa for the purpose of bringing the Arabs together on the basis of Islam. In order to achieve its goal, it undertook the task of including the independent amirs of Arabia in its membership.[8]

Although ʿAbdullāh became an adherent of the Arab nationalist movement, it seems unlikely that he did so before the first half of 1914. ʿAbdullāh undoubtedly minimizes his contact with the nationalists to too great an extent, but all other sources except Antonius slight the role of the nationalists and speak of ʿAbdullāh's joining an Arab society only as before July, 1914, and place his conversion to revolt just before the outbreak of war.[9] Furthermore, what is known of the activities of Muḥammad Rashīd Riḍa and his associates seems to support this view. They did not begin their efforts with the Arabian rulers until the spring of 1912, when Rashīd Riḍa made a trip to India and on his return journey approached the princes of the Persian Gulf region and sent envoys to Ibn-Suʿūd and to Sayyid al-Idrīsi. The Imam of the Yaman was not approached at this time and apparently was not approached until early 1914. The available evidence is completely silent about any negotiations with Ḥusayn or his sons. In addition, one member of the group believed on April 24, 1913, that they should provoke al-Idrīsi to march on Mecca; this fact implies that Ḥusayn was then regarded as no friend of the Arab movement.[10] At the turn of 1914, contemporary observers regarded

7. ʿAbdullāh, pp. 23–24.

8. Amīn Saʿīd, *al-Thawrah al-ʿarabīyah al-kubra* [*The Great Arab Revolt*], 3 vols. (Cairo: ʿĪsa al-Bābi al-Ḥalabi, [1934?]), I, 49–50.

9. E.g., Saʿīd and Lawrence, all based on information from ʿAbdullāh and Fayṣal which is older than the interviews of Antonius.

10. See the testimony of the Arab nationalists arrested by the Turks and the documents published in Turkey, Fourth Army, *La Vérité sur la question syrienne* (Stamboul: Tanine, 1916), pp. 102–103. The letter of Fuʾād al-

the Hijaz as the only Arab area of the Empire loyal to the Sultan and Ḥusayn, at least, as completely pro-Turkish. Although conflict between Ḥusayn and the Young Turks had been frequent after 1909, until 1914 Ḥusayn had had his way in the Hijaz and had reduced the Ottoman governor to insignificance.[11] But at the beginning of 1914 the Turks sent out a new governor, who was also the military commander, with reinforcements and orders to apply the new provincial law to the Hijaz and to extend the railroad. The Amir of Mecca and the people of the Hijaz opposed this new Turkish policy, and relations between the government and the Amir of Mecca had become strained. It was during this crisis that ʿAbdullāh, en route to Constantinople to attend Parliament, stopped in Cairo early in 1914.[12] It seems most likely that ʿAbdullāh's decision to abandon Ottomanism completely was made as a result of this crisis.

The exact nature and course of ʿAbdullāh's contacts with British officials are extremely difficult to determine from the available evidence. Extant contemporary documentary evidence is limited to certain communications by Kitchener about a meeting with ʿAbdullāh on February 5, 1914, and it seems unlikely that additional contemporary records will be found.[13] All other information regarding such conversations is memoir

Khaṭīb reproduced as Facsimile No. 31, from which an extract is quoted in translation on p. 103, is dated April 24, 1913. Muḥammad Rashīd Riḍa left Cairo for India about March 3, 1912; see *Revue du Monde Musulman,* XIX (1912), 287–288.

11. "X", "Les courants politiques dans le milieu arabe", *RMM,* XXV (1913), 279–280; Memorandum of Sir Louis Mallet (dated Mar. 18, 1914), Great Britain, Foreign Office, *British Documents on the Origin of the War,* ed. G. P. Gooch and Harold Temperly, X, pt. 2 (London: H.M.S.O., 1938), 828–829; compare the judgment of the Saudi Arabian diplomat Ḥāfiẓ Wahbah, *Jazīrah al-ʿarab fi-al-qarn al-ʿishrīn* [*The Arabian Peninsula in the Twentieth Century*], 2nd ed. (Cairo: Maṭbaʿah li-Jannah al-Taʾlīf wa al-Tarjamah wa al-Nashr, 1946), pp. 199–200. See also above, pp. 14–15.

12. ʿAbdullāh, pp. 77–80; Saʿid, I, 54–55, 125–126.

13. *Brit. Doc.*, X, pt. 2, 826–831. According to the editors a careful search of Foreign Office records was made and all relevant documents published, and Kitchener's biographer, Sir George Arthur, replied negatively to a query about the existence of additional documents about pre-war meetings between Kitchener and Arab leaders.

material written long after the event.[14] ʿAbdullāh, directly and indirectly, has left three different accounts which differ significantly from each other in detail, even though they are in general agreement.[15] Kitchener's principal communication and Storrs's account give the impression that the first meeting between ʿAbdullāh and Lord Kitchener occurred in 1914 and that ʿAbdullāh, having already decided that a break with Turkey was inevitable, sought out Lord Kitchener and felt him out about possible British support. This is the contemporary interpretation of Sir Louis Mallet.[16] However, ʿAbdullāh's story is that Lord Kitchener, whom he first met in 1912 or 1913, took the initiative and sounded him out concerning the state of relations between the Amir of Mecca and the Turkish government, thus indicating British interest and stimulating him to inquire regarding Britain's stand in the event that the Ottoman authorities should attempt to remove the Amir of Mecca. Antonius, apparently disregarding the results of his interview with ʿAbdullāh, decided in favor of the interpretation of Mallet.[17] Yet there is nothing inherently incredible in ʿAbdullāh's story, and it is made plausible by what is known of Kitchener's attitude toward British relations with Turkey during the period in which he was British Agent in Egypt.

The Hashimite Amir first met Lord Kitchener either in the spring of 1912 or at the beginning of 1913.[18] While ʿAbdullāh, en route to Constantinple,[19] was in Cairo as the guest of the

14. The account in Sir Ronald Storrs, *Memoirs* (New York: G. P. Putnam's Sons, 1937), p. 135, is based on memory; Storrs's papers were burned in 1931 (pp. vii–viii).

15. The first, as told to Amīn Saʿīd in 1933, in Saʿīd, I, 125; the second, as told to George Antonius in 1936, in *Brit. Doc.*, X, pt. 2, 831–832; the third, in ʿAbdullāh, pp. 71–74, 81. Hereafter referred to as Saʿīd, Antonius, and ʿAbdullāh respectively.

16. *Brit. Doc.*, X, pt. 2, 827, 829.

17. Antonius, *Arab Awakening*, pp. 126–128.

18. Saʿīd gives 1913, Antonius, spring of 1912 (hereafter in this article "Antonius" alone designates Antonius's notes in *Brit. Doc.*), and ʿAbdullāh dates it in the grand vizierate of Saʿīd Pasha, i.e., in the spring of 1912, but also one year before the appointment of Wahīb Pasha, i.e., at the beginning of 1913.

19. But Antonius relates that ʿAbdullāh was returning from Constantinople.

Khedive at ʿAbdīn Palace, Kitchener, accompanied by Sir Ronald Storrs, called upon him unexpectedly.[20] ʿAbdullāh did not wish to meet Kitchener, but the Khedive insisted "as if he were in previous agreement with Lord Kitchener." [21] After greetings and introductions, Kitchener said, "I have taken advantage of the opportunity of your passing through Egypt and have come to convey the gratitude of my government for what the Indian pilgrims, our subjects, have received in the way of attention of your father and his subjects during their sojourn in performance of the duty of the pilgrimage, and we are extremely happy at this change in the treatment of the pilgrims." [22] After the latter's departure, the Amir went to the Turkish commissariat and told the Turkish High Commissioner about the meeting with the resquest that he inform the Sublime Porte about it so as to avoid misunderstanding and misinterpretation.

The next morning ʿAbdullāh, having purposely picked a time at which Kitchener was certain to be absent, paid a visit to the British Residency to leave his calling card and thus satisfy the requirements of etiquette.[23] At this point the three accounts by or on the authority of ʿAbdullāh diverge strikingly. According to Saʿīd, Lord Kitchener being absent as expected, the Amir left his card and departed as planned. But according to ʿAbdullāh, Kitchener was waiting at the door of the Residency. Antonius also relates that ʿAbdullāh later met with Kitchener at the British Residency, and quotes ʿAbdullāh as saying, "Kitchener displayed a marked interest in Hijaz affairs and questioned me as to the form of its administration, the relations between Vali and Sherif, and the degree to which

20. Thus Saʿīd and Antonius; but ʿAbdullāh relates that ʿAbdullāh was with the Khedive in the Saray al-Qubbah when Kitchener arrived unexpectedly and the Khedive introduced the two men, after which ʿAbdullāh went to ʿAbdīn Palace, where, after an hour and a half, Kitchener and Storrs called upon him.

21. Saʿīd; ʿAbdullāh ascribes this to the previous meeting at the Saray al-Qubbah; Antonius does not mention it.

22. Quotation from Saʿīd; the other two versions agree, but ʿAbdullāh adds, "I request that [you] communicate to his Highness the Sharif this information and that his Majesty's Government will not be satisfied with any change there."

23. So Saʿīd and ʿAbdullāh; Antonius is silent.

the Turkish officials tried to exercise control in purely religious matters. I did not feel at liberty to answer his penetrating questions as fully as I should have liked, yet tried to give him a general idea of our fears and anxieties." ʿAbdullāh's own versions describes the conversation at the Residency in terms much closer to Antonius's account of the 1914 meeting with Kitchener; it probably is a description of the latter meeting.

ʿAbdullāh is explicit in all three versions that at some time before early 1914 Lord Kitchener called upon him and expressed the appreciation of the British government for the improvement in the conditions of the pilgrimage which had taken place since Ḥusayn became Amir of Mecca. There is evidence that as early as the spring of 1912 Kitchener was already concerned with the decay of Turkey and was beginning to believe that British interest might require Britain to support Arab separatist aspirations. In 1908 Kitchener, who had always been interested in the Eastern question, believed that in order to protect the British position in both India and Egypt England should support Turkey and assist her in reorganizing her army and thus forestall the extension to the Persian Gulf area of both German and Russian influence; but before he became British Agent in Egypt, he had seen Germany achieve predominance at Constantinople and British influence reduced to zero.[24] He regarded the collapse of the Turks in the Italo-Turkish War as complete, and the further partition of the empire as being only a matter of time. He wrote to Grey on November 3, 1912, "However much Turkey may be bolstered by the Powers, her former position in Europe and elsewhere is apparently gone. . . . I think that we must expect trouble later in other parts of the Ottoman Empire, now that the central Government has received such a severe blow." [25] Kitchener's true feelings about the matter were even stronger than he would communicate to Grey. At least as early as April, 1912, Kitchener believed that Europe could not permit an Ottoman victory over Italy, since

24. Sir George Arthur, *Life of Lord Kitchener,* 3 vols. (New York: Macmillan, 1920), II, 281–282, 306.
25. *Brit. Doc.,* IX, pt. 2 (London: H.M.S.O., 1934), 88.

such a victory by a Moslem country over a European power would galvanize the entire Moslem world and make the British position in Asia and Africa impossible. Moreover, "Ici meme on commence a etre inquiet et nerveux: il y a du malaise, et en mème temps des espoirs latents chez les arabes." [26] Kitchener thus was convinced that the Ottoman Empire could no longer maintain itself, that England could not assist the Empire to preserve itself, and that the Arabs of the Empire certainly would seek independence. Since he at the same time believed that the Arab lands were vital to the British position in Egypt and India, he was attracted to the idea of Britain's providing some measure of support to an Arab independence movement.[27]

It seems most likely that the British Agent in Egypt, expecting the Ottoman Empire to disintegrate, would have taken special efforts to sound out the attitude of so important an Arab as the son of the Sharif and Amir of Mecca. Such a move would have been in complete conformity with the general attitude of a man who spoke both Turkish and Arabic and believed that speaking the local language, i.e., speaking personally and directly with local leaders, gave him "rather a pull in seeing what was going on behind the scenes." [28] Kitchener,

26. See report on a conversation between Kitchener and M. Defrance, French ambassador to Cairo, in France, Ministère des Affaires Étrangères, Commission de publication des documents relatifs aux origines de la guerre de 1914, *Documents Diplomatiques Francais (1871–1914)*, 3rd ser. (Paris: Imprimerie Nationale, 1931), II, 445, n. 1; III, 18, n. 1.

27. Arthur, III, 153 writes: "When Turkey drew the sword there was revived in Kitchener's mind a long-cherished idea of founding an independent Arab State in Arabia and Syria." At the end of September, 1911, Kaiser William II believed (apparently on the authority of Max von Oppenheim) that Kitchener would certainly take advantage of the Italo-Turkish war to establish an Arab Caliphate under Anglo-Egyptian protection; see Germany, Auswärtige Amt, *Die Grosse Politik der europäischen Kabinette, 1871–1914,* ed. Johannes Lepsius, A. M. Bartholdy, and Friedrich Thimme, XXX, pt. 1 (Berlin: Deutsche Verlagsgesellschaft für Politik und Geschichte, 1926), 50–51; see also statement regarding Kitchener's activities in Syria, in letter from German ambassador to London dated June 2, 1913, *ibid.,* XXXVII, pt. 2 (1926), 485 (also printed in XXXVIII, 61). For Arab allegations and French fears concerning British activities among the Arabs during 1913 and 1914, see *La Vérité,* pp. 58–59, 127–129, 145–151.

28. Arthur, II, 281, n. 2; 333.

with his awareness of the great importance of Islam as a political force [29] and with his Indian background, almost certainly would have thought it worthwhile to express appreciation to the Amir of Mecca for the improved conditions enjoyed by the Indian pilgrims. British diplomatic officials in the area had in fact noticed an improvement in the public security of the Hijaz insofar as the personal safety of the Indian pilgrims was concerned as early as 1912, even though there was a deterioration in internal security at the end of this year.[30] In view of Kitchener's known opinions of the Arab-Turkish question and of his habitual diplomatic practices, then, there is no reason to discount the general outlines of ʿAbdullāh's account of his first meeting with Lord Kitchener.

A second meeting between ʿAbdullāh and Lord Kitchener took place in February, 1914, and the question of the British attitude toward a possible Arab revolt was definitely raised. Kitchener reported the matter on February 6 to Grey in a communication which began:

> The Sherif Abdullah . . . is now staying in Cairo on a short visit and called upon me yesterday.
>
> He begged me to convey to you his father's compliments, and said that affairs in the Hedjaz were not going as well as could be wished. . . .

The Amir, according to the report, went on to describe the position of the new governor, who combined civil and military functions and was not in sympathy with the people of the Hijaz, and inquired whether, if the Arabs resisted Turkish attempts to remove the Sherif, Great Britain would use good offices to prevent such a move by the Turks. If the Turks attempted to remove the Amir of Mecca, the Arabs would fight; it was to be hoped that the British would not allow reinforcements to be sent by sea against the Arabs. ʿAbdullāh closed by asking Kitchener if Grey would send the Sharif some message. Kitchener replied that such would be improbable.[31]

29. *Ibid.*, III, 153–154.
30. Memorandum by Mallet, *Brit. Doc.*, X, pt. 2, 828, 829.
31. *Brit. Doc.* X, pt. 2, 827.

The three accounts of the conversation of 1914 by or on the authority of ʿAbdullāh are mutually contradictory in detail, but even so they agree in presenting a narrative which is substantially different from that presented in Kitchener's communication. According to these versions, while ʿAbdullāh was in audience with the Khedive Lord Kitchener was announced, whereupon ʿAbdullāh greeted the British Agent and left. Later in the day Kitchener and Storrs visited ʿAbdullāh in his apartments at the royal palace.[32] Two days later ʿAbdullāh visited Lord Kitchener at the British Residency.[33] During the meeting in ʿAbdullāh's apartment Storrs gave ʿAbdullāh a letter to be delivered in Izmir to Mr. Fitzmaurice, First Translator of the British Embassy in Constantinople.[34] At the same time Kitchener and ʿAbdullāh discussed the political situation in the Hijaz.[35] Kitchener remarked that he had heard of the recent strengthening of the Turkish garrison there. ʿAbdullāh then described the situation in the Hijaz, and the "aims of the Arab movement as a whole."[36] Kitchener said that he had knowledge that it was the intention of the Turks to introduce fundamental changes in the Arab lands; he continued by asking if Ḥusayn would submit in case the Turks were to remove him.[37] ʿAbdullāh replied that the Sharif was an official whom the Sultan could appoint and remove as he saw fit.[38] Kitchener said that he thought the Turks would be reluctant to exercise this right.[39] ʿAbdullāh asked if Britain would aid Ḥusayn in

32. Antonius; but Storrs is not mentioned. Saʿīd says only that ʿAbdullāh met with Kitchener and Storrs and dates the incident in July; ʿAbdullāh makes no mention of any meeting with Lord Kitchener in 1914.

33. Antonius only.

34. Saʿīd; ʿAbdullāh, p. 81, relates the incident as a visit by Storrs alone; Antonius is silent.

35. Saʿīd does not specify the place. The fact that, according to Antonius, ʿAbdullāh concludes his account with "Kitchener laughed and rose to depart. As he was leaving . . ." indicates that the conversation here described took place during Kitchener's visit to ʿAbdullāh.

36. Antonius only.

37. ʿAbdullāh only; although the conversation is represented as having occurred in 1912, it is so nearly identical with Antonius's account and agrees to so great an extent with Kitchener's report that it is likely that it refers to the same conversation.

38. ʿAbdullāh and Antonius.

39. Antonius only.

case he decided to resist Turkish encroachment in the Hijaz, and Lord Kitchener replied that Britain's traditional friendship with Turkey did not permit her to interfere in Turkish internal affairs. ʿAbdullāh then pointed out that in the case of the Shaykh of Kuwayt Britain had not refrained from interfering in the internal affairs of Turkey.[40] At this Lord Kitchener remarked, "You have a clear memory,"[41] laughed, and rose to go,[42] saying that he would report the matter to his government.[43] To ʿAbdullāh's remark that the conversation was not worthy of reporting because it consisted merely of observations, Kitchener replied, "And if it were?"[44]

There are thus important differences between Kitchener's description of the conversation (or conversations) of February, 1914, and the general tenor of the three versions by or on the authority of ʿAbdullāh. It seems impossible to decide between the conflicting accounts. Kitchener's account has the authority of a contemporary document, and Antonius's version agrees that ʿAbdullāh, emboldened by the opportunity presented by Kitchener's call, visited the British Agent. But some fragmentary evidence lends some support to ʿAbdullāh's version. According to Antonius contemporary Cairo Arabic newspapers reported that on February 5, 1914, the Khedive received in audience ʿAbdullāh and then Lord Kitchener, and that on February 7 Kitchener visited ʿAbdullāh.[45] Although the press evidence cannot be regarded as decisive, taken together with ʿAbdullāh's own account it does indicate that Kitchener may

40. ʿAbdullāh and Antonius; Saʿid summarizes the conversation thus: "[Lord Kitchener] answered that England desired to maintain its friendly relations with the Turks and that she would aid the Arabs within this sphere, observing its ancient traditions." ʿAbdullāh quotes Storrs as saying, when he delivered the letter for Fitzmaurice, "Should the Sharif defend his rights in the Hijaz, the British Government, which has no right to interfere in the internal affairs of a friendly state, will never be satisfied with the continuation of any movement which Turkey might occasion against the existing tranquility in the land of the pilgrimage."

41. ʿAbdullāh.

42. Antonius.

43. ʿAbdullāh and Antonius.

44. ʿAbdullāh.

45. *Brit. Doc.*, X, pt. 2, 832. Apparently no other information relevant to the question could be found in the Cairo press.

not have been fully and accurately representing the facts when he reported to Grey, "The Sherif Abdullah . . . called upon me yesterday." Lord Kitchener did in fact later seek to modify the impression created by his first report. On April 4 he wrote to Grey, "[The statement] that the Sherif of Mecca sent his son . . . to me . . . does not . . . quite accurately represent what took place, as Abdullah Bey was actually on a visit to the Khedive and only called on me quite unofficially, and some time after his arrival in Cairo. . . ." In the same dispatch Kitchener also indicated his concern over conditions in the Hijaz by stating that, although care was necessary in dealing with the Arab question, it would have been unwise "to lose sight of the interests which Great Britain must always take in the Holy Places, owing to the annual pilgrimage which is attended by thousands of Indian Moslems and also by many Egyptians." He continued with the statement that the welfare and safety of the pilgrims were adversely affected by the dispute between Ḥusayn and the Turks, which was the result of the Turkish policy of centralization.[46] The newspaper evidence and Kitchener's dispatch of April 4 make credible ʿAbdullāh's assertion that he did not query the British Agent concerning support for an Arab break with Turkey until after Kitchener paid him a visit and opened the subject of relations between the Ottoman government and the Amir of Mecca.

Although the precise details of ʿAbdullāh's contacts with Lord Kitchener are obscure, the general course and nature of these contacts seem reasonably clear. ʿAbdullāh first met the British Agent in 1912 (or 1913), when the latter called on him and expressed his pleasure with Ḥusayn's administration as it affected the conditions of the pilgrimage. Lord Kitchener probably again took the initiative in 1914 and, during a visit to ʿAbdullāh, questioned him regarding the political situation in the Hijaz. ʿAbdullāh, taking advantage of and encouraged by Kitchener's expression of interest, brought up the question of the British attitude in the case of an Arab break with the

46. *Ibid.*, 830.

Turks. The British Agent stated that the British government could not give any support to an Arab rebellion.

In April ʿAbdullāh, returning from Constantinople, was again the guest of the Khedive in Cairo and called on Lord Kitchener. He seemed desirous of saying something, but he appeared unable to bring himself to say it. Kitchener, having been informed by Constantinople that the Turkish authorities had noticed the meetings with disapproval, ceased seeing the Amir, who then asked Storrs to call.[47] The latter called on ʿAbdullāh with instructions to inform him that "the Arabs of the Hedjaz could expect no encouragement from" Great Britain and that Britain's only interest in Arabia "was the safety and comfort of Indian pilgrims." ʿAbdullāh appeared to be disappointed with the results of his visit to the capital and with the determination of the government to build the railroad to Mecca.[48] After a two-hour conversation, ʿAbdullāh finally asked Storrs if England would present to the Amir of Mecca a dozen or a half-dozen machine guns; when asked for what purpose the guns would be used, the Amir replied that they were for defense against the Turks. Storrs answered that Britain could not supply arms for use against a friendly power. The two men parted on friendly terms.[49]

ʿAbdullāh's conversations with Kitchener and Storrs were undoubtedly important in leading him to advocate a break with the Turks. Even if Kitchener did not open the conversations, he did confirm the fact that Britain had an interest in the security of the pilgrimage. Kitchener's statement that England could not interfere in the internal affairs of a friendly state did not sound convincing to ʿAbdullāh, who, as he reminded the British Agent, could not forget British interven-

47. Storrs, p. 135. Kitchener's letter to Sir W. Tyrrell relates that ʿAbdullāh, on the way back from Constantinople, sent for Storrs and states, "I did not see him." *Brit. Doc.*, X, pt. 2, 831.

48. *Brit. Doc.*, X, pt. 2, 831.

49. Storrs, p. 135. Antonius, *Arab Awakening*, pp. 127–128, seems to be in error in dividing the above conversation between Storrs and ʿAbdullāh in two, placing one in February and the other in April.

tion in Kuwayt. The Amir also firmly believed that Britain had been supporting Ibn-Suʿūd, even though he did not remind Kitchener of it.[50] After Ibn-Suʿūd's expulsion of the Turks from al-Aḥsāʾ Province in May and June, 1913, the British government did mediate between the two parties, even though Great Britain had already recognized Ottoman sovereignty over the area.[51] Although ʿAbdullāh may not have known the exact facts about Britain's role as mediator, he undoubtedly knew that the Suʿūdi conquest of al-Aḥsāʾ had been preceded by a visit to Ibn-Suʿūd by a British political agent and that British agents were alleged to have visited Ibn-Suʿūd in January and March, 1914, because these visits were reported in the Arabic press of Baghdad.[52] At the time of ʿAbdullāh's talks with Kitchener and Storrs in 1914, moreover, Ibn-Suʿūd was still in unchallenged possession of the conquered territory. Finally, ʿAbdullāh's skepticism of Kitchener's disclaimer could only have been strengthened by British intervention on behalf of the Arab officer ʿAzīz ʿAli al-Miṣri, which was carried out between February 21 and April 12, 1914, primarily at the insistence of Kitchener. British intervention and Kitchener's role were widely publicized among the Arabs.[53] So impressed was ʿAbdullāh with the magnitude of British interest in Arabia (and not without justification) that he based his plan of action primarily on British intervention. ʿAbdullāh's conversations with Kitchener, then, were probably more a stimulus to ʿAbdullāh's deciding on a break with Turkey than the result of a decision already taken.

50. ʿAbdullāh, according to his memoirs (pp. 70–71), was told by the Grand Vizier in the spring of 1911 that the British Ambassador had protested the aid that Ḥusayn had given to one of Ibn-Suʿūd's rebellious kinsmen.

51. On the Suʿūdi conquest of al-Ahsāʾ, see *Die Welt des Islams,* II (1914), 46, 328–329. On British mediation, see *Brit. Doc.*, X, pt. 2, 829–830, and Philip Graves, *The Life of Sir Percy Cox,* 2nd ed. (London: Hutchinson and Co., [1941]), pp. 170–171.

52. *Welt Is.*, II (1914), 47, 302, 305, 328.

53. *Brit. Doc.*, X, pt. 2, 832–838; *The Near East,* VI (May 1, 1914), 819, 820; and *La Vérité,* pp. 31–32.

THREE

Ideological Influences in the Arab Revolt

ALTHOUGH the Amir of Mecca al-Ḥusayn ibn-ʿAli began his revolt against the Ottoman government in June, 1916, after having reached agreement with representatives of Arab nationalist societies, a careful analysis of Ḥusayn's policy shows that until that time he had never been an advocate of Arabism. Ḥusayn rose in conjunction with the Arab nationalists only after the failure of his efforts to find some accommodation for his political interests within the framework of the Ottoman empire. Ḥusayn's son ʿAbdullāh became convinced of the necessity of armed revolt well before his father did and by July, 1914, had become a convert to Arab nationalism. Since these two men played by far the most important part in the origin of the revolt, an analysis of the ideological influences at work in creating the revolt can be made largely in terms of their political attitudes and ideas.

Before 1916 both Ḥusayn and ʿAbdullāh were primarily politicians, not theorists and publicists. The readily available material on their political ideas is not voluminous. Indeed, the work in which ʿAbdullāh's political ideas find their best expression was not published until nearly thirty years after the beginning of the revolt.[1] Yet it will be seen that the ideas expressed in this book are drawn from the welter of nationalist theories current before 1916 and are not the fancies of ʿAbdullāh's old age.

In ʿAbdullāh's mind the Arabs were an exceptional nation.

1. ʿAbdullāh ibn-al-Ḥusayn, *Mudhakkarāti* [*My Memoirs*], 1st ed. (Jerusalem: Maṭbaʿah Bayt al-Muqaddas, 1945). The translation by G. Khuri, *Memoirs of King Abdullah of Transjordan* (New York: Philosophical Library, 1950), is not reliable and omits some important passages. In the discussion that follows, references to the Arabic text and to Khuri's translation will be given in parentheses in the text.

Even before the coming of Islam the Arabs had extraordinary qualities:

> The sudden torrent of the light of Islam from Mecca was the decisive sign for unification of the disunited tribes of the Arabs. The Arabs, by virtue of the geography, extreme heat, and aridity of their land, had no inclination to form powerful governments to put their affairs in order; rather, for these reasons, their inclination was to live scattered and disunited, engaging in battles and raids, with irreligiousness, idolatry, and the errors of the *Jāhilīyah.* Therefore, it was not easy for them to take their place in the world as a nation (*ummah*) possessing its government, integrity, and territory. Despite this, none of the great neighbouring nations was able to conquer them and to occupy their country. The Ḥimyarites had in al-Yaman an independent state, and a renowned government, but their achievement was restricted to al-Yaman and did not extend outside it.
>
> It must be said that the Arabs, if they were as described above, were free from the burdens placed on the shoulders of the [other] nations by the demands of civilization and submission to order. They were known for bravery and courage, haughtiness and pride, fidelity, the eloquence of their tongue, the excellence of their poetry, the wisdom of their orators, and the great strength of their valour. In politics they were like a nation (*qawm*) in the age of youth ready to do all that was expected and demanded of them. At that time, when God honoured them by sending the Prophet, they were the neighbours of two states, Persia and Rome, both of which had grown old and shown signs of decay, just as God . . . remarked on that, saying, "Decay has appeared on land and on sea with respect to that which the hands of man have acquired" [Koran 30 : 41]. (Appendix, p. 73.)

However, the Arabs were unable to realize complete nationhood until God blessed them with the religion of Islam:

> Accordingly and as a result of their existence as a single element having a single tongue, they were unified, converted to a single faith, and turned in a single direction. So they were made capable of reaching maturity and of occupying the world

> position which they merit. Thus, by the grace of God, the creator prepared for this fortunate nation (*ummah*) these advantages and honoured it with the "seal" of the prophets and messengers. It was the prophetic age, the age in which the Arabs were converted to the clear religion, in which they were unified so that they could carry out their obligation to form a single unit and to abandon the customs of the *Jāhilīyah* and the dispersion. Then they became a compact building, strengthening each other, no censurer finding them at fault before God. (Appendix, pp. 73–74.)

The Arabs have a special position in the world deriving from their Prophet. As long as Islam in accordance with the Koran and the sunnah prevails, the Arabs cannot but enjoy completely their natural rights, and there is no real need for the Arabs to exercise complete sovereignty:

> The Arab nation (*al-ummah al-ʿarabīyah*), the possessor of history and the master of a noble past, to whose Prophet the Koran descended and which conquered the East and the West in less than a quarter century, which produced a religious and cultural renaissance and the requisites of human brotherhood, is a nation (*ummah*) that cannot be a servile colony, but which is a free, independent, and leading nation. As to its remaining under the shadow of non-Arab, but Moslem, governments, this resulted from the submission of those nations to Islamic teachings and the Muḥammadan brotherhood. Then the teachings of the Koran and the sunnah prevailed, and the Arab at that time had equity whether his sultan was Arab or was a non-Arab from among the Moslems. Thus the Arab nation used to regard the sultans of Islam as an honour given it by God, like the honour which He had bestowed upon the Arab Prophet. . . . (Pp. 237–238; Khuri, pp. 243–244.)

The Arabs, then, are a special nation, blessed by God with the "seal" of the prophets. The requirements of Arabism are fulfilled by membership in an Islamic state which enforces the Koran and the sunnah, rather than by possessing a separate, independent Arab state. These ideas are made even more clearly when ʿAbdullāh discusses the reason for the Arab break with the Ottoman empire. The Arab desire for independence was born when the Turks began to replace fundamental Islamic institutions with the reforms of the *tanẓīmāt:*

> But in the last century and earlier, there occurred some of the changes which shook this unifying bond between the Arabs and the non-Arabs. The decree of the *tanẓīmāt* issued in the time of Sultan Maḥmūd II was the first step in the revolt against the Arab teachings handed down from their Koran and the sunnah of their Prophet in favour of the alien Western form which its devotees themselves did not understand. Then there were reversals, contradictions, falterings in progress, and dilatoriness in action. Among these were the sudden change in the form of the army and administration, the extermination of the Janissary corps and the creation of the troops called the "New Army". . . . (P. 238; Khuri, p. 245.)

ʿAbdullāh then describes (pp. 238–239; Khuri, pp. 244–245) the achievements of Muḥammad ʿAli and the efforts of the Sharif and Amir of Mecca, ʿAbd al-Muṭṭalib, to form an independent amirate as "the first independent Arab tincture," i.e., as the birth of Arabism, and makes it clear that the Arabs began to desire independence because the Turks had deviated from the "Arab teachings" of the Koran and the sunnah.

The primary fault of the Ottoman statemen consisted in their failure to execute the *sharīʿah* and their abandonment of the caliphate. In one passage (appendix, pp. 116–117) ʿAbdullāh speaks favourably of the *tanẓīmāt* reforms and makes it clear that he had no objections to the adoption of Western military and administrative techniques. But when the Young Turks went on to attempt the replacement of the caliphate with a Western constitutional and nationalist regime, the Arabs, as Moslems, had no alternative to rebellion:

> With the last Ottoman revolution [of 1908], as a result of which the Constitution of 1293 [A.D. 1876] was restored, the regime of the sultans was transformed into a national (*millīyah*) regime monopolized by the element of which the sultan was a member, and the other elements and countries became the servants of the ruling element. It [the Turkish ruling element],

perceiving the existence of other races in the empire greater in number [than the Turks] and professing Islam, began the Turkification of the other elements in order to change their national (*qawmīyah*) character and [thus] ward off danger from the Turkish constitutional sultanate. Various parties and numerous associations began to be organized for each nation (*ummah*), to take shape, and to contend for their privileges and [the realization of their] demands. The Turkish Union and Progress faction exerted pressure in the elections for the Ottoman parliament, so that no one won membership in the parliament unless he was a Turk or a Unionist. The Arabs and the other elements in the empire felt that they were in danger of extinction. So revolts took place in Albania, Jabal al-Durūz, and al-Karak; the famous Sāmi Pasha al-Fārūqi took charge of the suppression of the Arab revolt; then there was the revolt in ʿAsīr, which the amir of Mecca, the Sharif al-Ḥusayn ibn-ʿAli, suppressed, and the revolt of the Yaman, which the Mushīr ʿAbdullāh Pasha and the Mushīr ʿIzzat Pasha suppressed.

At that time the sharif was holding fast to the Ottoman bond, favouring it and looking toward its continuation, preferring it to dissolution and partition, whose extent was unpredictable, whose consequences were unassured. Finally, when Unionist self-centredness reached its apex, the necessity for the Arabs to separate from the Turks, who had threatened, scorned, and made enemies of all but themselves, became apparent. (Pp. 239–240; Khuri, pp. 245–246.)

Another passage makes it clear that the threat to the "national character" of the Arabs was the abandonment of the caliphate-sultanate by the Turks and not merely their repression of the Arabs and the other ethnic groups within the empire:

The Arabs are nothing except Islam, and it is one of their duties that they strive to restore their greatness, their right, and their caliphate. The last Arab rebellion which was raised by the great deliverer [i.e. Ḥusayn], may God be gracious to him, and his companions from among the notables of the Hijaz, and by the decision of their *ʿulamāʾ* and also the notables of Syria and Iraq, [was] a legitimate rebellion for the defence of Islam and for the Arabs to take the place which God had allotted to them exclusively when He said in his precious book, "You were the best nation created among mankind to command the good and to prohibit abominations" [Koran 3:110]. May God send to this nation (*ummah*) one who will know the location of the malady in it and cut it out, and the nature of the medicine and use it, before it is said: Woe, woe!

Republican revolution had been ardently desired by the Young Turks since the time of Midḥat Pasha, who did not see that the Ottoman sultanate was solidified in its boundaries, on the east, on the west, on the north, and on the south, only after it assumed the character of the caliphate, and that with the casting off of this character, the Arabs would be cast off as a matter of course. [You ask:] Have you not seen that they are stronger and more stable and modern today than they were yesterday? [I reply:] But where is their renown of yesterday and the influence they had when their sultan was "commander of the faithful," and caliph of the Messenger of the Lord of the Universe? In truth they have become weak and small today, while they were great and powerful yesterday. Thus I say that if a thing abandons its foundation, it becomes unsound. (P. 22; Khuri, p. 57.)

ʿAbdullāh thus holds the view that the special distinction and position of the Arabs results from Islam. The Arabs are a unique nation because God blessed them with the "seal" of the prophets. Conversely, the heart of Islam consists of "the Arab teachings handed down from their Koran and the sunnah of their Prophet." The Arabs, therefore, are pre-eminent among the Moslem peoples, but their pre-eminence is guaranteed by the enforcement of the Arabic Koran and sunnah, not by Arab independence. The Arab nation thus gives loyal allegiance to any sultanate which possesses the character of the caliphate and executes the Koran and the sunnah, whether its sultan be Arab or non-Arab. When the Ottoman government began to abandon the Koran and the sunnah and to replace the caliphate with an alien Western regime, reverses for it and for Islam were the inevitable result. The Arabs then naturally were compelled to oppose Ottoman policy, first to restore Islam and second to regain the position which God had allotted to the Arabs.

The principal indication of Ḥusayn's political ideology is the series of four proclamations which he issued between June 10, 1916, and March 5, 1917. The second, third, and fourth proclamations were published in Ḥusayn's official journal, *al-Qiblah;* there is therefore no question of their authenticity.[2] There is some doubt about the authorship of the first proclamation, which was published in Egypt. Amīn Saʿīd published a very long text which he claims is the original document sent by Ḥusayn to Egypt; Saʿīd further asserts that the text actually published in Egypt was greatly modified by the British before publication. "G.," on the other hand, asserts that the text published in Egypt was the proclamation sent by Ḥusayn. According to "G.," Ḥusayn's agent in Egypt was not satisfied with the proclamation and therefore had it revised by the editor of *al-Manār,* the well-known theologian and publicist Muḥammad Rashīd Riḍa; but Ḥusayn rejected the revised proclamation, which had been printed in Cairo, and insisted on the publication of the proclamation as he had written it.[3] The contents of the published proclamation and the suppressed version are much the same, with one important exception: the suppressed version embodies a theory of Arabism which is entirely lacking in the published proclamation. It is therefore important to determine the authorship of the two texts.

There are several indications that the published version is the work of Ḥusayn, the suppressed text the work of Muḥammad Rashīd Riḍa.[4] In the first place, it is difficult to think of any reason for the British to have suppressed the longer text,

2. For the Arabic texts and French translations of these proclamations, see "G.," "Textes historiques sur le réveil arabe au Hedjaz", *Revue du Monde Musulman,* XLVI (1921), 1–22; XLVII (1921), 1–27; L (1922), 74–100.

3. Amīn Saʿīd, *al-Thawrah al-ʿarabīyah al-kubra* [*The Great Arab Revolt*], 3 vols. (Cairo: ʿĪsa al-Bābi al-Ḥalabi, [1934?]), I, 149–157; *RMM,* XLVI (1921), 10–11.

4. Ettore Rossi, *Documenti sull' origine e gli sviluppi della questione araba, 1875–1944* (Rome: Istituto per l'Oriente, 1944), p. 53, n.1, accepts Saʿīd's assertion without discussion.

as asserted by Saʿīd. Second, the published version seems stylistically closer to Ḥusayn's other proclamations, agreeing with them in the very frequent use of long construct phrases composed of verbal nouns, while the suppressed text frequently employs relative clauses. However, this is merely an impression, and there do not seem to be any decisive stylistic criteria. In the third place, Ḥusayn's fourth proclamation, dated March 5, 1917, contains the clause: "What their breasts harbour toward the pure Islamic *sharīʿah,* as we said in line twenty-five of our first proclamation." [5] Line twenty-five of the published first proclamation contains the phrase: "What their breasts harbour toward the religion [of Islam] and the Arabs." This phrase does occur in the suppressed version, but it is very improbable that it was in line twenty-five, since the suppressed text is much longer than the published proclamation.[6] In his fourth proclamation Ḥusayn therefore seems to be confirming his authorship of the published proclamation. Finally, the theory of Arabism embodied in the suppressed text but lacking in the published proclamation is different from the theory of Arabism embodied in Ḥusayn's other proclamations, whose authorship is beyond question.

The theory of Arabism embodied in the suppressed proclamation is similar to ʿAbdullāh's. The distinctness and greatness of the Arabs derive from Islam: "the Islamic and the Arab interest (and they are two, mutually necessary for each other). . . ." [7] Moreover, the Arabs occupy a special position in Islam, for from the Prophet's "true tradition we have learned, 'If the Arabs are weak, Islam is weak' " (I, 155). In addition, "It is no secret that to kill the Arabic language [as the C.U.P. was trying to do] is to kill Islam itself, for in truth Islam is an Arab religion in the sense that its book was sent down in the Arabic language and [that fact] put the worshippers to reading it, reflecting upon it, and understanding it, not in the sense

5. *RMM,* L (1922), p. 93, ll. 12–13 (Arabic text), p. 79 (translation).

6. *RMM,* XLVI (1921), p. 21, l. 9 (Arabic text), p. 8 (translation); Saʿīd, I, 155.

7. Saʿīd, I, 156. In this paragraph, the rest of the references to the proclamation will be given in the text.

that it pertains to the Arabs exclusively . . ." (I, 152). Finally, the Moslems "used to have great, powerful states, the best of them being the states of our Arab ancestors" (I, 155).

The published version of Ḥusayn's first proclamation scarcely mentions the Arabs. It does, however, contain two passages which imply that "nationalism" is an independent motivating force: Ḥusayn says that the bombardment of Mecca is "proof of what their hearts harbour toward the religion and the Arabs," and he later says, "We cannot leave our religious and national (*qawmi*) existence in the hands of the Unionists." [8] In Ḥusayn's undoubtedly authentic proclamations such words as "national" occur in only one, the third proclamation, issued in November, 1916, which was signed by Ḥusayn as "Sharif of Mecca and King of the Arab Country." Here Ḥusayn speaks of "the duties the faithful execution of which are imposed on us by the obligations of religion, of nationality (*qawmīyah*), and of humanity"; of his "responsibility in the hands of God . . . and then before the patriotic (*waṭanīyah*) and national (*qawmīyah*) duty"; and of "the national and the patriotic interest." [9]

Ḥusayn's statement that the revolt was the result of "patriotic" and "national" duty as well as of religious obligations raises two questions. What is the "patriotic" and "national" duty as distinct from the religious duty, and what is the theoretical and legal basis for the existence of the *patria* and the "nation"? The primary "national" and "patriotic" duty seems to be identical with the religious duty of the Moslems, i.e., to follow the *sharīʿah.* Whenever the revolt is described as a revolt by the *ummah* or as the result of "patriotic and national duty," the accompanying particulars actually describe it as a revolt against "the heedless ones who . . . took the religion of God as an amusement and as a game." [10]

8. *RMM,* XLVI (1921), p. 21, ll. 9, 15 (Arabic text), pp. 8, 9 (translation).

9. *RMM,* XLVII (1921), p. 24, col. 1, ll. 4–5 (Arabic text), p. 15 (translation); p. 25, col. 1, l. 16 (Arabic text), p. 16 (translation); p. 27, col. 1, l. 1 (Arabic text), p. 20 (translation). On the title, see above, pp. 46–47.

10. *Ibid.,* p. 25, col. 1, ll. 1–3 (Arabic text), pp. 14–15 (translation).

"National duty" is, however, something more than the simple duty to defend and to follow the *sharīʿah.* Ḥusayn's ideas concerning the "nation" are given their fullest and clearest expression in the following passage:

> One of the things which increased my responsibility in the hands of God . . . and then before the patriotic (*waṭanīyah*) and national (*qawmīyah*) interest, is the unendurable hardship which befell my nation (*qawm*) and my countrymen. . . .
>
> Then we sought the protection of God . . . to rise against the oppressive criminals and the apostate vandals, escaping punishment in his [Muḥammad's] word: [Ḥusayn here quotes four *ḥadīths* justifying action against oppressors or heretics and concludes with the *ḥadīth:* "The best among you is the one who defends his tribe (*ʿashīrah*)".] And God selected us to arouse our nation (*ummah*), to restrain the unjust, and to banish the insolent ones, the heretics, from the land and from among the true worshippers, requesting for them what we request for ourselves, namely to make us desire to follow what he . . . [Muḥammad] brought [i.e., the *sharīʿah*], and to drive the evil from our tribes and our Arab communities (*jamāʿāt*), to whose race, language, customs, comforts, and pleasures these heedless ones showed enmity, explicitly and implicitly, in word and in act.[11]

The emphasis is unmistakable. The right and the duty of the "nation" "to rise against the oppressive criminals and the apostate vandals," and "to restrain the unjust and to banish the insolent ones, the heretics," is derived from the sunnah of the Prophet. The goal of the "nation" is to be able "to follow what he . . . brought." And herein lies the legal basis for "national" existence and duty. The first word used in this passage to denote "nation" is *qawm,* which means "tribe," or perhaps "the fighting men of a tribe." The "nation" ("tribe") has the right and the duty to defend its "race, language, customs, comforts, and pleasures," because the Prophet said, "The best among you is the one who defends his tribe." "National" existence and "national" duty is thus based on the *sharīʿah.* In this

11. *Ibid.,* p. 25, col. 1, l. 1; p. 24, col. 2, l. 1; p. 25, col. 2, l. 7 (Arabic text), pp. 16–17 (translation).

argument Ḥusayn was on sound legal ground, for among the Sunnites it was established at an early date that all Moslem "tribes and peoples" were equal.[12]

Even though Ḥusayn argues that a "nation" has the right to exist, he does not assert that nationhood entails the right to statehood. One passage does associate "the nation" and "independence":

> We express to our sincere nation (*ummah*) our pleasure with its Islamic zeal and its Arab fervour, and we thank it for the bravery, manliness, and Arab pride which it has thus far shown, and for its active co-operation in expelling the heretical conquerors from the hearth of our house and the fortresses of our land; for with that it began a new golden page in the history of the glorious Arab land, and it merited that it be the possessor of the greatest honour through regaining permanent complete independence for its land. . . .[13]

This passage might be interpreted as implying that a nation has the right to political independence in its own land; however, the correct interpretation would seem to be that Ḥusayn's nation merited independence because it had expelled the heretics from its land. In short, Ḥusayn is appealing to the Islamic doctrine of the obligation of the ruler to enforce the *sharīʿah* and of the implied right of rebellion against a ruler who violates the *sharīʿah,*[14] not to the doctrine of national self-determination.

Ḥusayn in fact apparently attributes no great social or political significance to ethnic sentiment. In exhorting his nation to work together for the cause, he relies on Islam: "And the most important thing to be expected from the nation (*ummah*) is sincerity of intention, the exchange of good advice, mutual

12. C. Snouck Hurgronje, "L'Islam et le problème des races," *RMM,* L (1922), 8–21.

13. *RMM,* XLVII (1921), p. 26, col. 1, ll. 5–8 (Arabic text), pp. 18–19 (translation).

14. For these doctrines, see David Santillana, *Istituzioni di diritto musulmano malichita,* 2 vols. (Rome: Istituto per l'Oriente, [1925–38]), I, 21–26; H. A. R. Gibb and Harold Bowen, *Islamic Society and the West,* vol. I: *Islamic Society in the Eighteenth Century,* pt. 1 (London: Oxford University Press, 1950), pp. 28–29.

aid, and the defence of the right and of national (*qawmīyah*) and patriotic (*waṭanīyah*) interest." Ḥusayn then quotes three *ḥadīths* concerning the duty of Moslems to aid one another and adds: "Thus our true Islamic religion commands us, so let us be true Moslems." [15]

The proclamation does not explicitly identify Ḥusayn's "nation" and "land." Although one would assume that this "nation" was the "Arab nation," the term *al-ummah al-ʿarabīyah* (or al-*qawn al-ʿarabi*) is not used. Ḥusayn associates the term "Arab" with the term "nation" in two passages only, quoted in full above, and then only indirectly. In the first passage his "nation" certainly includes "tribes and Arab communities"; in the second his "nation" possesses "Islamic zeal and Arab fervour" and "bravery, manliness, and Arab pride" and is the inhabitant of the "glorious Arab land." All that can be concluded from this is that Ḥusayn's "nation" is "Arab." There is no necessary implication that his "nation" includes all the Arabs.

Whenever such terms as "nation" or "national" are used with reference to a specfic region or people, the Hijaz and its inhabitants are meant. The opening paragraph of the third proclamation makes this clear: "Now the time has come for us to speak to the sons of our land . . . about . . . the duties the faithful execution of which are imposed on us by the obligations of religion, of nationality, and of humanity." Here "our land" must be the first region referred to: "Perhaps the soil of the two noble sanctuaries was smitten by their [the Unionists'] blows and corrupt acts less than any of the Ottoman territories, not because . . . they love the Hijazis more than the inhabitants of Rumelia, Anatolia, Syria, and Iraq. . . ." [16] Besides identifying "our land" with the Hijaz, the passage also refers to the Hijaz as a country distinct and separate from the two Arab territories, Syria and Iraq. These two regions are mentioned in only one other passage, with a parallel, though not so clear, meaning: "Behold the people of Medina . . . did

15. *RMM* XLVII (1921), p. 27, col. 1, ll. 1–8 (Arabic text), pp. 20–21 (translation).

16. *Ibid.*, p. 24, col. 1, l. 3; p. 25, col. 1, l. 7 (Arabic text), pp. 14–15 (translation).

not escape oppressive and unjust blows like those which they [the Unionists] inflicted on the Arabs of Syria and Iraq. . . ." There follows a recital of the oppressive acts against the people of Medina.[17] Another identification is given when Ḥusayn speaks of the famine and want created in the Hijaz as the "unendurable hardship which befell my nation and my countrymen." [18] Ḥusayn's *waṭan,* then, is the Hijaz, and his *ummah* or *qawm* is the people of the Hijaz.

Ḥusayn's third proclamation thus does not embody the theory of Arabism found in the suppressed version of his first proclamation and in the writings of his son. Ḥusayn used "nationalism" only in a localized sense and did not appeal to the entire Arab nation. Surely if Ḥusayn believed in, or desired to use, the theory of Arab pre-eminence among the Moslems exemplified in ʿAbdullāh's writing and in the suppressed version of the first proclamation, he would have utilized it in the proclamation in which he assumed for the first time the title, "the King of the Arab Country." Ḥusayn, therefore, was neither the author of the suppressed first proclamation nor an advocate of its theory of Arabism.

Ḥusayn's proclamations make it clear that to him the lawful state is not a national state but a Moslem state, a caliphate, embracing as much of the community of the faithful as possible: "The first of the Moslem governors and amirs to recognize the Sublime Porte were the amirs of Mecca the Blessed, desiring them [*sic,* i.e., the Ottoman rulers] to unify the Moslems and to strengthen the bonds of their community (*jamāʿah*) through its sultans from the exalted Ottoman family . . . acting steadfastly in accordance with the Book of God and the sunnah of His prophet . . . and through their zeal in executing their prescriptions." [19] In a similar vein, Ḥusayn spoke of "the sole bond between the Sunnite Ottoman sultanate and all the Moslems of the world; is it not clinging fast to the Book and

17. *Ibid.,* p. 25, col. 2, l. 8; p. 26, col. 1, l. 4 (Arabic text), pp. 17–18 (translation).

18. *Ibid.,* p. 25, col. 1, l. 16; p. 24, col. 2, l. 4 (Arabic text), p. 16 (translation).

19. *RMM,* XLVI (1921), p. 20, ll. 1–2 (Arabic text), p. 4 (translation).

the sunnah?"[20] When these conditions prevailed, the Ottoman sultanate was a caliphate: "Their [the Unionists'] violation of the conditions which the Moslems stipulate for the caliphate requires their repudiation."[21] As long as the Ottoman government held fast to the *sharīʿah,* it was more than just one caliphate; it was the true "state (*dawlah*) of Islam,"[22] that is, the state of all Moslems.

Ḥusayn's description of the reasons for the Arab break with the Ottomans is much the same as ʿAbdullāh's. The break was necessary because the Turks had ceased to execute the *sharīʿah* and thus to fulfill the conditions of the caliphate. Of special significance are Ḥusayn's attacks on Unionist measures which represented the process of modernization and Europeanization. Thus Ḥusayn attacked the Unionists for measures designed to improve the legal status of women,[23] for freeing soldiers from the fast of Ramaḍān,[24] and for modernizing the law of evidence.[25] He also attacked constitutionalism: "They have extinguished the power of the most mighty sultan and robbed him even of the authority to choose the chief secretary of the *Ma-bayn* of the noble sultanate, or the chief of his honoured, exalted Privy Chamber, let alone to attend to the affairs of the Moslems and the interests of the land and of the true believers."[26] One of Ḥusayn's most striking and interesting specific charges against the Unionists, a charge made in three of his four proclamations, is the charge of having caused the loss of territory by the "state of Islam"; for this, every Moslem must hate them.[27]

20. *Ibid.,* p. 20, ll. 9–10 (Arabic text), p. 5 (translation).
21. *Ibid.,* p. 20, l. 15 (Arabic text), p. 6 (translation).
22. The phrase occurs twice; *ibid.,* p. 20, l. 6 (Arabic text), p. 5 (translation); XLVII (1921), p. 13, ll. 7–8 (Arabic text), p. 10 (translation). In both cases, the "state" is used in connection with "all Moslems" and the "Moslems of the world."
23. *RMM,* XLVI (1921), p. 20, ll. 11–12 (Arabic text), p. 6 (translation); XLVII (1921), p. 13, col. 2, ll. 10–12 (Arabic text), p. 10 (translation).
24. *RMM,* XLVI (1921), p. 20, ll. 12–13 (Arabic text), p. 6 (translation).
25. *Ibid.,* p. 21, ll. 1–2 (Arabic text), p. 7 (translation).
26. *Ibid.,* p. 20, ll. 14–15 (Arabic text), p. 6 (translation).
27. *Ibid.,* p. 20, ll. 4–5 (Arabic text), p. 4 (translation); XLVII (1921), p. 13, col. 1, ll. 12–17 (Arabic text), p. 7 (translation); p. 25, col. 1, ll. 3–4

The theory of the state accepted by both Ḥusayn and ʿAbdullāh is the modern Sunnite theory of the caliphate, which was established by the end of the fifteenth century. According to this theory, the true universal caliphate, possessed by a sole legitimate caliph, had existed for only a short time after the death of the Prophet; thereafter, only sultanates existed among the Moslems. However, any Moslem sultanate whose sultan enforced the *sharīʿah* was a legitimate government and worthy of being designated a "caliphate." This designation carried no implication that such a sultanate was the sole caliphate to which all Moslems owed allegiance; accordingly, the title "caliph" was rarely applied to its head.[28] This theory is clearly reflected in the words of both ʿAbdullāh and Ḥusayn: the Ottoman sultanate was a caliphate as long as, and only as long as, it enforced the *sharīʿah.* Similarly, although the empire is designated a "caliphate," its head is called "caliph" only once by ʿAbdullāh, and not at all by Ḥusayn. In the one instance of the word "caliph" in Ḥusayn's proclamations, Ḥusayn refers to the fact that the Unionists called ʿAbd al-Ḥamīd II "caliph"; he does not himself apply the title.[29]

The use of the modern theory of the caliphate by Ḥusayn and ʿAbdullāh helps to illuminate one of the striking features of nineteenth-century Near Eastern history, i.e., the Pan-Islamic movement centered in the Ottoman Empire. The Ottoman government applied the title "caliphate" to itself and sought popular support among the Moslems of the world. Under the modern theory of the caliphate, the Ottoman government had a perfectly valid claim to the title as long as it enforced the *sharīʿah.* ʿAbdullāh and Ḥusayn obviously regarded the Ottoman government's claim to the title as genuine, and just as obviously

(Arabic text), p. 15 (translation); p. 25, col. 1, l. 12 (Arabic text), p. 15 (translation).

28. On the modern theory of the caliphate see H. A. R. Gibb, "Some Considerations on the Sunni Theory of the Caliphate," *Archives d'Histoire du Droit Oriental,* III (1948), 401–410, and Gibb and Bowen, I, pt. 1, pp. 26–38.

29. *RMM,* L (1922), p. 94, l. 18; p. 96, l. 1 (Arabic text), p. 81 (translation). Ḥusayn's proclamation (Texte VII) is continued on p. 96, which should be labeled "Texte VII (Page 3)" rather than "Texte VII (Page 4)"; p. 95, labeled "Texte VII (Page 3)," is not part of Ḥusayn's proclamation.

believed that most Moslems shared their opinion. Thus the ridicule of the Ottoman caliphate by some European Islamists on the ground that the Ottomans did not possess the qualifications for the classical caliphate was beside the point.[30] Any Turkish pretensions to the classical caliphate were for the benefit of Europeans, not for that of Moslems.

The universal caliphate, however, remained the ideal of sensitive Moslems, even though Moslem legal theorists had long since held that it was a thing of the past. In the nineteenth century, as Islam was subordinated politically, economically, and intellectually to Europe, everywhere Moslems began to long for a great Moslem state which could withstand Europe and preserve Islam.[31] By the end of the nineteenth century, the Ottoman empire was the last hope of Moslems who thought in this way. Ḥusayn probably sincerely shared this opinion when he termed the Ottoman Empire "the state of Islam." He certainly believed that most Moslems regarded the Ottoman state in such a light, for he obviously thought that the charge of having allowed the territories of Islam to diminish was one of the most telling charges which he could level against the Unionists.

The theories of nationalism contained in the writings of ʿAbdullāh and of Ḥusayn are different. ʿAbdullāh was an advocate of the theory of Arab pre-eminence among the Moslems. This theory, in two different forms, was developed and popularized around the turn of the century by Muḥammad ʿAbduh and his pupil Muḥammad Rashīd Riḍa, on the one hand, and by ʿAbd al-Raḥmān al-Kawākibi on the other. All three men agreed that the Arabs were the pre-eminent Moslem people because the Prophet was an Arab and the Koran was an Arabic book; the Arabs, therefore, were the Moslems best qualified to lead in the restoration of Islam to its position of greatness, and an Arab revival was the necessary first step in a general Islamic revival.

30. See, e.g., C. Snouck Hurgronje, *The Holy War Made in Germany* (New York: G. P. Putnam's Sons, 1915), pp. 16–29, 61–63.

31. For an example of this desire in an eighteenth-century Arab jurist, see Gibb and Bowen, I, pt. 1, p. 35. On the nineteeth century, see below, pp. 128–138.

But the first two were never able to subordinate Islam to Arabism, and they did not develop a theory of Arab statehood separate and distinct from Islamic statehood, unlike al-Kawākibi, who gave political content to Arabism and advocated the establishment of an Arab caliph in the Hijaz as the spiritual, but not temporal, head of all the Moslems.[32] In this respect ʿAbdullāh's theory is in agreement with that of ʿAbduh and Rashīd Riḍa. Moreover, ʿAbdullāh's description of Arab pre-eminence exhibits strong similarities to those of ʿAbduh and Rashīd Riḍa, and it lacks the characteristic features of al-Kawākibi's exposition of this subject. Thus ʿAbdullāh borrowed his theory of Arabism from Muḥammad Rashīd Riḍa, with whom he was on close terms before 1914.

Ḥusayn, unlike his son, did not adopt any modern theory of nationalism. It is true that he spoke of his *ummah* and his *qawm,* and he used the adjectives *qawmi* and *waṭani,* and the noun *qawmīyah,* all words used by modern Arab theorists to denote "nation," "national," "patriotic," and "nationalism." Ḥusayn's usage of *ummah* and *qawm,* however, finds its parallel in the usage of his ancestors, not in the usage of the modern nationalists. In classical Arabic, *ummah* was used to denote "a man's *people, community, tribe, kinsfolk,* or *party,*" as well as the larger Islamic *ummah* encompassing the totality of the Moslems; according to Meninski, *qawm* had the meaning of "familia, tribus, consanguinei, *Popolo, gente, nazione. . . .*" While the adjective *waṭani* is not given in the classical dictionaries, the *ḥadīth* "Love of the *waṭan* is a part of faith" was current well before the beginning of the nineteenth century.[33] Ḥusayn thus was using traditional terms, and in his proclamations he used them in accordance with traditional political theory.

32. See below, pp. 133–140. See also Charles C. Adams, *Islam and Modernism in Egypt* (London: Oxford University Press, 1933), p. 85, and *al-Muʾtamar al-ʿarabi al-awwal* [*The First Arab Congress*] (Cairo, 1331H/1913), pp. *alif-jīm.*

33. Edward W. Lane, *An Arabic-English Lexicon* (London, 1863), I, *s.v.* "ummah"; Francisci a Mesgnien Meninski, *Lexicon Arabico-Persico-Turcicum,* 4 vols. (Vienna, 1780–[1802]), *s.v.* "qawm," "waṭan"; Sylvia G. Haim, "Islam and the Theory of Arab Nationalism," *Die Welt des Islams,* n.s., IV (1955), 127–140, 142.

The ideological influences which affected the two principal leaders of the Arab Revolt, or which were used by them to gain popular support, originated in the general Moslem reaction to European domination which began in the nineteenth century. Ḥusayn and ʿAbdullāh agreed in desiring above all to preserve the independence and integrity of Islam and of its fundamental institutions, the *sharīʿah* and the caliphate. Beyond this point, however, their views were divergent. Ḥusayn held fast to traditional Sunnite Islam, while ʿAbdullāh joined ʿAbduh, Rashīd Riḍa, and in a general way the Arab nationalists in advocating an Arab revival as the necessary precursor of the restoration of Islam.

FOUR

Hashimite Aims and Policy in the Light of Recent Scholarship on Anglo-Arab Relations during World War I

SINCE the completion and first publication of the preceding essays, the progressive opening of the private and official papers of British statesmen has led to a number of studies which bear on British relations with the Hashimites and the Arabs. All these studies set the elucidation of British policy as the principal goal, but most consider Arab behavior to some degree. Some concern themselves primarily with European diplomacy or focus on the post-1918 period: Zeine N. Zeine, *The Struggle for Arab Independence: Western Diplomacy and the Rise and Fall of Faisal's Kingdom in Syria* (Beirut: Khayat's, 1960), Jukka Nevakivi, *Britain, France, and the Arab Middle East, 1914–1920* (London: The Athlone Press, University of London, 1969), Aaron S. Klieman, "Britain's War Aims in the Middle East in 1915," *The Journal of Contemporary History,* III, no. 3 (July 1968), 237–251, and the same author's *Foundations of British Policy in the Arab World: The Cairo Conference of 1921* (Baltimore: Johns Hopkins Press, 1970). Hashimite and Arab activities during World War I receive much more attention in Elie Kedourie, "Cairo and Khartoum on the Arab Question, 1915–18," *The Historical Journal,* VII (1964), 280–297 (reprinted in *The Chatham House Version and Other Middle-Eastern Studies* [London: Weidenfeld and Nicolson, 1970]); A. L. Tibawi, "Syria in the McMahon Correspondence" and "Syria in War Time Agreements and Disagreements," *Middle East Forum,* XLII, no. 4 (1966), 5–31, and XLIII, nos. 2–3 (1967), 77–109 (which are included in his *A Modern History of Syria, Including Lebanon and Palestine* [London and New York: Macmillan and St. Martin's Press,

1969]); and Isaiah Friedman, "The McMahon-Hussein Correspondence and the Question of Palestine," with comments by Arnold Toynbee and a reply by the author, *The Journal of Contemporary History,* V, no. 2 (1970), 83–122; V, no. 4 (1970), 185–201. The research in all is admirable, all provide extensive documentation, and those published since 1964 have been able to take advantage of the sudden opening of British official records to the public. Kedourie, Tibawi, and Friedman are especially valuable for their thoroughgoing expositions of important theses with full citation and ample quotations of sources. It is the nature of scholarship, unfortunately, that points of disagreement tend to overshadow points of agreement, even when the latter are more numerous and more significant than the former. The views which are presented here, whether justified or baseless, could not have been formed save for the labors of those who have mined the unpublished records with such energy, judgment, and skill and presented their discoveries in so fair-minded a manner.

The unpublished sources have not yielded evidence counter to the view that Ḥusayn converted to Arabism when the conditions of World War I made Arabism more useful to the Amir of Mecca than Ottomanism. Nor do the new studies show that Ḥusayn took his new ideology lightly. In particular, nothing in the new evidence suggests that the caliphate, rather than Arab kingship, was the object of Ḥusayn's ambition. Similarly, nothing supports the view that the new claimant to leadership of the Arab nation had only slight interest in securing the national territories.

That the British suggested from late 1914 on that Ḥusayn might assume the caliphate has never been in doubt. The only question concerns Ḥusayn's response to the hint. The weight of the new evidence is the same as that of the old—namely, that Ḥusayn attached no importance to the British hint of the caliphate other than as an argument in favor of his claims to Arab kingship. Kedourie still ascribes great importance to the caliphate, but the only new piece of evidence from the unpublished documents is another account of the Sharif's informing a British officer that the British had offered him the caliphate without any expression of interest on his part.[1] In this conversation Ḥusayn pretty surely was using the British suggestion as an argument for British recognition of his kingship, just as he unquestionably was in the two similar incidents which have long since been attested to by two published documents. There still is no reason to believe that Ḥusayn took the caliphate question seriously, in view of the absence of evidence that he was in any way an adherent of the nineteenth-century secularist heresy that the caliphate was a kind of papacy, and in view of his specific remarks to Lawrence.[2]

Ḥusayn's territorial objectives and his action on their behalf remain the center of debate. Kedourie doubts that "the sharif was really much interested in territorial commitments."[3] Both he and Friedman believe that Ḥusayn accepted some British reservations and that the Arabs later went back on Ḥusayn's agreement. Palestine especially continues to be controversial. Tibawi insists that Ḥusayn and the Arabs made no concessions. The old shadow over British honor persists, with Tibawi repeating the charge of betrayal and Kedourie and Friedman absolving the British of guilt. British behavior is not the subject of this essay, but in examining Hashimite activity it is crucial to determine precisely what promises and commitments the British and Ḥusayn made to each other. To achieve this end it will be necessary not only to consider the relatively few contemporary sources which have been summarized and quoted by recent researchers, but also to examine in detail the extensive subsequent commentaries on the war-time contacts between the British and the Hashimites.

It remains absolutely clear that when McMahon received Ḥusayn's terms in July, 1915, the British had abundant evidence to confirm that the Amir's territorial demands embodied

1. Kedourie, *Chatham House Version*, pp. 18, 23–24.

2. See above, pp. 40–45, 81–83. For material concerning the new view of the caliphate as papacy, which was circulated chiefly by intellectuals, civil servants, and politicians, not *ʿulamāʾ*, see Bernard Lewis, "The Ottoman Empire in the Mid-Nineteenth Century: A Review," *Middle Eastern Studies,* I (1965), 291–294.

3. Kedourie, *Chatham House Version,* pp. 22–24.

the claims of all Arab nationalists. One could, of course, question seriously the importance of the Arab national movement, but the relative strength of a political movement and its aspirations are entirely different matters. The British in Cairo had plentiful contacts with Arab nationalists, and all claimed precisely the boundaries demanded by Ḥusayn.[4] The Amir of Mecca was transmitting a proposal on behalf of the Arab nationalist movement, not presenting his own personal demands.

It remains equally clear that the British never committed themselves to the full Arab nationalist program as presented by Ḥusayn. The British commitment is essentially contained in McMahon's letter to Ḥusayn dated October 24, 1915,[5] about which so much debate has raged. The letter contains a few ambiguities, but the only truly disputable point is whether or not Palestine was excluded from the territory which the British pledged to recognize as the area of Arab independence. A great amount of heat has been generated by McMahon's statement, "Portions of Syria lying to the west of the districts of Damascus, Homs, Hama and Aleppo cannot be said to be purely Arab, and should be excluded from the limits demanded." The debate hinges on the word "districts," which was rendered by *wilāyāt* in the Arabic translation sent to Ḥusayn.[6] In response to Arab assertions that McMahon had not excluded Palestine from the area of Arab independence, from 1921 on the British goverment argued that *wilāyāt* could only have its most usual meaning, the plural of the term used to designate the Ottoman administrative unit of the highest rank, the vilayet. Accordingly, the British argued, the resultant phrase "lying to the west of the Vilayet of Damascus" was a clear formal implicit exclusion of Palestine, which was a separate Ottoman administrative unit lying to the west of the Vilayet of Damascus, which

4. Tibawi, *Mod. Hist. Syria*, pp. 220–221, 223, 224, 225–226; Kedourie, *Chatham House Version*, p. 19.

5. Text in Great Britain, Foreign Office, *Correspondence between Sir Henry McMahon . . . and the Sherif Hussein of Mecca, July 1915–March 1916*, Cmd. 5957 (House of Commons Sessional Papers, 1938–39, vol. 27), pp. 7–9.

6. For the official Arabic text see Ḥāfiẓ Wahbah, *Jazīrah al-ʿarab fi-al-qarn al-ʿishrīn* [*The Arabian Peninsula in the Twentieth Century*], 2nd ed. (Cairo: Maṭbaʿah li-Jannah al-Taʾlīf wa al-Tarjamah wa al-Nashr, 1946), p. 155.

extended southward to Maʿān. The Arabs countered that the only possible interpretation of the word *wilāyāt* was as "environs, vicinities, regions," and that Palestine could not have been excluded by the phrase since it lay to the south of the vicinity of Damascus and not west of the specified region.[7] The question has been illuminated and the controversy renewed by Isaiah Friedman's bringing to light from unpublished official records the basic texts of the later British position. The official exegesis evidently had its birth in an opinion regarding "districts"/*wilāyāt* which Hubert Young set forth in 1920, and it reached maturity in a memorandum written in 1930 by W. J. Childs, an official in the Foreign Office. An entirely different exegesis had already been advanced by Arnold Toynbee, who, when he was an official in the Foreign Office in 1918, interpreted the phrase in the same way that Arab spokesmen were later to do. Friedman opts for the British official position, which rejects the arguments of Toynbee and the Arabs. Toynbee, however, reaffirms his stand.[8]

The later British official interpretation of the phrase is virtually impossible on both linguistic and documentary grounds. Linguistic and logical considerations are decisive. From the material now published, it appears that the British official position is based on a misconception of the linguistic problem. The proponents of the British official position fail to understand that the argument turns on interpreting the Arabic word *wilāyāt* as "vilayets" instead of "environs," and that McMahon's own "districts" is inconsequential. A second misconception is the belief that the problem is one of deciding whether McMahon "would have resorted to ambiguous wording in the Arab vernacular in preference to accepted terminology in which both Hussein and his son Abdullah were well versed," and that since a High Commissioner was unlikely to have used the

7. Great Britain, Colonial Office, *Correspondence with the Palestine Arab Delegation and the Zionist Organization*, Cmd. 1700 (House of Commons Sessional Papers, 1922, vol. 23), pp. 11, 16, 20, 25–26, 30.

8. *Journ. Cont. Hist.*, V, no. 2 (1970), 103–122; V, no. 4 (1970), 185–200. On Young, Childs, and Toynbee specifically, see V, no. 2, 112–116; V, no. 4, 185–186, 191, 194, 198.

vernacular, the term can only mean vilayets.[9] The problem is not one of a difference in meaning which depends upon the use of the term as vernacular or accepted terminology and thus can be settled by deciding on non-linguistic grounds whether or not the author was likely to have used vernacular or accepted terminology. Instead, the problem is the universal linguistic one of single words having multiple meanings with the precise meaning being determined by the linguistic context. Arabic *wilāyah,* the singular of *wilāyāt,* can mean vilayet or vicinity. The linguistic context of *wilāyāt* in McMahon's letter makes it certain that the author (1) either meant environs or (2) was so ignorant of Arabic and of Ottoman administrative geography that he stated a crucial limitation in a totally self-contradictory way. In McMahon's letter, the wording is "districts/*wilāyāt* of Damascus, Homs, Hama, and Aleppo," and if Vilayet of Damascus is meant, then the vilayets of Homs, Hama, and Aleppo must also be meant, which is absurd since there were no Ottoman vilayets of Homs and Hama and the western border of the Vilayet of Aleppo was the Mediterranean. To believe that McMahon intended to entail the exclusion of Palestine by the phrase is to believe that he or his drafting officer devoted conscious thought to the choice of the words. It is most difficult to believe that any British official in Cairo would have deliberately sought to imply the exclusion of Palestine by a statement so obviously incapable of supporting the desired inference.

The English text presents no great mysteries or difficulties. The actual English term "district," whether interpreted as "an administrative division" or as "region, tract," is much too general to serve as the equivalent of "vilayet," i.e., an Ottoman administrative unit of the highest rank. Unlike "vilayet," "district" usually does not signify a specific administrative unit unless further bound by an attributive term, and "district" was not used in English to designate any of the Ottoman administrative divisions. Both Damascus and Aleppo were the centers

9. Friedman, *Journ. Cont. Hist.,* V, no. 2 (1970), 114, 120 (quotation, 114); no. 4 (1970), 198, n. 10.

of three Ottoman administrative districts, while Homs and Hama both were the centers of two. McMahon's phrase, on the usual construction of the English, would suggest the exclusion of the region to the west of a belt of territory running from Damascus in the south to Aleppo in the north. This obvious meaning of "districts"/*wilāyāt* was quite naturally the one given to it in all official British commentaries which antedate 1920. In view of the contrary claim of the later British official explanation, the problem must be taken up in detail.

The British official position that *wilāyāt* meant vilayets appears to have been first formulated in the fall of 1920 by Hubert Young. Rather surprisingly, no one seems to have attributed this exegesis to the two officials who wrote the letter, McMahon and Clayton, or to officials who worked with them in Cairo, such as Hogarth and Ormsby-Gore, though all are among those who are cited as having later declared that the exclusion of Palestine from McMahon's pledge had certainly been intended.[10] It may be that all these officials did espouse the official exegesis, but if none of them did in fact appeal to the interpretation, as appears to be the case, then they were not relying on that phrase when they declared that Palestine had been exluded. Whatever the case, the later official exegesis is highly suspect. As Toynbee [11] points out, it was advanced after the Palestine mandate had been assigned to Britain and the mandate had been challenged by Arabs. The exegesis is thus intrinsically self-serving, by its very nature subject to serious question.

While the later official interpretation of "districts"/*wilāyāt* is linguistically and logically almost impossible and highly suspect under the rules of evidence, the linguistically normal one is supported by contemporary British official commentaries which have much greater evidential weight than the post-1920

10. *Journ. Cont. Hist.*, V, no. 2 (1970), 104, 108, 116; V, no. 4 (1970), 197; Great Britain, Colonial Office, *Report of a Committee Set up to Consider Certain Correspondence between Sir Henry McMahon . . . and the Sharif of Mecca in 1915 and 1916*, Cmd. 5974 (House of Commons Sessional Papers, 1938–39, vol. 14), pp. 8, 30.

11. *Journ. Cont. Hist.*, V, no. 4 (1970), 191–192.

explanations. According to his testimony, Toynbee in 1918 quite naturally read the phrase as referring to a region to the west of a line running from Damascus to Aleppo. Two years earlier an important official in Cairo, D. G. Hogarth, had read McMahon's phrase in exactly the same way. Toynbee's claim that his interpretation was entirely independent may well be true and cannot be rejected on any logical grounds. At the same time, it may well have been unconsciously influenced by Hogarth's earlier interpretation, which Toynbee apparently had read and to which he had access in any event. Nevertheless, Toynbee's interpretation was not self-serving, since he at the time did not believe that Palestine should be included in the area of Arab independence and he was not opposed to Jewish colonization. His exegesis of 1918 thus is at least evidence that Hogarth's earlier reading of McMahon's phrase was not unnatural to one who was linguistically qualified and without any non-linguistic bias. Hogarth himself obviously regarded his interpretation as the linguistically natural one. He spent no time pondering the meaning, and his reading was not the result of a desire to have Palestine included in the area of Arab independence, for, as will be seen below, elsewhere in the same memorandum, on different grounds, he held Palestine to have been excluded from the area of Arab independence.[12] Hogarth's interpretation may indeed have been influenced by the two authors of the phrase, Clayton and McMahon.

In a document dated two days after his letter to Ḥusayn, McMahon made it clear that the word "districts" could have meant nothing more than environs or vicinities. Writing to Foreign Secretary Grey on October 26, 1915, the High Commissioner said, "I have been definite . . . in excluding . . . those districts on the *northern* coast of Syria, which cannot be said to be Arab and where I understand that French interests have been recognized."[13] In this passage McMahon explicitly makes "those districts on the northern coast of Syria . . .

12. *Journ. Cont. Hist.*, V, no. 2 (1970), 112–114; no. 4 (1970), 187–189, 193–196.

13. Friedman, *Journ. Cont. Hist.*, V, no. 2 (1970), 109; Tibawi, p. 233. Italics added.

where . . . French interests have been recognized" the equivalent of "portions of Syria lying to the west of the districts of Damascus, Homs, Hama and Aleppo." Palestine cannot be in the area covered by the phrase, unless the northern coast of Syria is considered as beginning at Gaza. And so Ḥusayn interpreted McMahon's letter in precisely the same way when in protest, he replied, "The two *vilayets* of Aleppo and Beirut and their sea coasts are purely Arab *vilayets*. . . ."[14] In the same explanation to Grey, McMahon also indicates the meaning of "districts." When he writes "while recognizing the *towns* of Damascus, Homs, Hama and Aleppo as being within the circle of Arab countries,"[15] he makes "the towns of Damascus, Homs, Hama, and Aleppo" the equivalent of "the districts of Damascus, Homs, Hama and Aleppo," and "town" cannot mean vilayet. Two days after writing the letter to Ḥusayn, McMahon stated that he had intended to exclude "districts on the northern coast of Syria" from and to include "the towns of Damascus, Homs, Hama and Aleppo" in "the circle of Arab countries." In view of McMahon's explicit explanation, one may wonder why the official exegesis was ever put forward. Nevertheless, the exegesis was advanced, and its other parts must be considered.

The British government itself never had a great deal of confidence in the interpretation of "districts"/*wilāyāt*. As a result of the argument made by the Palestine Arab Delegation in 1922, the Colonial Office gave up its plans to base its case on a formal inference from the supposed occurrence of "Vilayet of Damascus" and rested content with the simple statement, "But this promise was given [by McMahon to Ḥusayn] subject to a reservation made in the same letter, which exluded from its scope, among other territories, the portions of Syria lying to the west of the district of Damascus. This reservation has always been regarded by His Majesty's Government as covering the vilayet of Beirut and the independent Sanjak of Jerusa-

14. Ḥusayn to McMahon, Nov. 5, 1915, Cmd. 5957, p. 9.

15. Tibawi, p. 233, italics added. Friedman, *Journ. Cont. Hist.*, V, no. 2 (1970), 109, omits this passage from his quotation of this document.

lem."[16] In 1930 W. J. Childs held fast to Young's exegesis, and in 1939 the British government began its talks with the Arabs at the London Palestine Conference with a weak reaffirmation of the exegesis. But the British quickly retreated. The formula was never renounced, but its frailty was now admitted. The British government then, following a lead given by the Palestine Royal Commission in 1937, based its claim that McMahon had excluded Palestine largely on McMahon's general reservation in respect of French interests.[17]

A final and more enduring point in the later official exegesis is that the phrase, instead of originating with McMahon, had been used by Muḥammad Sharīf al-Fārūqi, an alleged representative of Ḥusayn, in the course of some conversations with McMahon and Clayton early in October, 1915, just before McMahon wrote his letter. But here the argument concerning the meaning of the phrase becomes involved in the assertion of much broader claims. The Fārūqi episode must be examined as a whole, though it will be well to separate the various issues involved rather than leave them entangled.

When Fārūqi, an Arab officer in the Ottoman Army who had deserted to the British lines at Gallipoli, arrived in Cairo in 1915, the military position of the Allies had begun to worsen. Fārūqi claimed to be a member of the Arab secret societies and painted a vivid picture of the great strength which the Arabs were about to let loose against the Turks. The British military in Cairo and in London began to urge that agreement be reached with Ḥusayn in order to create an Arab diversion against the Turks.[18] Fārūqi's claims undoubtedly influenced the military, but, in view of the military situation, the British military were looking for assistance wherever they could find it. It is reasonable to believe that the British military would have shown increased interest in Ḥusayn's letter even if Fārūqi or

16. Cmd. 1700, pp. 20, 25–26, 30 (quotation, p. 20).

17. Cmd. 5974, pp. 7, 10, 24–28, 45–46; Great Britain, Palestine Royal Commission, *Report*, Cmd. 5479 (House of Commons Sessional Papers, 1936–37, vol. 14), pp. 19–20.

18. Friedman, *Journ. Cont. Hist.*, V, no. 2 (1970), 89–93; Tibawi, pp. 229–232.

any other Arab revolutionary officer had never appeared in the British camp. Similarly, McMahon would have had to come to grips with Ḥusayn's demands sooner or later, even without any additional contact with the Arab underground. Nevertheless, Fārūqi's appearance in Cairo did stir the British to action at the time and certainly had an influence on McMahon's reply to Ḥusayn.

The full official British interpretation of the Ḥusayn-McMahon correspondence added to Young's interpretation of the phrase "districts," etc., an attribution of the phrase to Fārūqi. The argument goes on to claim that Fārūqi, a representative of Ḥusayn, agreed to the exclusion of Palestine and the Syrian coast from the region of Arab independence. Indeed, the official version goes much further by attributing the initiative to Fārūqi and by representing both McMahon's letter to Ḥusayn and the Sykes-Picot agreement as terms formulated by the British as a result of and in order to conform to Fārūqi's statement of Arab goals and demands. This final version evidently was first set forth by W. J. Childs in 1930 and was still an important part of the British case at the London Palestine Conference of 1939.[19] There are substantial differences between Fārūqi's account of his talks and those written by Clayton, McMahon, and Sykes. Nevertheless, it is possible to draw some conclusions which do not permit much doubt. Even the quoted parts of the British records do not support the British official interpretation.

To begin with the most narrow question, the meaning of the phrase in McMahon's letter, the ostensible evidence for its attribution to Fārūqi seems to be McMahon's October 18, 1915, report to Grey, in which the High Commissioner summarized Fārūqi's opinions as follows: "The occupation by France of the purely Arab districts of Aleppo, Hama, Homs and Damascus would be opposed by the Arabs by force of

19. Friedman, *Journ. Cont. Hist.*, V, no. 2 (1970), 105, 113, 114; V, no. 4 (1970), 198; Cmd. 5974, pp. 23–24, 26–27; Elie Kedourie, *England and the Middle East: The Destruction of the Ottoman Empire, 1914–1921* (London: Bowe and Bowes, 1956), pp. 37–38, also accepted the British official interpretation of the Fārūqi conversations.

arms, but with this exception, they would accept some modifications of the northwestern boundaries proposed by the Sharif of Mecca."[20] From this Childs and subsequent British officials, followed by Friedman, have inferred that Fārūqi was the author of the phrase and that he must have been referring to the Vilayet of Damascus, not merely the environs of Damascus. There really is no evidence that Fārūqi used the words "districts." But this aspect of the British position is not based on the meaning of "districts." Instead, quite another chain of inference is followed. Since Fārūqi is reported to be specifying the places for which the Arabs would fight, it is further assumed that "districts" must have entailed "Vilayet of Damascus," for otherwise Fārūqi would have been abandoning all of Transjordan as a part of the Arab state. The reasoning is specious. No evidence is cited as indication of Fārūqi's territorial claims other than the phrase itself. The assumption is based on an unstated premise that Fārūqi would have sought to retain as much territory as possible, and from this premise it follows that Fārūqi was not willing to exclude any territory at all from the area of Arab independence.

There is no evidence that Fārūqi used the word "district" and none that the word meant vilayet, whoever used it first. Clayton, reporting the same conversation with Fārūqi, spoke only of "the inclusion of Damascus, Aleppo, Hama and Homs in the Arab confederation."[21] McMahon's report to Grey has no greater intrinsic credibility than does Clayton's account. The latter's use of the mere names of the four cities indicates that whatever the origin of the word "districts," it was not used in the talks with Fārūqi to mean vilayets. The same conclusion is indicated by a confidential letter which McMahon wrote for the record in 1922. The former High Commissioner declared that he had intended to exclude Palestine and asserted that Ḥusayn had never given him reason to believe that the Sharif failed to understand that Palestine was excluded. But

20. Friedman, *Journ. Cont. Hist.*, V, no. 2 (1970), 105 (quotation). Tibawi, p. 228, gives a summary only; Cmd. 5974, pp. 23–24, 26–27.
21. Tibawi, p. 228.

McMahon ignored the official British argument. He connected his letter to Ḥusayn and the talks with Fārūqi in the following manner:

> My reasons for restricting myself to specific mention of Damascus, Homs, Hama and Aleppo in that connexion in my letter were: (1) that these were places to which the Arabs attached vital importance and (2) that there was no place I could think of at the time of sufficient importance for purposes of definition further south of the above.

Later in the letter, McMahon develops his explanation for lack of specifics with respect to Palestine by asserting that he thought it best to leave the actual frontier of Palestine to future negotiations and that "at that moment, moreover, very detailed definitions did not seem called for." [22] McMahon does not mention the Vilayet of Damascus. Indeed, he once again omits the word "districts" from the crucial phrase and merely names the four cities which he describes as "places to which the Arabs attached vital importance." Once again, "places," like "towns," indicates that McMahon was not thinking of vilayets. The word "districts" was probably McMahon's, not Fārūqi's. Even if the word "districts" was Fārūqi's own, the phrase must be interpreted by the same linguistic, logical, and documentary standards as the phrase in McMahon's letter, and these once again point to a zone of territory from Damascus in the south to Aleppo in the north; this could not be included in the territory lying to the west where, the British said, French interests were decisive. Palestine, as McMahon wrote in 1922, did not figure prominently in his thinking in 1915.

The phrase "districts of Damascus, Homs, Hama and Aleppo" in McMahon's letter to Ḥusayn and its analogue in his report to Grey on the conversation with Fārūqi refers to a zone running from the region of Damascus in the south to the environs of Aleppo in the north. The two documents and other contemporary evidence agree with McMahon's confidential memoir of 1922. This territory had figured prominently in the

22. Friedman, *Journ. Cont. Hist.*, V, no. 2 (1970), 108.

British talks with Fārūqi, so much so that McMahon did not think any other region or place was important enough to specify. But the evidence thus far considered establishes nothing more than that this was McMahon's view. Why McMahon held this opinion is a question which has yet to be explored.

McMahon and Clayton do agree with the later British official interpretation in strongly implying that Fārūqi came forward without prompting to inform the British that the Arabs would be content with no more than the "districts of Aleppo, Hama, Homs and Damascus." This view is not supported by the unpublished evidence quoted or summarized in the recent studies. It is difficult to imagine that Fārūqi would, in full knowledge of the Arab territorial demands already presented to the British, start bargaining by reducing the price even before the British had made their first counter-offer. And the evidence indicates that whatever Fārūqi said, he said it in response to some British questions about specific pieces of territory. According to Clayton, Fārūqi asserted, "Our scheme embraces all the Arab countries, including Syria and Mesopotamia, but if we cannot have all, we want as much as we can get." [23] Clayton also quotes him as saying that "a French occupation of Syria would be strenuously resisted by the Mohammadan population. They would, however, no doubt seek England's good offices towards obtaining a settlement of the Syrian question in a manner as favorable as possible to their views. . . ." [24] The only likely interpretation of these statements is that they are summaries of the trend of the conversations, and imply that Fārūqi began by reiterating the Arab claims in full, and then admitted that if forced to do so the Arabs would accept whatever modifications they were not able to prevent. Even so, this is a decidedly self-serving British record. Fārūqi himself related that the British outlined French claims and indicated the reservation to him. "After they had acquainted me with this proposal," he wrote, "they asked me my personal opinion and I answered them in a personal ca-

23. Quoted by Friedman, *Journ. Cont. Hist.*, V, no. 2 (1970), 105.
24. Quoted by Tibawi, p. 288.

to limited Arab rule under British tutelage in Iraq and Palestine.[30]

It has been alleged that Fārūqi stated that the Arabs had "not included the places inhabited by a foreign race in the territories which they demand" and that the statement excluded Palestine by implicitly referring to the existing Jewish population. The statement occurs in a message which McMahon sent to Grey in October, 1915, but the message apparently was separate from the one which includes the statement about the four cities.[31] It is likely that McMahon took the phrase itself not from Fārūqi, but from the statement in Ḥusayn's letter dated September 9, that the Arabs "within these limits have not included places inhabited by a foreign race" and that "these limits include only our race." Fārūqi, by his own account, said that he "was unaware of a non-Arab country west of the Damascus-Aleppo line. . . ." Whatever Fārūqi said, his intention was undoubtedly the same as Ḥusayn's in his letters of September 9 and November 5—that is, to reaffirm Arab claims, not, as has been argued, to relinquish them.[32]

Fārūqi's alleged acceptance of limitations on Arab territorial claims did not originate with him but was made in response to a direct approach by the British. He at most acknowledged that the Syrian coast from Lebanon to Alexandretta would be left to the French. He appears to have included Palestine with Iraq in an Arab area which was to be under British tutelage rather than fully independent. But there is no need to believe that Fārūqi went quite this far. Clayton's own report depicts him as saying that the Arabs would try to get all that they could. At most, Clayton describes Fārūqi as realizing that the

30. Tibawi, p. 228. Friedman (*Journ. Cont. Hist.*, V, no. 4 [1970], 199) says, "Al-Faruqi specifically mentioned Palestine by name when excluding it, as well as the Syrian littoral, from the area destined to become an Arab state." It is not clear whether this refers to Fārūqi's conversations in October, as does Tibawi's statement, or to a November conversation between Sykes and Fārūqi.

31. Friedman, *Journ. Cont. Hist.*, V, no. 2 (1970), 105–106, 107; V, no. 4 (1970), 199.

32. Ḥusayn's letters in Cmd. 5957, pp. 6, 9; Fārūqi's statement in Marmorstein, p. 163.

Arabs might not be able to obtain all that they asked for. Fārūqi was perhaps telling the truth when he wrote Ḥusayn that he had insisted to the British that the Arabs could not renounce any territory.

Fārūqi's second set of statements on Arab aims was explicitly the result of British direct queries. As a result of urging from Grey, Sykes called on Fārūqi in mid-November. Sykes obviously set aside for the occasion his own belief that Palestine should be British and clearly told Fārūqi what apparently had not been said a little more than a month earlier, i.e., that both Palestine and northern Syria were in the sphere of French influence. According to Sykes, Fārūqi agreed that in the entire area west of a line running from Dayr al-Zawr to Darʿa and then along the Hijaz Railway to Maʿān, France should have a monopoly of economic concessions, a privileged position with respect to educational institutions and activities, and the sole right to provide European advisers and employees. Even so, Fārūqi said, the Arabs would dispense with the Europeans if they were able to do without them.[33]

Sykes's conversation with Fārūqi has been used by Friedman (V, no. 2, 106–107, 114, n. 97) in an attempt to bring Palestine within the territory lying to the west of Damascus, Homs, Hama, and Aleppo which was to be absolutely excluded from the area of Arab independence. The reasoning is faulty. Two false propositions compose the argument. First, Friedman here says that the region under discussion is the territory lying to the west of the Hijaz Railway from Darʿa to Maʿān and of the districts of Damascus, Homs, Hama, and Aleppo—i.e., the Syrian littoral and Palestine. Second, the entire territory is said to be totally excluded from the area of the Arab independence, like the territory lying to the west of the districts of Damascus, Homs, Hama, and Aleppo in McMahon's letter to Ḥusayn and in the McMahon-Clayton conversation with Fārūqi. The first proposition is contradicted by Sykes's report

33. Nevakivi, pp. 28–29; Friedman, *Journ. Cont. Hist.*, V, no. 2 (1970), 106.

of his conversation as summarized by both Nevakivi and Friedman. There is no doubt that the territory under discussion is all of Syria and Palestine, not just the Syrian littoral and Palestine. Friedman himself (p. 106) says that Fārūqi agreed to recognize French privilege in the area which Fārūqi called "Syria and Palestine"—i.e., in the entire region, not just the Syrian littoral and Palestine. Furthermore, Friedman describes the area where Fārūqi recognized French interests as being "bounded by the Euphrates in the north running south to Deir Zor, and to Deraa and along the Hedjaz Railway to Maan." The districts of Aleppo, Homs, Hama, and Damascus lie to the west, not to the east, of a line from Dayr al-Zawr to Darʿa. It would seem unquestionable that Sykes was describing to Fārūqi the eastern frontier of the French zone which was set forth in the de Bunsen Committee report and extending it from Darʿa to Maʿān. The falsity of the proposition that the region in question consisted of Palestine and the area west of Damascus-Aleppo destroys the logical basis for the second proposition, i.e., that the region in question was the region which was to be excluded from the area of Arab independence as in McMahon's letter to Ḥusayn. Since Palestine is included in the same region as the Damascus-Aleppo zone, Palestine cannot be in the region which was totally excluded from the Arab area.

The second proposition is doubly false. Once again, Friedman's statement is contradicted by his own summary of Sykes's report, which explicitly says (p. 106) that the region was one in which the Arabs agreed to a French monopoly of concessionary enterprises and of European advisers and employees and to a special position for French educational institutions and activities. It is clear then that Palestine is not said to be an area of absolute exclusion from Arab independence, like the Syrian littoral, which is not even referred to in this conversation. All that is involved is a reputed agreement to accept French advisers and concessions in Syria and Palestine, just as Fārūqi had agreed to accept British advisers and concessions in Iraq.[34] Nothing whatever was said about areas which were to be totally excluded from the Arab area.

At most, then, the British had obtained from Fārūqi admission that the Arabs might accept certain British proposals, i.e., the exclusion of the north Syrian coastal region in favor of France and the grant to Britain and France of a special position in the rest of the Arab countries outside Arabia. With regard to Palestine, Fārūqi accepted a proposal for a French special position as he had earlier accepted the proposal that England have special status.

The British conversations with Fārūqi and McMahon's letter to Ḥusayn of October 24 are part and parcel of the same policy. The modifications of Arab claims which Fārūqi is reported to have accepted originated with the British officials, not with Fārūqi. These modifications were included in McMahon's letter to Ḥusayn. McMahon excluded from the area of Arab independence the hinterland of the northern coast of Syria. He did not explicitly or implicitly exclude Palestine by any clear specific reference. But McMahon did include another reservation in his letter to Ḥusayn dated October 24, 1915. Immediately following the paragraphs in which the Syrian littoral was excluded, the High Commissioner said, "As for those regions lying within those frontiers wherein Great Britain is free to act without detriment to the interests of her ally, France, I am empowered . . . to give the following assurances. . . ." This reservation limited British assurances to those territories where France had no claim. It surely covered Palestine, which, along with the rest of Syria, was an area of acknowledged French interest. This was recognized by D. G. Hogarth in 1916 when he wrote his memorandum on British commitments. He saw that McMahon's one specific territorial exclusion left Palestine

34. Cf. Toynbee on this point and Friedman's refutation, *Journ. Cont. Hist.*, V, no. 4 (1970), 189–190, 199. The question here is what Fārūqi said to Sykes, and of the evidence to which Friedman appeals in answer to Toynbee, only Sykes's report is relevant to this question. No one has depicted McMahon, Clayton, Nicolson, or Grey as having participated in Sykes's conversation with Fārūqi and thus qualified to give testimony concerning it. As has been shown, Friedman's inference from this conversation is contradicted by what he himself ascribes to Sykes, the sole qualified witness.

within the independent Arab area, but he also saw that the area so defined was "subject to these undefined reservations": that Britain had not committed itself to "Arab independence . . . in any portion of the Arab area in which we are not free to act without detriment to our ally France," and, conversely, that Britain had obligated itself only with respect to "those portions of the Arab speaking area in which we are free to act without detriment to the interests of France." Not surprisingly, when Hogarth included the Sykes-Picot agreement in this commentary, he did not consider it (even the provision to internationalize Palestine) to be contradictory to McMahon's letter to Ḥusayn.[35]

The applicability to Palestine of McMahon's general reservation in respect of French interests was challenged by the Arab delegations to the London Palestine Conference of 1939. The Arab argument was that Palestine was not an area of French interest because the British government, urged on by Kitchener, was allegedly opposed to assigning Palestine to France in 1915. The argument has no legal weight, for, as the British representatives pointed out, British desire to deny the claims of an ally would not set aside those claims unless the ally agreed.[36] The Arab contention, it turns out, is also factually false. Kitchener and other British officials did wish to exclude France from as much of the Arab world as possible, but the British government always recognized French interests, and in fact the only formal agreement which Britain concluded with respect to the Arab territories, the Sykes-Picot Agreement, was concluded with France.

The British government's official recognition of France's special position in Syria, including Palestine, created considerable dissension among British officials during 1915. There is no doubt that men like Kitchener, Wingate, Clayton, and McMahon preferred the total exclusion of France. Nevertheless, all knew that something must be left for France. On this basis Kitchener, far from seeking Palestine, which he regarded as

35. Friedman, *Journ. Cont. Hist.*, V, no. 4 (1970), 194–196.
36. Cmd. 5974, pp. 6, 7, 12–13, 27–28, 42, 46.

strategically negligible, favored assigning it to France as compensation for the British acquisition of Alexandretta, which France claimed and which Kitchener thought strategically vital.[37] As most British officials believed that France would never give up Alexandretta, British predominance in Palestine came to be regarded as necessary, with the Jerusalem and the religious shrines being left to international control. The de Bunsen Committee recommended against partition, and the cabinet did not adopt any decision. Nevertheless, McMahon, Clayton, and Sykes obviously were proceeding on the assumption that in the end Britain would replace France in Palestine, if not in the better part of Syria.

The desire of some British officials to limit or exclude the French did not change British policy. Foreign Secretary Grey, responding to McMahon's opinion that the British should replace the French in all of Syria except Lebanon, warned Cairo in March that England was not to be the competitor of France in Syria.[38] McMahon took his government's policy into account when formulating a response to the Arab nationalist movement. In proposing to Grey in October that Britain negotiate with Ḥusayn about boundaries, the High Commissioner added the limitation "in so far as England is free to act without detriment to the interests of her present Allies." When Grey replied and authorized McMahon to proceed, the Foreign Secretary stressed the need to take French sensitivities into account. Both McMahon and Grey were thinking about a general reservation which applied to the entire area claimed by Ḥusayn. Grey replied to McMahon, "You can give cordial assurances on the lines, and with the reserve about our allies, proposed by you. . . . The general reserve you propose is however necessary more especially for the north-western boundaries. . . ." [39] Both McMahon and Grey, then, believed it necessary to enter a

37. Nevakivi, pp. 15–16, 19–22; Klieman, *Journ. Cont. Hist.*, III, no. 3 (1968), 241–242; Friedman, *Journ. Cont. Hist.*, V, no. 2 (1970), 111–112.

38. Nevakivi, p. 26.

39. Friedman, *Journ. Cont. Hist.*, V, no. 2, 92, 110 (first quotation, McMahon to Grey, 92); Tibawi, pp. 231–232 (second quotation, Grey to McMahon, p. 232).

general reservation in behalf of French interests; in writing to Ḥusayn, McMahon did so.

Cairo still wished to change the official policy with respect to French interests. As late as November 15, 1915, Sykes was proposing a British protectorate over Palestine.[40] McMahon appears to have used his letter to Ḥusayn as a means of attempting to lead Grey to a new position. The High Commissioner's explanation to Grey of the general reservation in respect of French interests in the letter to Ḥusayn was disingenuous. McMahon began by saying, "I am not aware of the extent of French claims in Syria, nor of how far His Majesty's Government have agreed to recognise them," but he proceeded immediately to inform Grey that his general reservation was intended to apply to the Damascus-Aleppo region, not Palestine or Syria in general, by declaring, "Hence, while recognizing the towns of Damascus, Homs, Hama and Aleppo as being within the circle of Arab countries I have endeavoured to *provide for possible French pretensions to these places by a general modification* to the effect that His Majesty's Government can only give assurance in regard to those territories in which Great Britain is free to act without detriment to the interests of her ally France." [41]

The Foreign Office prevailed over Cairo. Grey kept insisting to McMahon that Britain should neither seek to replace France in Syria nor indicate to the Arabs any desire to do so. As a result, Fārūqi was approached once more, this time by Sykes, in mid-November. The British officials in Cairo now did what they seem to have neglected a little more than a month earlier. Fārūqi was told that all of Syria, including Palestine, was an area of French interest. Fārūqi reportedly stated in turn that the Arabs would recognize certain French privileges in the region.[42]

40. Tibawi, pp. 234–235.

41. Quotation in Tibawi, p. 233 (italics added). Friedman (*Journ. Cont. Hist.*, V, no. 2 [1970], 109) omits the crucial "while recognizing the towns of Damascus, Homs, Hama and Aleppo as being within the circle of Arab countries."

42. Nevakivi, p. 28; Tibawi, p. 243; cf. Friedman, *Journ. Cont. Hist.*, V, no. 2 (1970), 106.

In his letter to Ḥusayn McMahon excluded Palestine by the general reservation in respect of French interests. This meaning would have been clear to any politically active Arab at the time, for France's claim to special status in Palestine and Syria as a whole was common knowledge. However, the first conversations with Fārūqi did create a basis for some ambiguity, since Palestine evidently was not mentioned as being in the area of French interest. This might have been used to argue that Palestine was not covered by the general reservation. But the possibility of this interpretation was destroyed when Sykes informed Fārūqi in the second conversation that Palestine was an area of French interest. If Fārūqi's conversations did create any Arab misunderstanding of British promises, the responsibility was Fārūqi's.

The British in Cairo never offered unconditional independence to Ḥusayn or to any other Arab. In McMahon's letter to Ḥusayn the British reserved special status in certain areas for themselves, excluded the hinterland of the northern Syrian coast totally from the area of Arab independence, and entered an unspecified reservation on behalf of French interests wherever they might exist. Above all, the British provided no basis whatever for an Arab claim that the British had guaranteed the independence of all or most of the territory desired by the Arab nationalists and Ḥusayn.

The Arabs reserved their freedom as much as did the British. Even if Fārūqi said all that the British officials attributed to him, he was not unequivocal. The British reports relate that Fārūqi said the Arabs would resist French occupation and would dispense with European advisors insofar as possible. More importantly, Fārūqi did not bind any other Arab by his words. His British interviewers quote him as having said that "he was accredited by the committee [of either *al-ʿAhd* or of its joint committee with *al-Fatāh*] and that through him the reply of England [to the Sharif's offer] may be given," [43] but this carries no necessary implication beyond his being a mem-

43. This and the following quotation, including the bracketed insertions and the ellipsis, are from Tibawi, p. 227.

ber of the committee who could pass on a message from the British to the committee. The same sources furthermore quote Fārūqi as having said, "I am not authorized to discuss with you officially our political programme. . . ." It is clear, then, that Fārūqi did not claim to be an authorized agent of either Ḥusayn or the societies. Nor did Ḥusayn ever acknowledge that Fārūqi was his representative in October-November, 1915. The Sharif's letter to McMahon of January 1, 1916, merely adduces Fārūqi as evidence that the Sharif was representing the Arabs and not acting purely from self-interest: "Your honour will have realised, after the arrival of Mohammed (Faroki) Sherif [*sic*] and his interview with you, that all our procedure up to the present was of no personal inclination or the like, which would have been wholly unintelligible, but that everything was the result of the decisions and desires of our peoples, and that we are but transmitters and executants of such decisions and desires in the position they (our people) have pressed upon us."[44] The letter decidedly does not give Ḥusayn's approval to Fārūqi's alleged concessions. Instead, the letter specifically repeats Ḥusayn's refusal to admit French claims. This would constitute a rejection of Fārūqi if the Amir had known of his alleged concessions; it cannot possibly be counted an approval of Fārūqi's alleged modifications, in view of the total absence of any reason for the British to have believed that Fārūqi's concessions had been reported to Ḥusayn. It happens that Fārūqi had reported to Ḥusayn, although there is no evidence that the British knew it. In a letter dated December 6, 1915, Fārūqi wrote the Amir that he had told the British that the Arab nationalist territorial demands were not subject to revision but that England and France could be granted economic privileges and the right to provide administrative guidance.[45] It is thus doubly impossible to interpret Ḥusayn's letter to McMahon as approval of the alleged concessions of Fārūqi.

The only agreement reached by Ḥusayn and the British was

44. Cmd. 5957, p. 13; cf. Friedman, *Journ. Cont. Hist.*, V, no. 2 (1970), 107.

45. Kedourie, *Eng. and Mid. East*, p. 36, n. 3, p. 37; Marmorstein, pp. 163–164.

that they would suspend negotiations concerning their conflicting claims until the end of the war. Neither promised the other anything more than this. This agreement, embodied in Ḥusayn's letters of January 1 and February 18, 1916, and in McMahon's letter of January 25, 1916, was never modified thereafter.[46] But the post-war settlement was discussed on several occasions thereafter during the war by Ḥusayn and British officials. The British cannot be accused of keeping the Arabs in the dark, and in any event the talks with Fārūqi and the letters to Ḥusayn gave the British an enormous degree of freedom to determine the post-war settlement. But neither can it be shown that Ḥusayn, who was the only individual recognized by anyone as the spokesman of the Arabs, ever gave his assent to any modification of Arab demands beyond those set forth in his letters to McMahon.

In May, 1917, Sykes and Picot discussed the future with Ḥusayn. It is perhaps too strong to say, as Kedourie does, that when Sykes and Picot saw the King they "put the Agreement in his hand." There is even less justification for Tibawi's saying that "even the existence of an Anglo-French agreement regarding the future of Syria and Iraq was never mentioned." [47] The statement may be technically true, but the intent is not legitimate. Whether or not the existence of a formal Anglo-French agreement was mentioned, Ḥusayn had been apprised of British respect for French interests in the only formal British commitment to the Arabs, McMahon's letters. Furthermore, whatever was said in the conversations in Jidda, French claims and plans were discussed. Once again, Ḥusayn did not accept French claims. According to Sykes, the King declared "That His Majesty the King of Hejaz learned with satisfaction that the French Government approved of Arab aspirations on the Moslem Syrian littoral as the British did in Baghdad." [48] This, of course, represented a victory for the Arabs, as Ḥusayn told

46. See above, pp. 31, 32–33.

47. Kedourie, *Chatham House Version*, p. 26; Tibawi, p. 260.

48. Quoted in Kedourie, *Eng. and Mid. East*, p. 97. Nevakivi, p. 60, ends the statement with "Arab aspirations," which is followed by a semicolon and an ellipsis.

Lawrence, since the French and McMahon had always insisted on the absolute exclusion of the "Moslem Syrian littoral" from the area of Arab independence.[49] Ḥusayn gave up little. He followed his expression of satisfaction with the French recognition of Arab rights by a declaration that "as he had confidence in Great Britain, he would be content if the French Government pursued the same policy towards Arab aspirations on the Moslem Syrian littoral as the British did in Baghdad." [50] Ḥusayn had conceded little to the British in Baghdad and Basra. In his reply to McMahon dated November 5, 1915, the Sharif said, "As the Iraqi *vilayets* are parts of the pure Arab Kingdom . . . they are greatly valued by all Arabs far and near, and their traditions cannot be forgotten by them. . . . But in order to render an accord easy, and taking into consideration the assurances mentioned in the fifth article of your letter to keep and guard our mutual interests in that country as they are one and the same, for all these reasons we might agree to leave under the British administration for a short time those districts now occupied by the British troops without the rights of either party being prejudiced thereby (especially those of the Arab nation; which interests are to it economic and vital), and against a suitable sum paid as compensation to the Arab Kingdom for the period of occupation, in order to meet the expenses which every new kingdom is bound to support. . . ." [51] That he still envisaged a minimal role in the future Arab state for Britain and France is indicated in Sykes's own report. The King made it clear that he would strive to limit European political rights to the fullest extent possible, and that European advisers would be advisers only, without executive authority.[52] Ḥusayn, far from approving the Sykes-Picot agreement, thought that he had obtained from Picot a reduction of French claims in the Syrian littoral from possession in full sovereignty to such privileges as the right to provide advisers and teachers.

The final formal exchange of views between Ḥusayn and a

49. Kedourie, *Eng. and Mid. East.*, p. 97.
50. Nevakivi, p. 60; the ellipsis is Nevakivi's.
51. Cmd. 5957, p. 10; see also p. 13 (Ḥusayn to McMahon, Jan. 1, 1916).
52. Tibawi, p. 261.

British representative (Commander D. G. Hogarth in January, 1918, in this case) was equally devoid of any renunciation of Arab claims by the King. When Hogarth, according to his account, reminded the King of Britain's reservations with respect to French interests, he responded with a joking reference to Fashoda. But Ḥusayn had no need to protest. Hogarth brought with him a message which came closer to guaranteeing Arab independence than any words hitherto communicated to any Arab by any English statesman, for Hogarth delivered a message from the British government which opened by asserting, "The *Entente* Powers are determined that the Arab race shall be given full opportunity of once again forming a nation in the world. This can only be achieved by the Arabs themselves uniting and Great Britain and her Allies will pursue a policy with this ultimate unity in view." Hogarth, according to his own account, also said, "France had come to see eye to eye with us in Arab matters . . . took the view . . . that people should have the government they desire, and wished only to protect and assist the development of independent Government in Syria." The review of the Palestine question by the two men was also quite satisfactory to Ḥusayn. Point two of the British government's message specified that the religious shrines in Palestine (Moslem, Jewish, and Christian) required "a special régime to deal with these places approved of by the world," but that "the Mosque of Omar" should "be considered as a Moslem concern alone" and should "not be subjected directly or indirectly to any non-Moslem authority." Furthermore, even the future administration of religious shrines was to be subject to the condition "that no people shall be subject to another." It is not surprising that Ḥusayn readily agreed. In the third point of the message the British government declared, "Since the Jewish opinion of the world is in favour of a return of Jews to Palestine . . . His Majesty's Government are determined that in so far as is compatible with the freedom of the existing population, both economic and political, no obstacle should be put in the way of the realisation of this ideal." In commenting on this point, Hogarth "explained [to Ḥusayn] that His Majesty's

Government's resolve safeguarded existing local population." Ḥusayn, according to Hogarth, "seemed quite prepared for [the] formula and agreed enthusiastically, saying he welcomed Jews to all Arab lands." Ḥusayn was not agreeing to very much, since the government's statement and Hogarth's explanation had envisaged only the right of Jews to immigrate to Palestine and, while pointedly omitting any specification of Jewish economic or political rights, had guaranteed the economic and political rights of the existing population. As Hogarth recorded, "The King would not accept an independent Jew State in Palestine, nor was I instructed to warn him that such a State was contemplated by Great Britain." Hogarth's retrospective summary of the conversation is an accurate description of Ḥusayn's interpretation of his agreement with Britain. Writing specifically about "international control of the Palestine Holy Places," but then extending his remarks to every question discussed, Hogarth said, "The King left me in little doubt that he secretly regards this as a point to be reconsidered after the Peace, in spite of my assurance that it was to be a definitive arrangement. He compared ourselves and himself . . . to two persons about to inhabit one house, but not agreed which should take which floor or rooms! Often in the course of our conversations he spoke with a smile of accounts which he would settle after the war, pending which settlement he would press nothing. . . . I have no doubt that in his own mind he abates none of his original demands on behalf of the Arabs, or in the fullness of time, of himself." [53]

The newly available sources provide no support either for those who insist upon British perfidy or for those who cry Arab perversity. Both British and Hashimites knew that the other had not accepted their demands, and each deliberately proceeded

53. Great Britain, Foreign Office, *Statements Made on Behalf of His Majesty's Government during the Year 1918 in Regard to the Future Status of Certain Parts of the Ottoman Empire,* Miscellaneous no. 4 (1939), Cmd. 5964 (House of Commons Sessional Papers, 1938–39, vol. 27), pp. 3–4. The text of the message which Hogarth delivered, but not of his notes and memorandum, was also published in Cmd. 5974, pp. 48–49; cf. Kedourie, *Eng. and Mid. East,* pp. 98, 109, Friedman, *Journ. Cont. Hist.,* V, no. 2 (1970), 117; V, no. 4 (1970), 196–197; and Tibawi, pp. 262–263.

to put into effect an agreement which in important respects was an agreement to disagree. The reciprocal undertakings of the British and the Arabs have no legal expression except in the McMahon-Ḥusayn correspondence. Whatever was said by Fārūqi and Ḥusayn in conversations with British officials, nothing was ever put in writing by Ḥusayn or an authorized agent which seriously modified the position which the King took in his letters. The same is true of the British. The British records of the Anglo-Arab conversations in fact indicate that both Arabs and British held to their positions throughout the war. Ḥusayn never agreed to the British exclusion of any territory except Cilicia. He did accept, in his letters, a special British position in Iraq and British assistance, including advisers, everywhere. He probably did, in his talks with Sykes and Picot, accord the same position to France in Syria. The King probably also told Hogarth that he welcomed Jewish immigrants in every Arab country. But it is also clear from Ḥusayn's letters and the British records of the conversations that Ḥusayn's conception and the British and French conception of the British and French roles were miles apart. Nor was the idea of a Jewish political entity or of mass colonization even suggested in the conversation with Hogarth. Both sides stated their positions frankly. In 1915–1916, the problems confronting both the Arabs and the British led them to proceed deliberately as allies, even though both knew that their positions on the vital issues were possibly irreconcilable.

The ultimate settlement was the result of the interaction of Britain, France, and the Arabs after the war. We are very fortunate in having this interaction so well illuminated from differing points of view by Kedourie, Zeine, Nevakivi, Klieman, and Tibawi. There is no reason for the outsider to ascribe duplicity or bad faith to any one of the three sides. The Arabs had been told at the outset that Britain would have to assign first priority to French friendship. As Kedourie has long since made clear, some British officials were always (and the British government was sometimes) opposed to French claims. Not unnaturally, the Arabs attempted to utilize this rivalry to secure their own objectives, but in taking this path they assumed a risk that military action would be the result and that the Arabs would gain less by opposing than they would by agreeing with France. In the end, as the Arabs refused to reach agreement with either Britain or France, British and French military strength prevailed. When two sides have agreed to disagree and a settlement is unilaterally imposed by force, it is pointless to ascribe to either side the faithless betrayal or the sincere execution of a solemn covenant. One may make a moral choice if one wishes, but it cannot be made on the ground of betrayal of or fidelity to an ally.

It cannot even be said with certainty that the Arabs lost. The Arabs probably gained more than they lost by Ḥusayn's refusal to reach agreement with Britain and France during the war. Actually, the British and French mandates can be viewed as preferable to the terms offered in McMahon's letters. McMahon offered full French sovereignty in the Syrian littoral, virtual British colonial rule in Basra and Baghdad, and British or French protectorate everywhere else. These terms Ḥusayn never accepted. He refused the exclusion of the Syrian littoral and conditioned his acceptance of the other terms on an interpretation that made them meaningless from the British and French points of view. The mandates were closer to Ḥusayn's conditions. No part of Syria or Iraq was excluded. The British and French had the power to rule, but not as full sovereigns and not as protectors. At best, under McMahon's pledge the British and the French would have limited themselves voluntarily to assisting the Arabs to develop self-governing institutions. But such action would have been at the will of Britain and France, and they would have been answerable only to themselves. Under the mandates Britain and France were charged with ruling by a higher authority, and their rule was made conditional and temporary. Unsatisfactory as the mandates were from an Arab nationalist point of view, they were preferable to the terms of McMahon's letters.

Ḥusayn's policy contributed in a major way to what successes the Arab nationalists achieved. This was not because Ḥusayn's policy aroused the Arabs or contributed to their physical strength. Rather, the contribution lay in the fact that Ḥusayn's diplomacy enabled the Arabs to take advantage of an entirely new situation which had emerged by the end of World War I. Under the new conditions, the European Powers were no longer willing to behave in quite the same way that they had previously. Consequently, smaller or dependent nationalities who refused to accept rule by the Powers were in a much better position than previously.

The decisive element in 1918 was the new principle of international politics. Arab military strength was of minor significance. The British and the French defeated the Arabs but still settled, legally, for less than they had asked at the beginning of negotiations with Ḥusayn. Part of the reason for this was, as Kedourie has pointed out, the revolution in European thinking about international politics which occurred during World War I. The McMahon letters and the Sykes-Picot agreement were written by men who believed Great Powers had the right and the duty to maintain order and stability throughout the world. The belief became disreputable with the triumph of the principle of national self-determination. The belief that Great Powers were different persisted, however, and Powers continued to act as Powers. Consequently, Britain and France now had to justify their world positions in terms consistent with national self-determination. And so the Arab countries became mandated territories, not colonies, protectorates, or spheres of influence.

The failure of British and French imperialism in the Arab countries has resulted from world forces, the most important of which center in Europe and North America, but Arab utilization of the forces was necessary. Ḥusayn perhaps prepared the way for the Arabs to insure that Britain and France would disguise their rule in non-imperialist clothing and thus to hasten their ultimate departure. Once again Ḥusayn did not by his action provide a model or rally the Arabs. The political classes of the Fertile Crescent would have organized a nationalist movement against Britain and France in any event, and those who led were often as not only slightly less bent on excluding the Hashimites than the British or the French. What Ḥusayn had done was to give credibility to Arab nationalism in the Western countries and to encourage those in France and, much more important, Great Britain who for one reason or another were opposed to French or British imperialism. By carrying out the Arab revolt the Hashimites had provided an Arab claim to recognition as a nation and as an ally of Britain and France. Accordingly, the exact nature of the agreement between the Arabs and the British had great importance for political opinion, especially in Britain. Perhaps there is no better reflection of the contribution of the Hashimite movement to Arab nationalist achievement than in the way in which the British tried to justify their mandates.

The new principle was especially important in Great Britain. Here a wide range of political activists, including imperialists who thought it possible to exclude the French by means of British cooperation with Arab nationalism, immediately took up the Arab charge of betrayal, each for different reasons. In meeting the charge of duplicity and perfidy, the British for two decades would not avail themselves of the best defense—namely, that they had never promised the Arabs unconditional independence free of special position for Britain and France. The trouble was that a policy devised by honorable men in 1915 was totally dishonorable under the views which prevailed after 1918. As Kedourie has indicated, McMahon's promises were based on the same principles as the discredited Sykes-Picot agreement. If Ḥusayn had agreed to McMahon's demand that Britain and France have special status in the future Arab state or states, the charge of imperialism could have been turned aside on the ground of Arab consent. But Ḥusayn never gave his approval to McMahon's reservations. Therefore, the McMahon-Ḥusayn letters would have convicted the British of imperialism while acquitting them of betrayal. Surely this was one of the major reasons for the deep reluctance of the British to publish the letters.

Great Britain adapted its policies to the new theory with remarkable facility. In Iraq the British went a long way by granting the Arabs at least the semblance of self-government. Palestine was another matter, however. Here British special obligation to Zionism and its supporters throughout the world precluded an Iraqi solution except in an incomplete fashion in Transjordan. But a nationalist solution was devised for Palestine. The answer was found in the patently unsatisfactory exegesis of the phrase "districts of Damascus, Homs, Hama and Aleppo" instead of the impeccable reservation in respect of French interests. This was partly the result of reluctance to take note of French claims growing out of the continuation of the old rivalry with France. But even more it was produced by the feeling that it was immoral or impolitic to base British rule on such old-fashioned principles. McMahon's letter of October 24 provided just the answer needed. "Portions of Syria lying to the west of the districts of Damascus, Homs, Hama and Aleppo," McMahon told Ḥusayn, "cannot be said to be purely Arab, and should be excluded from the limits demanded." Here and here alone in McMahon's letter, the reservation is based solely on national self-determination, and if the phrase could be interpreted as covering Palestine, then the British position could be made entirely consistent with the principle of nationality. Better yet, since the territory was excluded on the ground that it was not purely Arab, Ḥusayn's acceptance was not even required to justify the British mandate. Thus for twenty years the British government chose to reveal only this much of the McMahon-Ḥusayn letters and to base its position in Palestine exclusively on this passage. In no other way could British imperial interests be made to harmonize with the new political ethics.

Al-Ḥusayn ibn-ʿAli ibn-ʿAwn, Amir and Sharif of Mecca and King of the Hijaz, worked zealously for his newly found cause, Arabism. In his dealings with the British, Ḥusayn was careful never to concede any basic Arab claims. Ḥusayn's diplomacy would have had little effect under the political ethics of 1915, but after the great revolution in ideas of international morality which took place during World War I, Ḥusayn's diplomacy had placed the Arabs in position to utilize the new concepts to their own advantage.

FIVE

From Ottomanism to Arabism: The Origin of an Ideology

SINCE 1918 the doctrine that the Arabs are a nation and that nationality is the basis of politics has come to be accepted by a very large majority of Arab political leaders and of at least the lay intellectuals. The espousal of this doctrine by a people who are predominantly Moslem in religion is a development of revolutionary significance, since for many centuries Moslems viewed the state in terms of religion and dynasty. Moslems have recognized the existence of distinct peoples or nations since the time of Mohammed. Indeed, Islam in its first century or so was the peculiar religion of the Arab nation, and to become a Moslem was to join the Arab nation as a dependent person. This system proved unworkable, however, and in the end Islam became the supreme bond which superseded nationality.[1]

The state in Moslem theory existed to enforce the *sharīʿah,* the law which God had sent to man through His messenger, Mohammed. Originally, it was held, the totality of the Moslems constituted a congregation, who ought to be joined together under the rule of one monarch, the caliph, or successor to the Prophet Mohammed, who was God's first viceroy on earth under Islam. After some centuries during which actuality was close to theory, the caliphate broke up, leaving the Moslems governed by a variety of dynasts or sultans. In theory, the *sharīʿah* remained to give unity to the Moslem congregation, and any ruler who enforced the *sharīʿah* was a legitimate ruler, regardless of how he had attained power.

Such was the nature (in theory) of the Ottoman Empire, the state sovereign in most of the Arab lands after 1517. The

1. A. N. Poliak, "L'Arabisation de l'Orient sémitique," *Revue des Études Islamiques,* 1938, pp. 37–40; Ignaz Goldziher, *Muhammedanische Studien,* 2 vols. (Halle, 1889–1890), I, 101–176.

Arabs of southwestern Asia and of Egypt accepted the rule of the Turkish Ottomans, at least nominally, for four centuries. But by the end of the nineteenth century a few Ottoman Arab intellectuals had put forward theories which denied the right of Turks to rule Arabs. These intellectuals created a new ideology, Arabism, and offered it as a solution to the problems of the day. One might simply assume that the antique Arab consciousness was revivifying itself, that these Arabs were returning to the ways of their ancestors in reasserting the primacy of their nationhood. Such an assumption, however, would leave unanswered the question of why the Arab national consciousness was reactivated after a millennial slumber.

Interest in nationality as a political principle was rekindled among the Moslem peoples by contact with the West. At the turn of the nineteenth century, a few Turks and Egyptian Arabs who had resided in Europe began to become aware of the European ideas of fatherland and nation. By the middle of the new century, terms for these and related concepts existed in both Turkish and Arabic.[2] One of the most influential persons in spreading the new ideas was an Egyptian, Rifāʿah Rāfiʿ al-Ṭahṭāwi, who spent the years 1826–1831 in France and described his experiences in a book published in 1834. This book enjoyed great popularity among both Arabs and Turks; it was reissued in 1848, and in 1840 a Turkish translation appeared.[3] The importance of European ideas in stimulating the thinking of these men is shown by their concern with the idea of patriotism. Love of one's place of birth or of one's homeland was a well-established virtue among the Moslems, but they did not give it political significance. Nor did the Moslems consider nationality to be connected with territoriality. Ṭahṭāwi and his

2. Bernard Lewis, "The Impact of the French Revolution on Turkey," *Journal of World History,* I (July 1953), 107–108.

3. J. Heyworth-Dunne, "Rifāʿah Badawi Rāfiʿ aṭ-Ṭahṭāwi: The Egyptian Revivalist," *Bulletin of the School of Oriental and African Studies* (London University), IX (1939), 961–967; X (1940), 400–401. The long-standing need for a systematic and comprehensive treatment of modern Arab intellectual history has now been satisfied by Albert H. Hourani's masterful *Arabic Thought in the Liberal Age, 1798–1939* (London: Oxford University Press, 1962; rpt. Oxford Paperback, 1970).

contemporaries did. Ṭahṭāwi spoke frequently of nations and countries and made it clear that a nation was intimately bound to a specific country. To him Egypt was a country and the Egyptians a nation which should love its fatherland.[4] After he returned to Egypt, in the course of a long career as educator and author, he explicitly introduced the new concepts in poetry.[5]

Ṭahṭāwi and his Turkish counterparts of the early nineteenth century were not mere mimics who copied for the sake of imitation. The European notions had no obviously necessary application to the Ottoman situation. Different men, in fact, applied the general idea in different ways. While Ṭahṭāwi talked of Egyptian patriotism, the Ottoman reformers sought to create a sense of Ottoman patriotism.[6] None of these men went deeply into the European theories of nationalism. They accepted without question the traditional Islamic dynastic state. They rendered the new concepts with Arabo-Turkish words which had long since been used in both Arabic and Turkish with meanings not far removed from their new significations.[7]

Of course, contact with strange ways is never a guarantee that the strange ways will be imitated. At the beginning of the nineteenth century, the peoples of the Ottoman Empire had a long history of close contact with Europe, throughout which they had shown no desire to imitate Frankish customs. Instead, even at the beginning of the nineteenth century most Ottomans

4. Rāfiʿ al-Ṭahṭāwi, *Kitāb talkhīṣ al-ibrīz ila talkhīṣ bārīz* [*The Book of the Distillation of Pure Gold, Even the Distillation of Paris*] (Cairo, 1323H/1905), pp. 5, 7, 14, 19, 20–21, 55–58, 258, 260, 262.

5. Walther Braune, "Beiträge zur Geschichte des neuarabischen Schrifttums," *Mitteilungen des Seminars für Orientalischen Sprachen zu Berlin,* XXXVI (1933), 119–123; Heyworth-Dunne, *BSOS,* X (1939), 399–400, 403, 404. For examples of his patriotic poems, see ʿAbd al-Raḥmān al-Rāfiʿi, *Shuʿarāʾ al-waṭanīyah* [*The Poets of Patriotism*] (Cairo: Maktabah al-Nahḍah al-Miṣrīyah, 1373H/1954), pp. 8–12.

6. Roderic H. Davison, "Turkish Attitudes Concerning Christian-Muslim Equality in the Nineteenth Century," *American Historical Review,* LIX (1954), 852. For more recent scholarship, see below, n. 17.

7. The same was true of much later writers on nationalism; see Sylvia G. Haim, "Islam and the Theory of Arab Nationalism," *Die Welt des Islams,* n.s., IV (1955), 127–140 and above, pp. 77–85.

regarded the ways of the Franks with repugnance.[8] As good Moslems, the Ottomans regarded Mohammed as the final, the perfect, and the best of the messengers whom God had sent to make His will known to man. The Mohammedan revelation contained all that man needed to know for this life and the next. The Moslem *sharīʿah,* or law, was perfect and unchangeable. The Moslems, then, were the best of peoples and had no need to learn from the infidels.

Yet Ṭahṭāwi and the Ottoman *tanẓīmāt* reformers, despite their having been nurtured by traditional Moslem Ottoman culture, obviously were interested in European patriotism and sought to apply the notion to their own country. When the Turks noted the zeal of patriotic Frenchmen in battle and their fidelity to the French state, they doubtless recognized the usefulness of such patriotism to the Ottoman state. Perhaps they also shared the impression which Ṭahṭāwi stated clearly when he attributed the remarkable progress and well-being of France to patriotism. In describing the wonders of Paris, he remarked, "Without the astronomy [i.e., science] of the people of Paris, their wisdom, their accomplishments, their good administration, and their concern with the interests of their land, their city would be nothing at all." He went on to describe their efforts and said, "If Egypt took care and the tools of civilization were applied copiously there, then it would be the sultan of cities and the chief country of the world." Ṭahṭāwi then presented a long patriotic poem about Egypt, probably the first poem of this new type in the Near Eastern languages.[9]

To men like Ṭahṭāwi and his Turkish counterparts of the early nineteenth century, patriotism was just another element of Frankish civilization which appeared to be useful to the Moslems. These men were acutely aware that the East had something to learn from the West. To understand what they, and their successors, meant by patriotism and nationalism and what value they believed it to possess for the inhabitants of the

8. For an example, see Lewis, p. 118, n. 35.
9. Ṭahṭāwi, pp. 54–55.

Ottoman Empire, one must comprehend their views on the value of the West to Islam.

The traditional Ottoman view of Europe was shaken by the unbroken string of military defeats which the Ottomans suffered throughout the eighteenth century and the first half of the nineteenth. The French expedition to Egypt made Ottomans even more aware of European progress. Quite naturally those in charge of the Ottoman state came to realize the importance of borrowing from the West in order to defend the Empire. Just as naturally the same men saw that their personal positions within the Empire could be bolstered by using the techniques of the West. Thus the Ottoman statesmen and Mehmed Ali, the governor-general of Egypt, began to carry out military and administrative reforms. In order to implement the reforms, Turks and Egyptians had to be sent to Europe in increasingly larger numbers. In Europe these young men became acutely conscious of the differences between the East and the West. As a result, a new element was added to their thinking: aware of the progress of the West, they began to desire progress for its own sake, not merely for the sake of defending the Empire from the advances of the Christians. To this second generation of Ottoman Westernizers belonged Ṭahṭāwi and the Ottoman *tanẓīmāt* reformers such as Reshid, Âli, and Fuad.

The overwhelming majority of the Ottoman people saw no need to imitate the West. The Islam of their fathers was good enough for them. Theologically and culturally most Ottoman Moslems remained conservatives. The early reforms were pressed through only by ruthless measures on the part of the rulers against the stubborn opposition of vested interests and Moslem conservatism. For the new situation created deep disturbance in the minds of Ottoman Moslems, the depth of which is indicated by the fact that the early Ottoman Westernizers, including those of the *tanẓīmāt* period, were in basic outlook just as conservative as the anti-Western majority.

Ṭahṭāwi and the *tanẓīmāt* reformers knew that in some ways the West had surpassed the East. At the same time, they felt that Islam and the Ottoman way of life were fundamentally sound. All that was necessary, they thought, was to borrow certain things from the West and the gap could be closed.[10] "In the time of the caliphs," Ṭahṭāwi wrote, "we were more perfect than the other lands, because the caliphs used to appoint learned men and masters of the arts, etc.," but then the Moslems declined and the Franks made progress.[11] "The lands of the Franks," he said, "have reached the highest stage of excellence in mathematics and the natural and physical sciences. . . ." On the other hand, Ṭahṭāwi was confident that Islam was still sound, far superior to Christianity. The Franks, for all their progress in the arts and sciences, he wrote, "have not been guided to the straight path, and they have not followed the course of salvation at all. Just as the Islamic lands have excelled in the sciences and application of the *sharīʿah* and in the rational sciences and have neglected the wisdom sciences entirely . . . so the Franks . . . admit that we were their teachers in the other sciences and our precedence over them. . . (p. 8). God was with the faithful, thought Ṭahṭāwi, for "if Islam had not been succored by the decree of God . . . then there would have been nothing to compare to their [the Franks'] power, multitudes, wealth, and excellence" (p. 9). Accordingly, although the Moslems have "neglected the wisdom sciences entirely, and thus need the Western lands to acquire what they do not know" (p. 8), Ṭahṭāwi did "not approve of [borrowing] anything except what does not contradict the text of the Mohammedan *sharīʿah*" (p. 5).

The Westernizing conservatives like Ṭahṭāwi and the Turkish *tanẓīmāt* reformers recognized the necessity of reforming on the European model. At the same time, they retained the traditional Moslem's calm assurance that Islam and Eastern culture were inherently superior to Christianity and Europe and were in no need of reformation in fundamentals. The Mos-

10. For suggestive remarks, see Niyazi Berkes, "Historical Background of Turkish Secularism," *Islam and the West*, ed. Richard N. Frye (The Hague: Mouton and Co., 1957), pp. 48–62, and Davison, pp. 849–853. For more recent works, see below, n. 17.

11. Ṭahṭāwi, p. 9. In this paragraph, other references to this work will be given in the text.

lems and the East, they admitted, were in danger and had lost some of their previous greatness and glory, but this lamentable situation could be treated simply by borrowing whatever was necessary of the practical wisdom of the Europeans. By the middle of the nineteenth century, this comfortable self-assurance had been shaken. Thereafter the situation grew progressively more intolerable to the proud and sensitive Moslem who knew something of the world.

Although the Near East made material progress throughout the nineteenth century (even striking progress in some areas), by the middle of the century it had been far outdistanced by the astounding progress of Europe, and by the end of the century left far behind. At the same time, the progress of Europe was made manifest to a much larger number of Ottoman subjects than ever before. Many more young men spent some time in Europe. Western teachers in state and missionary schools made others acquainted with the world outside the Empire. That the ways of the infidel were attractive to Moslems was obvious. The upper classes aped Frankish dress and manners. Rulers borrowed large sums of money from Europeans to spend, in part at least, on public improvements *à la française*. Worst of all in the eyes of the orthodox was the attraction that study in Europe and in the infidel missionary schools held for the youth.

It was equally obvious that the infidels held the basic precepts and institutions of Islam and the Ottoman state in disdain. Alien and infidel courts, operating outside the *sharīʿah*, favored the Christian over the faithful. When Christian subjects engaged in disorderly or treasonable conduct (so the Moslem Ottomans believed), the European powers used pressure, even armed force, to insure special privileges and sometimes independence for the rebellious Christians. Perhaps worst of all were the charges of Christian missionaries and the belittling remarks of Europeans about Eastern civilization. Even learned European Orientalists passed judgments that, when stripped of subtle nuances of phrasing, reduced in the Moslem's view to Lord Cromer's "reformed Islam is Islam no longer."

With the new situation there was a change in the thinking

of Ottoman intellectuals. Gone was the old calm confidence that Islam was inherently superior to other religions and Moslem Ottoman civilization basically sounder than European. Whereas the older intellectuals had merely asserted Moslem and Ottoman superiority, the new ones made impassioned defenses of the true faith and vehement refutations of the false. The defense of Islam and of the East became the overriding concern of Ottoman intellectuals. All were obsessed with the denial that Islam and the East were inferior to Christianity and Europe. In mode of denial, however, the Ottoman intellectuals differed from each other. Some simply denied that in their day Islam and the Ottoman lands were behind the West. Others admitted it, but explained it away.

Some (probably most) Ottoman intellectuals remained conservative and merely reaffirmed with renewed vigor the traditional belief that Islam was the best of all possible ways of life. The production of apologetics and polemics in both Arabic and Turkish became notable after 1860.[12] The most popular and widely read of them was the book *Iẓhār al-Ḥaqq* by the Indian Moslem Raḥmatullāh al-Hindi, which was published in Arabic at Constantinople in 1867 and soon translated into Turkish.[13] In all this there was nothing new. Islam was affirmed and Christianity attacked with the traditional arguments of early Islam. The remarkable thing is the great increase in quantity after 1860. Similarly newspapers in both Turkish and Arabic took up the defense of Islam and the East. There were many, but the most notable was the Arabic *al-Jawā'ib,* which was published in Constantinople following 1860 by Aḥmad Fāris al-Shidyāq.[14]

Some of these men were concerned with more than the de-

12. *Journal Asiatique,* 7th ser., XIX (1882), 169–170; 8th ser., V (1885), 244; IX (1887), 360.

13. Ignaz Goldziher, "Ueber Muhammedanische Polimik gegen alh al-kitab," *Zeitschrift der Deutschen Morgenländischen Gesellschaft,* XXXII (1878), 343–344; C. Snouck Hurgronje, *Mekka in the Latter Part of the Nineteenth Century,* trans. J. H. Monahan (Leiden: E. J. Brill, and London: Luzac and Co., 1931), p. 173.

14. C. Brockelmann, "Fāris al-Shidyāḳ Aḥmad b. Yūsuf," *Encyclopaedia of Islâm,* [1st ed.], II, 67–68; M. Hartmann, "Djarīda," *ibid.*, I, 1019.

fense of a religion, Islam. They also took upon themselves the defense of a civilization. They compared European society unfavorably to Ottoman. Shidyāq, who had lived in England and France, was willing to admit that the West was superior in material wealth. But in words suggestive of Western attacks on the monotony and materialism of modern industrialism, he insisted that the East still was superior in insuring true happiness, culture, and morality to man.[15] He summed up his attitude with the remark (p. 603), "Without doubt, the peasants of our country are more fortunate than those people." He was outraged by the assertion of a European Orientalist that the Europeans "had all necessary knowledge of the Eastern languages" and that European scholars had "become the professors of the Persians and the teachers of the Arabs." Shidyāq, applied eighteen synonyms for "lie" to this assertion and made a violent assault on the errors and vanities of Orientalists.[16] Shidyāq, and those like him, were strong defenders and advocates of the Ottoman Empire. We may refer to them as Ottoman conservatives.

In the minds of other Ottoman intellectuals, the traditional apologetics and polemics were not adequate for the defense of Islam. These intellectuals, unlike the conservatives, admitted that in their day Islam was in a deplorable state. They agreed with the conservatives, however, that Islam and the East were inherently superior to other religions and to the West. True Islam, they argued, was not incompatible with advanced civilization like that of Europe. The Moslems were in such a sad condition because true primitive Islam had been corrupted and, as a result, the Moslems had not been able to continue the remarkable progress of their early years. The remedy was simply to restore Islam to its pristine purity so that the Moslems, by adopting and adapting the necessary elements of modern

15. Aḥmad Fāris al-Shidyāq (Faris El-Chidiac), *Kitāb al-sāq ʿala al-sāq fi-ma huwa al-faryāq* (*La Vie et les aventures de Fariac*) (Paris, 1855), pp. 597–605, 641–644, 659–660, esp. pp. 603–605, 659 for denial of true civilization to the Europeans.

16. Appendix, pp. 1–2. The contrast between the new conservatives like Shidyāq and the older ones is well illustrated by the contrast between this appendix and the remarks of Ṭahṭāwi (pp. 68–75) concerning Orientalists.

civilization, might regain their former greatness. We may therefore designate them modernists, in contrast to the conservatives, and since they, like the conservatives, were advocates of a strong Ottoman state, as Ottoman modernists. Among the Turkish element of the Empire, the point of view is exemplified in the New Ottomans who became active in the 1860's. This group now explicitly adopted the ideas of Ottoman patriotism and the Ottoman fatherland.[17] During the 1870's, very similar ideas became widespread in Egypt as a result of the activities of Jamāl al-Dīn al-Afghānī.[18] Primitive Islam, said Afghāni (pp. 165–167), required its followers to exercise reason and examine

17. T. Menzel, "Kemāl Meḥmed Nāmiḳ," *Encyclopaedia of Islâm,* [1st ed.], II, 849–850; Davison, 861–864; Niyazi Berkes, "Ziya Gökalp: His Contribution to Turkish Nationalism," *Middle East Journal,* VIII (1954), 379–480; Ettore Rossi, "Dall Impero Ottomano alla Repubblica di Turchia," *Oriente Moderno,* XXIII (1943), 364–366, 367–368, 369. Since the first publication of this essay, a number of major studies relating to nineteenth-century Turkish Ottoman intellectual history have appeared: Bernard Lewis, *The Emergence of Modern Turkey,* 1st ed. (London: Oxford University Press, 1961; 2nd ed., 1968); Şerif Mardin, *The Genesis of Young Ottoman Thought* (Princeton, N.J.: Princeton University Press, 1962); Roderic H. Davison, *Reform in the Ottoman Empire, 1856–1876* (Princeton, N.J.: Princeton University Press, 1963); Niyazi Berkes, *The Development of Secularism in Turkey* (Montreal: McGill University Press, 1964).

18. Jamāl al-Dīn al-Afghāni, *Réfutation des Matérialistes,* trans. A. M. Goichon (Paris: Paul Geuthner, 1942), pp. 121–130, 133–134, 152–171. Cf. Charles C. Adams, *Islam and Modernism in Egypt* (London: Oxford University Press, 1933), pp. 15–16. Afghāni has subsequently received new attention. Eile Kedourie, *Afghani and ʿAbduh: An Essay on Religious Unbelief and Political Activism in Modern Islam* (New York: The Humanities Press, 1966), primarily on the basis of the political activities of Afghāni and ʿAbduh, convicts both of unbelief, cynical opportunism, and the deliberate subversion of Islam. Nikki R. Keddie, *An Islamic Response to Imperialism: Political and Religious Writings of Sayyid Jamāl ad-Dīn "al-Afghānī"* (Berkeley and Los Angeles: University of California Press, 1968), concentrating the analysis on Afghāni's writings, handles the problem with care and subtlety. She concludes that Afghāni was "some kind of 'Islamic deist,' a believer in a creator who set the world in motion and made it operate according to natural law" (p. 96), who followed the old philosophical tradition of the Islamic world by which the Islam of the *ʿulamāʾ* was regarded as an instrument for managing the masses which, being a lower truth if not false, was both needless for and unworthy of the elite. Albert H. Hourani, reviewing Keddie in *International Journal of Middle East Studies,* I (1970), 90–91, 189, convincingly counters the more recent arguments and reaffirms the view pesented in his *Arabic Thought in the Liberal Age,* rpt., pp. 107–129, which had already drawn attention to the complexities of Afghāni's career as political revolutionary, religious reformer, and believing Moslem.

the bases of their faith. Quoting Guizot, he argued that European progress was the result of the appearance in Europe of a similar theology, Protestantism.

Although most of the modernists were Ottomanists, a few Syrian Christians who shared the general ideas of the modernists advanced a quasi-secular Arab nationalism. American and French missionary schools in Lebanon brought many Syrians, mostly Christians, into close contact with the West. By the 1860's these Arabs had contributed greatly to a revival of classical Arabic literature and to the diffusion of modern knowledge. One of the most important spokesmen for the group was Ibrāhīm al-Yāziji, who in 1868 called for an Arab national revival. He agreed with the Ottoman modernists that in his day the East was in a deplorable condition, even though it was the home of civilization. His concern, however, was with the Arabs alone. He recalled vividly the glory and greatness of the Arabs in the past. To him, the Arabs were the most remarkable of nations, because they had achieved more in a short period of time than any other people. The Europeans made their rapid progress only because they had been able to borrow directly from the Arabs. The Arabs had declined after the non-Arab (Turk) came to dominate them and reduced learning to the religious sciences and religion to bigotry and fanaticism. To Yāziji, the means for the Arabs to regain their rightful glory was for the Arab nation to cast off the foreigner and to rid itself of bigotry and fanaticism. Then the old vigor of the Arab nation would return and the Arabs would resume their former progress in civilization.[19]

The Christian version of Arabism was not to the liking of the Syrian Moslem Arabs. In fact, the Moslem Arabs of Syria were outraged at the spectacle of Christians assuming the air of masters of Arab learning. Attacks on the pretensions of Yāziji and other Christian Arab literary men were popular. The Moslem Arabs of Syria adopted the battle cry, "Arabic shall not be

19. See Ibrāhīm al-Yāziji's essay, "al-ʿUlūm ʿinda al-ʿarab [The Sciences among the Arabs]," and his poem "Tanabbahu wa istafīqu [Awake! Awake!]," in ʿĪsa Mikhāʾ īl Sāba, *al-Shaykh Ibrāhīm al-Yāziji, 1847–1906,* Nawābigh al-fikr al-ʿarabi, 14 (Cairo: Dār al-Ma ʿārif, 1955), pp. 49–50, 71–74.

Christianized."[20] Yāziji's secular Arabism found few followers, and Ottomanism, whether conservative or modernist, remained the dominant ideology within the Ottoman lands until 1914.

Ironically, the outlines of a Moslem theory of Arab nationalism were propounded by the greatest of the Arab Ottoman modernists, the Egyptian Muḥammad ʿAbduh, whose primary goal was the revival of Islam and who was himself, during his political phases, an advocate of the Ottoman state.

ʿAbduh reaffirmed the essential superiority of Islam. He recalled the past glories of Islam, its rapid spread, great empire, and splendid civilization.[21] Islam is the perfect religion because it is based on reason and demands that its followers exercise their rational faculties and know the bases of their belief. This is the cause of the great Moslem progress in the past (pp. 6–10, 194–223). Other religions are inferior to Islam. ʿAbduh developed Afghāni's use of Guizot and declared that Europe did not begin its amazing progress in civilization until the Europeans began to learn from the Moslems, and, having adopted a creed "which is in concord with Islam, except for the recognition of Mohammed's mission," "organized their lives in a fashion analogous to the precepts of Islam" (pp. 109, 131–32). The Moslems declined when Islam was perverted by intermixing science and religion, which ought to be kept separate, so that in the end the Moslems ceased to exercise reason (pp. 13–19).

ʿAbduh thus maintained the intrinsic adequacy and superiority of Islam as a way of life. The sad condition of the Moslems in his day was the result of deviation from pristine Islam. "The Moslems have spent an age in inflicting harm on their souls, they have passed the time in chipping away the mortar of their faith," he wrote in 1887, "and they have injured the bonds of their conviction, because of the shadows of ignorance

20. Ignaz Goldziher, *ZDMG*, XXVIII (1874), 167–168.

21. Mohammed Abdou, *Rissalat al Tawhid: Exposé de la religion musulmane,* trans. B. Michel and Moustapha Abdel Razik (Paris: Paul Guethner, 1925), pp. 123–130. In this paragraph, subsequent references to this work are given parenthetically in the text. This work, which was first published in 1897, is a reworking of lectures delivered in Beirut in 1885–1888.

of the roots of their faith which have covered them." He went on to attribute the decline in Moslem political fortunes to the corruption of true Islam:

> Weakness has followed corruption in morals, lapses in behavior, and the abasement of souls, so that most of the populace resembles cattle, whose only ambition is to live to the end of their days, eating, drinking, and reproducing, contending with each other in bestiality. After that it was all the same to them whether majesty was with God, His prophet, and His caliph or with whoever else was lord over them.[22]

ʿAbduh's prescription for the ills of Islam was the rejection of Western civilization and the return to pure Islam. He warned against sending Moslems to the schools of the missionaries, who were "foreign devils," whose "satanical whisperings" had "deceived a number which is not small." Primitive, uncorrupted Islam, not the teachings of the missionaries, was ʿAbduh's remedy. "In acquiring this vital knowledge," he wrote in 1886,

> we have no need to seek benefits from those who are foreign to us. Rather, it is sufficient for us to return to what we have abandoned and to purify what we have corrupted. This consists of our religious and humanistic books, which contain more than enough of what we seek, and there is nothing in books other than ours which adds anything to them except that which we do not need.[23]

Religious revival, ʿAbduh believed, was the only way for the Moslems to regain their political greatness. In 1887 he wrote:

> Anyone of Islamic faith who has a heart believes that the preservation of the high Ottoman state is the third article of faith after faith in God and His prophet, for it alone is the preserver of the dominion of religion, the guarantor of its possessions,

22. Muḥammad Rashīd Riḍa, *Taʾrīkh al-Ustādh al-Imām al-Shaykh Muḥammad ʿAbduh,* 2nd ed. (Cairo: al-Manār, 1344H/1925–26), II, 506.
23. *Ibid.,* pp. 507, 353.

> and the religion [of Islam] has no government [*sulṭān*] except it [the Ottoman state].

He went on to say:

> The Islamic caliphate has fortresses and walls, and whatever strengthens confidence in it and zeal to defend it in the hearts of the faithful strengthens its walls. Nothing instills confidence and kindles zeal in the hearts of the Moslems except what the religion [of Islam] sends to them. If anyone believes that the name of the fatherland, the interest of the country and other such resounding words can take the place of religion in raising ambitions and pressing on their realization, then he has strayed onto an evil path.[24]

Although ʿAbduh, during his days as a political activist in the 1880's, was a strong advocate of Ottomanism, his belief in the necessity of returning to Islam led him to formulate an idea which was implicitly contrary to Ottomanism. The cure for the disease of the Moslems was the restoration of the true, original Islam, and that meant the Islam of the Arabs. "The Koran is the source of the success of the Moslems," he wrote in 1887,

> and there is no power capable of reforming their affairs except returning to it. . . . The Koran must be taken in its strictest aspects in accordance with the rules of the Arabic language, so as to respond to it as did the shepherds and camel-drivers to whom and in whose language the Koran descended. The Koran is close to its student when he knows the Arabic language, the practices of the Arabs in disputation, their history, and their customs in the days of the revelation, and knowledge of these is the most excellent way to understand it.

ʿAbduh then went on to urge, as the basis of the necessary religious revival, the intensive revival of the classical Arabic literary and religous studies.[25]

ʿAbduh in his later years gave up the political activism of his

24. *Ibid.*, p. 506.
25. *Ibid.*, pp. 515–516.

middle years, but he never gave up his basic ideas. When Christians, Arab and European, charged that Islam was inherently inadequate to the problems of the modern world, ʿAbduh in vigorous replies reaffirmed that Islam was the perfect system and, if restored to its full vigor, completely sufficient for modern life. Having given up political activism, he stressed religious reform even more. And to the end he held that fundamental religious reform required a revival of Arabic studies.[26]

ʿAbduh's ideas were taken up by a close associate and devoted pupil, the Syrian Muḥammad Rashīd Riḍa, who, after March, 1898, spread them through his journal, *al-Manār*. Rashīd Riḍa also was concerned with the question of how Islam and the East were to regain their rightful glory. His answer was the same as ʿAbduh's: "Have we said . . . 'Is it possible to restore the glory of the East through the strength of Islam?' Yes! a thousand times yes!" He continued: "The roots of the Islamic religion and its true teachings and humanistic learning united the tribes of the Arabs, advanced them from the depths of barbarism to the apex of excellences, honored them over the states of the world with sovereignty and suzerainty, and guided them to the sciences and the arts." Echoing ʿAbduh, he declared that in Islam, God had sent "a true *sharīʿah* . . . through which the kingdoms of Europe became glorious and mighty, which Europe acquired only from Islam." The diagnosis and prescription was the same as ʿAbduh's:

> It is beyond dispute that the deviation of the Moslems from its highway robbed them of their achievements and that returning to it will bind their hearts together, unite them, and return to them their sovereignty. . . . If . . . [the Moslem men of learning] set the Koran before themselves and revive its meanings intelligently . . . then the spirit of union will fall on the [Moslem] congregation from Heaven, and the Easterners and

26. See ʿAbduh's *al-Islām wa al-naṣrānīyah maʿ al-ʿilm wa al-madanīyah* [*Islam and Christianity Compared with Respect to Science and Civilization*], ed. Muḥammad Rashīd Riḍa, 7th ed. (Cairo: al-Manār, 1367H/1947–48), esp. pp. 62–64 (for Islam as the final and perfect religion), and pp. 81, 119–121, 151–154 (for Arab revival as the foundation of Islamic revival). This book, which was first published in 1902, is a compilation of articles which had previously been published in periodicals.

> Westerners [of the congregation] will be united and they will return to the East its glory.[27]

Rashīd Riḍa, like ʿAbduh, was led by his doctrine of primitive Islam to stress the priority of the Arabs. The return to primitive Islam inevitably stressed an Arab revival. Rashīd Riḍa's reform was to be carried out by the Ottoman sultan, as caliph, following the advice of a society of learned men which had its seat in Mecca. One of the specific proposed reforms was the revival of Arabic studies, which was indeed at the root of the matter. "It is necessary to spread the Arabic language rather than Turkish," said Rashīd Riḍa, "since it [Arabic] is the language of religion, and so its revivification is the revivification of it [religion] and its [Arabic's] spreading is the means of spreading it [religion] and of understanding it." [28] Rashīd Riḍa soon went on to make it even clearer that an Arab revival was the only way to restore Islam.

> To be filled with passion for the history of the Arabs, to strive to revive their glory, is the same as working for Islamic union, which in the past was achieved only through the Arabs and which will not be regained in this century except through them. . . . The basis of this union is Islam itself, and Islam is nothing but the Book of the Omnipotent and the *sunnah* of His prophet. . . . Both are in Arabic; no one can understand Islam if he does not understand them both correctly, and no one can understand them correctly if he does not understand their noble language.

From this, it was an easy step to glorifying the Arabs: "The greatest glory for the Moslem conquests belongs to the Arabs and . . . the religion grew and became great because of them. Their foundations are the most solid, their light is the clearest, they are in truth the best nation born into the world." [29]

27. *Al-Manār,* I, no. 40 (1 Shaʿbān 1316/Dec. 24, 1898, 2nd printing 1327H/1909), 799, 800, 800–801, 885. Rashīd Riḍa had already expounded these ideas at length in a series of articles: *ibid.*, 606–610, 628–633, 649–655, 670–679, 696–704, 722–730.

28. *Al-Manār,* I, 764–771, 788–793 (quotation on 770).

29. Quoted in Sylvia G. Haim, "Intorno alle origini della teoria del panarabismo," *Oriente Moderno,* XXXVI (1956), 415, 416. The passages were published in May and July, 1900.

Rashīd Riḍa thus developed to completion Abduh's emphasis on the necessity of Arab revival as the foundation for a general Moslem revival. At the same time, Rashīd Riḍa made explicit the notion that the Arabs were the best of the Moslems. Nevertheless, for a long time he retained his hope that his reform would be carried out under the patronage of the Ottoman sultan and his loyalty to the Ottoman state. It remained for another Syrian Arab, an associate of Rashīd Riḍa, to add political content to the theory. This was done by ʿAbd al-Raḥmān al-Kawākibi, who came to Cairo in 1898.

Kawākibi believed that in his time "confusion and weakness had encompassed all the Moslems." [30] He still took pride, however, in the past greatness of Islam and maintained its superiority to other ways of life. The non-Moslems had excelled the Moslems only in the "empirical sciences and arts" (p. 9). Islam remained "a straight, firm, correct, well-founded religion which is not surpassed, and not [even] approached by any other religion in wisdom, in order, and in solidity of structure" (p. 15; cf. p. 67). In fact, the Christians did not make progress in the arts and sciences until Protestantism, which is similar to true Islam, appeared, after which Orthodoxy and Catholicism remained "favored by the masses, but dwindled away entirely among the educated, because science and Christianity do not agree at all." The one who follows true pure Islam, however, increases his faith whenever he increases his science or exercises thought, for . . . he will not find in it [true Islam] anything which reason rejects or scientific investigation refutes" (p. 124; cf. pp. 92–94).

Accordingly, Kawākibi rejected blind imitation of the West. He vehemently criticized the Moslem upper classes as "weaklings" who saw "perfection in foreigners, as children see perfection in their fathers." The foreigners deceived the Moslems and made them falsely ashamed of their religion and their customs (p. 160). Kawākibi's diagnosis of the disease was that of the Ot-

30. ʿAbd al-Raḥmān al-Kawākibi, *Umm al-qura* [*The Mother of Villages* (one of the names for Mecca)] (Cairo: al-Maṭbaʿah al-Miṣrīyah bi-al-Azhar, 1350H/1931), p. 3. Subsequent references to this book in this and the following paragraphs will be given in the text.

toman modernists. "Is there still anyone who doubts," he wrote, "that the existing religion . . . is not the religion by which our ancestors were distinguished over the worlds? Nay, unfortunate changes have fallen upon the religion which have changed its foundation" (p. 60). Thus, "the cause of the langour [of the Moslems] is religious defectiveness" (p. 200). The remedy was also the same:

> We should rely upon our knowledge of the clear [word] of the Book, the sound [parts] of the *sunnah* [the customary usage of Mohammed], and the confirmed [provisions] of the *ijmāʿ* [the consensus of the early congregation] . . . for the creed of the ancestors is the source which the congregation will not discard, nor will it reject returning to it (p. 12; cf. p. 67).

Kawākibi, like ʿAbduh and Rashīd Riḍa, was led by his diagnosis of the ills of Islam to underline the pre-eminence of the Arabs and their unique role in the revival of Islam. A return to true Islam meant a revivification of Arab Islam, for the Koran and the *sunnah* could be understood only through knowledge of "the Arabic language, which is the language of the Koran . . ." (p. 71; cf. pp. 95, 170). Like Rashīd Riḍa, Kawākibi made much of the pre-eminence of the Arabs in Islam (pp. 195–198), and concluded that ". . . the Arabs are the sole medium for religious unification—Nay! for Eastern unification" (p. 198). Kawākibi went beyond his predecessors in singling out the Arabs of Arabia as the best of the Arabs because they were the closest to the original Moslems (pp. 12, 193–195). He also made political proposals. He respected the Ottoman Empire as "the greatest state, whose affairs concern the generality of the Moslems" (p. 142) and made proposals to reform its administration (pp. 142–148). He loved "the Ottomans [sultans] for the kindness of their dispositions and their elevation of religious rites" (p. 210). On the other hand, he believed that "every nation within the population of Turkey should attain administrative autonomy" (p. 143, n.). Moreover, he criticized the opportunism of Ottoman policy toward the Moslems and their caliphate policy (pp. 211, 201–207). Finally, Kawākibi proposed the establishment of an Arab "caliphate" in Mecca, not as a successor to the historical caliphate, but as a means of facilitating the reform of Islam and the formation of a great Pan-Islamic federation (pp. 207–210).[31]

The theory of Arab nationalism thus grew out of the modernist diagnosis of Moslem decline and prescription for Moslem revival. The Arab nationalist theorists were Arabist modernists in distinction to their close relatives, the Ottomanist modernists. Both varieties of modernists shared one characteristic with the conservatives. All were unwilling to admit that the East was inferior to Europe; instead, all maintained that Islam and the culture of the East were intrinsically superior to Christianity and Western civilization. The conservatives simply denied inferiority and reaffirmed superiority. The modernists, both Ottomanist and Arabist, admitted inferiority in their day but explained it away by making their backwardness the result of deviation from true Islam, which was inherently the perfect system. This attitude might be interpreted as simple religious bigotry. Yet these Moslem intellectuals were defending a civilization as much as a religion. Their attitude, moreover, was shared by many Christian intellectuals who, like their Moslem brethren, were unwilling to admit the inferiority of the East to the West.

Some Christian Arabs, such as Ibrāhīm al-Yāziji, put forward a theory which implicitly advocated a secular nationalism. As the Moslems could not accept the separation of Islam from Arabism, it is doubtful that Yāziji's ideas had much influence on the course of Arab nationalist thought. The subject remains to be investigated, but it seems likely that ideas such as Yāziji's contributed to the development of regional nationalisms among the Christians of Syria and Lebanon.[32]

Yet Yāziji agreed with the Ottoman modernists on one point.

31. For a discussion of al-Kawākibi's Arab caliphate, see Sylvia G. Haim, "Blunt and al-Kawākibī," *Oriente Moderno*, XXXV (1955), 132–143.

32. Relatively few Christians actually participated in the Arab political movement of the early twentieth century. They worked instead for Lebanese or Syrian nationalism. Al-Yāziji himself exhibits traces of Syrian nationalism in his essay, "Syria": Sāba, pp. 93–95.

The Easterners, or at least the Arabs, instead of being inferior to the Europeans, were the most remarkable of people, a people who had civilized the West. Yāziji, like the Ottoman modernists, was seeking a way to restore the past glory of the Arabs. He found it in a return to the true spirit of the Arab nation.

Other Christian Arab intellectuals shared Yāziji's desire to restore the greatness of the East but, unlike him, saw the East in broader terms. One was Adīb Isḥaq, a contemporary of Yāziji in Beirut and then an associate of Afghāni and ʿAbduh in Cairo during the late 1870's. Isḥaq maintained that the East was the "home of the seeds of the religious and political movements which changed the form of the earth and the conditions of man."[33] Isḥaq was outraged by the aspersions which Westerners cast on the East, which had taught civilization to the West (pp. 198–199; cf. p. 200). Yet Isḥaq admitted that in his day there had been a decline: the East is "the older brother of the West, which nursed it as an infant, fed it as a boy, supported it as a youth, and needs it as a mature man" (p. 473). The contrast between Eastern and Western civilization Isḥaq explained as the result of the casting aside of the true *sharīʿah* of the East and the consequent decline in spirit and learning (pp. 54, 111–112, 201–202). The East would revive, not through the efforts of foreigners, who had selfish designs of their own (p. 113–114), but through the efforts of sincere Eastern patriots who, after they had been moved to "reverence for the ancient glory and outrage with the new abasement, so that the fire of ambition and zeal will burn in [their] hearts" (pp. 174–175), would "expunge the shameful innovations and purify the true *sharīʿah*" (p. 202) and lead the East to the restoration of its past greatness (pp. 112, 202–203).

Isḥaq was led by the great problem of his day to identify himself with the "East," which was his favorite term for his "homeland." Specifically, however, he was an Ottomanist (pp. 96–97, 111–113, 128–129, 132, 382–384). He was proud of be-

33. Adīb Isḥaq, *Al-Durar* [*The Pearls*], ed. ʿAwni Isḥaq (Beirut: al-Maṭbaʿah al-Adabīyah, 1909), p. 105. In this and the succeeding paragraphs, further references to this work will be given in the text.

ing an Arab, but his pride in the Arabs was subordinate to his Ottomanism and Easternism (pp. 149–150, 200).

Other Christian Arabs identified themselves with the civilization of the East even more closely than did Isḥaq. The outstanding case was that of Aḥmad Fāris al-Shidyāq, who was born a Christian but converted to Islam shortly before 1860 and became one of the most famous of the Ottoman conservatives. Yāziji and Isḥaq, when confronted with the contrast between the East and the West, found hope in the past greatness of the East. In doing this, they necessarily recalled the past greatness of Moslems, not Christians. Shidyāq, even before his conversion to Islam, made this explicit by identifying Eastern civilization with Islam. In reply to the belittling remarks of a European Orientalist, he wrote, "Those [European] professors have not taken learning from its *shaykhs*, i.e., from Shaykh Muḥammad, Mulla Ḥasan, and *Ustādh* Saʿdi [i.e., Moslem scholars]; no, they have been parasites on it and have taken unfair hold [of it]. Whoever [of the Europeans] is educated at all in it is only educated by Priest Ḥanna, Monk Tūma, and Priest Matta. Then he puts his head in nightmares, and the nightmares enter his head, and he thinks that he knows something, but he is ignorant."[34] Other Christian Arabs were to follow Shidyāq, but without renouncing the religion of their birth.

By 1914, some Christian Arabs had gone a long way toward accepting the theory of Arabism which Rashīd Riḍa and Kawākibi had advanced. One was Nadrah Maṭrān, a Lebanese by origin. His nationalism had a racial basis. "Racial pride is a fundamental virtue," he said in 1913, "and I do not know a nation more strongly affected by its influences than the Arab nation." Nevertheless, he was willing to admit that Islam was one of the glories of the Arab nation. He described how, when the "Arab Moslem armies" were advancing against Damascus, the Arab Christian Ghassanids, "instead of fighting the Moslems and standing in their faces, were stirred by the sentiment of brotherhood and abandoned the religious bond and the political tie which made them the clients of the Romans and con-

34. Shidyāq, Appendix, p. 2; see also pp. 703–704.

tracted friendship with and fidelity to the speakers of their language, the sons of their father." It was good for the Christian Arabs of Syria to submit to the rule of the Moslems, for the latter "were Arabs who ruled an Arab country which had a right to glory in them and to pride themselves in their works and their conquests. . . ." Maṭrān went on to make the glory of Islam virtually equivalent to the glory of the Arabs.

> Religious fellow-feeling had become predominant with all the nations without exception, and so it was with the Moslems, and it is not strange if we saw them [the Moslem Arabs] submitting to the rule of the Seljuks, the suzerainty of the Ayyubids, and the dominion of the Ottomans, since they believed them capable of supporting the glory of Islam and of raising the banner of the caliphate. . . .[35]

It was good for the Christian Arabs to join the Moslems, because that brought glory to the Arabs. It was equally good for the Arabs to submit to the rule of non-Arab Moslems, because that maintained the glory of Islam. Moslem and Christian Arab ideas on Arabism had converged. The Arabs, said the Moslems, are the best of nations because God chose them to receive the perfect religion, Islam. Islam, said the Christians, is dear to all Arabs, because it made them great. A Syrian Christian contemporary of Maṭrān put the matter neatly: "Let everyone of us say I am Arab . . . and if being Arab is only possible through being Muslim, then let him say I am an Arab and a Muslim. . . ."[36]

Arabism, then, grew out of modernist Ottomanism and in response to the same stimulus. Both theories were primarily concerned with denying that Eastern culture was inferior to that of the West. They shared this trait with Ottoman conservatism. Something of the emotional make-up of all the theorists is revealed by Adīb Isḥaq, who admitted that he had

35. Text of Maṭrān's speech in *al-Muʾtamar al-ʿarabi al-awwal* [*The First Arab Congress*] (Cairo: al-Lajnah al-ʿUlya li-Ḥizb al-Lāmarkazīyah, 1331H/1913), pp. 58, 55, 56.

36. Sylvia G. Haim, "'The Arab Awakening': A Source for the Historian?" *Die Welt des Islams*, n.s., II (1953), p. 249, n. 1. For a later (1930) expression of the same idea, see *Oriente Moderno*, X (1930), 57.

"made love of the self the source of love of the fatherland and of the nation." In another place he explained: "Belonging to the fatherland connects it and the inhabitant with a firm bond of personal honor, and he [the inhabitant] is jealous of it and defends it, just as he defends his father who has begotten him, even if he is very angry with him." The abasement of Isḥaq's fatherland in comparison to the West thus humiliated Isḥaq personally. His great goal, like that of the other modernists, both Ottomanist and Arabist, was to deliver the East from its humiliation. "We have composed a history of the French Revolution," he wrote,

> only to make us remember it is an example and a lesson to a nation which remembers and reflects. And to instruct those who suffer tyranny, those who yearn for deliverance from humiliation, how people before them achieved this goal, and changed from weakness to strength, from humiliation to mightiness, from slavery to freedom, and raised their heads, and rejoiced their souls. . . .[37]

The gap between the general advancement of the Islamic East and that of the Christian West was the great innovator in Ottoman intellectual and political activity during the nineteenth century. That some of the ways of the alien and infidel West must be imitated was obvious to a minority of significant magnitude. The majority, perhaps, remained firmly orthodox and either opposed all innovations or left the great matters where they belonged, in the hands of the Omnipotent, but those who influenced and directed state policy were forced to look to the West. The necessity of imitating the infidel alien, however, was a heavy blow to their pride and self-esteem. Consequently, their advocacy of Westernization was mingled with the defense of Islam and of the East.

In the beginning, when the gap between East and West did not appear unbridgeable, the apologetics of the Westernizers were moderate and restrained. As the gap grew increasingly wider, the Westernizers came more and more to be primarily

37. Isḥaq, pp. 102, 454, 165.

apologists until the advocacy of Westernization was all but submerged in a flood of self-justification and anti-Westernism. Men who set out to show how the Islamic East could overtake the Christian West ended by devoting most of their energies to explaining that the East was really superior. Some, the conservatives, were content with showing the falsity of Christianity by means of the orthodox apologetics and polemics and with emphasizing the unpleasant aspects of European life. Others, the modernists, went on to show that the Europeans actually owed their progress to their having absorbed something of the true spirit of Islam, which the Moslems, alas, had forsaken.

Interest in patriotism and nationalism was one of the results of the Ottoman preoccupation with the humiliating differential between East and West and with means of erasing it. National patriotism, the Westernizing Ottomans believed, was one of the sources of European strength and progress and should therefore be adopted by the Ottomans just as military and administrative techniques should be adopted. This belief led to the appearance of a generalized Islamic Ottomanism within the Turkish element of the Empire and of a local Islamic Egyptian nationalism with Ottomanist overtones in Egypt. In general, the conservatives, like the *tanẓīmāt* reformers and Aḥmad Fāris al-Shidyāq, agreed with the modernists, like the New Ottomans, Afghāni, and the young Muḥammad ʿAbduh, in posing as the supreme interest the defense of the Ottoman Empire and of the Islamic East against the Christian West.

The modernist justification of the Islamic East created the basis of Arab nationalist theory. To show how the East could catch up with the West and to prove that the East was in fact superior to the West, the modernists dwelt on the perfect system, uncorrupted original Islam. To the modernists, the return to pure Islam was the answer to the problems of their day. But, as Muḥammad ʿAbduh was the first to note, emphasis on early Islam heightened the importance of the Arabs, their language, and their past to the defense and revival of Islam and the East.

Islam was as much the center of Arabism as it was of Ottomanism. Yet Arabism and Ottomanism were something more than recrudescences of religious bigotry and fanaticism. Both were defenses against the West, not against Christianity alone. Both were justifications of a civilization, the East, the worth and adequacy of which had been questioned by the progress of the West. Some Christian Ottomans, at least among the Arabs, shared the Moslem's sense of personal dishonor in the existence of the gap between Islamic East and Christian West. They joined in the defense of the East against the West, and they took pride in the past greatness of Islam.[38]

Arabism, like Ottomanism, was the result of preoccupation with the problem which the general progress of Europe posed for the inhabitants of the Ottoman Empire. This preoccupation led to the giving of political content to nationality in a region where religion and dynasty had been the twin pillars of the state. Nationality was incidental to a scheme of thought which was directed chiefly at expounding a plan for progress and at vindicating the worth of a way of life. The Ottomanists attempted to make a single nationality of the diverse ethnic elements which peopled the Ottoman Empire. The Arabists raised a single people, the Arabs, to a position of pre-eminence. The aim of both, however, was to defend the East and to further the glory of Islam in the face of the West. The common goal of Arabism and Ottomanism expressed the sentiment of identity which was shared by most Ottomans in a world dominated by European civilization. However much they disagreed, in moments of crisis all closed ranks around the fundamental necessity of maintaining their cultural identity and self-dignity.

But disagree they did. For though Arabism and Ottomanism, both conservative and modernist, were very similar responses to the same problem, the differences between the answers are significant. The question arises of how different people of sim-

38. Additional evidence of Christian Arab Ottomanism and resentment of the West, including Protestant missionary activity, is contained in A. L. Tibawi, *British Interests in Palestine, 1800–1901: A Study of Religious and Educational Enterprise* (New York: Oxford University Press, 1961), pp. 9–12, 21–28, 89–116, 175–177, and the same author's "The American Missionaries in Beirut and Butrus al-Bustānī," *St. Anthony's Papers*, no. 16 (Carbondale: Southern Illinois University Press, 1963), pp. 166, 170–173. See also Hourani, rpt., pp. 99–102, on Bustānī's thought.

ilar background in the same situation came to give divergent answers to the same problem. The question cannot be answered by anything in the content or the technical structure of the ideas under consideration. A modernist might be Ottomanist or Arabist, an Ottomanist either conservative or modernist. The ethnic sentiment of the Arabs is of little help as a clue, for, despite the obvious value of Arabist theory in bolstering Arab pride, most Arabs remained Ottomanists until 1918. The search for a complete explanation of the emergence of Arabism from Ottomanism must extend beyond the realm of ideologies. However, that poses a new problem which cannot be dealt with here. One conclusion can be proposed: Arabism developed from modernist Ottomanism and, like modernist and conservative Ottomanism, was a reaction against the failure of the Ottoman civilization to keep pace with Europe.

SIX

The Rise of Arabism in Syria

In the early days of the twentieth century, two ideologies competed for the loyalties of the Arab inhabitants of the Ottoman territories which lay to the east of Suez. The dominant ideology, Ottomanism, defended the continuation of the Ottoman Empire. The challenging ideology, Arabism, proclaimed that the Arabs were a special people who possessed peculiar virtues and rights. Nevertheless, the central concern of Arabism was identical with that of both the varieties of Ottomanism, conservative and modernist, which were current in political and intellectual circles within the Empire during the half century or so which preceded the outbreak of World War I. Arabism, as propounded by its creators and advocates, was, like Ottomanism, a defense and a vindication of Islam and the East in the face of the dominance of the Christian West. Both ideologies claimed to be the best way of restoring to the Islamic East the greatness which it had lost to the West. Arabism and Ottomanism, in short, were special manifestations of a general reaction against the failure of the Ottoman territories to keep pace with the advancement of Europe.[1]

If the goal of Arabism was the defense of the Islamic East, one might ask, why should the larger bond, Ottomanism, be forsaken for the lesser, Arabism? Perhaps many Arabs went over to Arabism from the feeling that Ottomanism was unable to achieve its goal, i.e., to close the gap between Islam and the West. As the first two and a half decades of the twentieth century unfolded, objective reality provided less and less sustenance for the hope that Ottomanism could promote the cause of the Empire and of Islam in the race with the West. The conservative Ottomanism of ʿAbd al-Ḥamid II and the modernist Ottomanism of the Young Turks both appeared ineffectual in

1. On the question of Christian Arab participation in the early Arab movement, see above, pp. 132–133, 140–143, and below, pp. 159–160.

the face of Europe. The failure of Ottomanism, however, was not obvious to all or even to a majority of Ottoman Arabs. Arabism remained a minority position among the Arabs of the Empire. The opinion may be ventured, purely tentatively, that the struggle between conservative and modernist Ottomanists was at least as important as that between Ottomanists and Arabists. Yet Arabism spread and became, especially after 1908, a political movement of increasing importance. Granted that the adherents of Arabism saw in it a way of defending their ethnic identity against the West, the question remains why some Arabs preferred Arabism to Ottomanism, which claimed to serve the same general goals as Arabism and at the same time enjoyed the support of most Arabs. To suggest an answer to the general question, we must delimit the spread of Arabism, identify those who acted on its behalf, and estimate their influence in its growth.

The earliest significant manifestation of political Arabism within the Ottoman Empire was the formation in 1908 of the Ottoman Arab Brotherhood in Constantinople. After this society was suppressed in 1909 its place was taken by the Arab Club of Constantinople. Before long, Arab deputies in the Ottoman Parliament were opposing the Young Turk governments and demanding Arab rights. Simultaneously newspapers which spoke for the Arab nation appeared in some of the major cities. The public movement for Arab rights soon was coordinated by the formation of the Ottoman Decentralization Society, which had its headquarters in Egypt and branches in Syria. The movement spread with the formation of the Reform Societies of Beirut and of Basra in 1912–1913 and culminated in the convening of the Arab Congress in Paris in June, 1913. None of these groups spoke openly for independence. Their expressed goal was reform which would insure Arab rights within the Ottoman Empire.[2]

2. Amīn Saᶜīd, *al-Thawrah al-ᶜarabīyah al-kubra* [*The Great Arab Revolt*], 3 vols. (Cairo: ᶜĪsa al-Bābi al-Ḥalabi wa Shurakāʾuhu, [1934]), I, 6–9, 13–31; Muḥammad ᶜIzzat Darwazah, *Ḥawl al-ḥarakah al-ᶜarabīyah al-ḥadīthah*

Although the public societies and activities of Arab nationalism were directed toward no more than the attainment of Arab rights within the Ottoman Empire, many who participated in the movement had independence in mind and covertly worked for this goal. Some even went so far as to seek the support of European governments for armed rebellion.[3] At the same time, these and other Arabs began to organize secret societies with a revolutionary program. There were several of these, but two came to dominate the movement and to include all but a few members for the secret societies. The two were the Young Arab Society (commonly known as *al-Fatāt*) and the Covenant Society (commonly known as *al-ʿAhd*).[4]

Despite such progress, the Arab nationalists had won no striking victories when the Ottoman government entered the war in October, 1914. With the war crisis, however, some nationalist leaders began to plot armed rebellion against the Turks. In particular, some Arabs began to negotiate with the Amir of Mecca. al-Ḥusayn ibn-ʿAli, with the aim of inducing him to lead the proposed revolution, and with the British to seek their support of the Arab nationalist cause. After protracted negotiations, the Amir of Mecca reached agreement with the Arab nationalists and the British, revolted in June, 1916, and formed an Arab army in Arabia. Then followed the Arab war made famous by T. E. Lawrence and the entry of the Arab army into Damascus as a part of the Allied forces. After the armistice the Arab army, commanded by the Amir Ḥusayn's son Fayṣal, was assigned the occupation of Transjordan and the interior of Syria. Meanwhile, a British force had advanced from the Persian Gulf to defeat the Turks in Iraq and occupy that country.

In the area occupied by Fayṣal's Arab army nationalism grew during 1919–1920. Political personalities rushed to join the

[*Concerning the Modern Arab Movement*], 6 vols. (Sidon and Beirut: al-Maṭbaʿah al-ʿAṣrīyah, 1950–[1951]), I, 22–25, 33–40; Turkey, Fourth Army, *La Vérité sur la question syrienne* (Stamboul: Tanine, 1916). Martin Hartmann, *Reisebriefe aus Syrien* (Berlin: Dietrich Reimer, 1913) contains much material on the public advocates of Arabism in 1913.

3. See *La Vérité sur la question syrienne, passim.*

4. Saʿīd, I, 9–11, 46–50; Darwazah, I, 25–33.

Arab nationalist societies (especially *al-Fatāt,* which enjoyed a great increase in membership) and founded new ones. The Arab movement culminated in the formation of an elected body, the Syrian General Congress, which claimed to be the spokesman for all of "Syria," i.e., Palestine, Lebanon, and Syria. At the same time, a Syrian government was formed. Both bodies accepted the theory of Arab nationalism from the start. Although the Congress claimed to represent only Syria, its pronouncements and resolutions referred to the Syrian people as members of the Arab nation. The sentiment of Arabism filled the declaration of independence which the Congress adopted on March 8, 1920. This declaration went explicitly to full Arab nationalism by declaring that Syria and Iraq "possess linguistic, historical, economic, natural, and racial bonds and ties which make the two regions dependent on each other," and demanded that "there be a political and economic federation between the two brother regions." [5]

Such were the external stages in the growth and fulfillment of Arab nationalism in the Arab lands east of Suez. It remains to define the connections between the stages of the movement and to isolate the influences at work in each. To this end, the identification and comparative study of the personnel of each stage must be undertaken.

The membership of the pre-1914 Arab nationalist movement can be identified by comparatively simple procedures. An Arab nationalist was one who worked for Arab nationalist goals. The membership must include, therefore, those Arabs who distinguished themselves as public advocates of Arabism. To these should be added those who were members of the societies which had Arab nationalist aims. Only three societies—the Ottoman Decentralization Society, *al-Fatāt,* and *al-ʿAhd*—can be so described. The Ottoman Arab Brotherhood aimed at strengthening Ottoman-Arab ties, and several of its founding Arab mem-

5. For the acts of the Syrian General Congress, see Sātiʿ al-Ḥusari, *Yawm Maysalūn* [*The Day of Maysalun*] (Beirut: al-Makshūf, 1945), pp. 246–273 (the quotation is from p. 265).

bers were prominent advocates of Arab loyalty to the Ottoman Empire in the period 1908–1914.[6] There were also several Lebanese societies which worked for Lebanese, not Arab, nationalist goals.The programs of the Beirut and Basra Reform Societies were of general reformist nature, not specifically Arab nationalist, and many members of the Beirut Society are known to have been Lebanese, not Arab, nationalists (the full membership of the Basra society is unknown). On the other hand, the Arab nationalist members of the two Reform Societies were also members of one or more of the purely Arab societies. Thus a complete list of the pre-1914 members of the Ottoman Decentralization Society, *al-Fatāt,* and *al-ʿAhd,* is a complete roster of the members of the Arab nationalist societies before 1914.

This investigation of the growth of Arabism has been limited to the territories which were to be included in the Syrian Republic. There are two reasons for this. In the first place, in Syria the various phases of growth of Arabism took forms which permit comparison with each other more readily than do the stages of the movement elsewhere. The earliest phase can be delimited everywhere by public advocacy of Arabism and membership in the nationalist societies. For the latest phase, however, only in Syria, Lebanon, Transjordan, and Palestine did Arabism take the form of a formally elected body, the Syrian General Congress, and of a regularly constituted government. The second reason for restricting the study to Syria is that more biographical information is available for the inhabitants of Syria than for those of the other eastern Arab lands.

Furthermore, the pre-war Arab movement in Syria is representative of the entire pre-war Arab movement. Only 126 men are known to have been public advocates of Arab nationalism or members of Arab nationalist societies before October, 1914. This number may be too large, since 30 of the men are only doubtfully to be regarded as having been active Arab nationalists before 1914.[7] Of the 126 Arab nationalists, 51 can be iden-

6. For example, ʿĀrif al-Māridīni, Shukri al-Ayyūbi, and Yūsuf Shatwān; see Saʿīd, I, 7, 14, 34, 53, and Hartmann, p. 19.

7. The names are given in the principal sources: Saʿīd, Darwazah, and Hartmann. Darwazah, who was secretary of *al-Fatāt* in 1919, gives a complete

tified as Syrian; one was Egyptian, 21 Lebanese, 18 Iraqi, 22 Palestinian and 13 unidentifiable as to place of origin or residence. Of the 30 who are only doubtfully identified as having been nationalists before October, 1914, 11 were Syrians, four Lebanese, five Iraqis and 10 Palestinians. (See Appendix I for the Syrian membership of the pre-1914 Arab movement.) Syrians thus predominated in the leadership of the pre-war Arab movement. Furthermore, the incidence of Arabism was at least as great in Syria as it was elsewhere. Using the only available population estimates for 1915, there were 3.5 Arab nationalist leaders per 100,000 of total population in Syria in comparison to 3.1 in Palestine and 2.4 in Lebanon.[8]

We may regard the 126 Arabs who were members of the Arab societies or prominent spokesmen for the Arab cause as the leadership of Arab nationalism. They also make up a significant percentage of the total number of known active par-

list for each of the various societies. The thirty whose Arabism before 1914 is regarded as doubtful are those listed by Darwazah as having joined a society before the end of World War I and about whom no other information is available. While we may regard them as nationalists, we cannot be sure that they joined before October, 1918, and in fact some men whom Darwazah lists as having joined before the end of the war are known to have joined only after the armistice.

8. The population statistics are from A. Ruppin, *Syrien als Wirtschaftsgebiet* (Berlin: Kolonial-Wirtschaftliches Komitee, 1917), pp. 8–9. In addition to the usual reservations which arise from faulty methods of collecting, these statistics are subject to an additional error which arises from the fact that the statistics are given by Ottoman administrative districts which cannot be exactly redistributed among the territories established after 1918. I have redistributed Ruppin's statistics so that the population is as follows: Syria, 1,416,644; Palestine, 689,275; Lebanon, 806,602; Transjordan, 131,788. The post-war statistics are uncertain, but for comparison the rate of incidence of Arabism using the number of Arab nationalists before 1914 and the post-war population statistics is as follows: Syria (1926), 3.8 (1,324,026 population), or 3.3 if the preceeding population total does not include an estimated 250,000 bedouin; Lebanon (1926), 3.5 (597,799 population, not including certain emigrees, who most likely were included in Ruppin's total); Palestine (1922), 2.9 (752,279 population); Iraq (1927), 0.6 (2,970,000 population). For the statistics, see France, Ministère des Affaires Étrangères, *Rapport sur la situation de la Syria et du Liban,* 1926, pp. 190–193, and 1922–1923, p. 8; Great Britain, Colonial Office, *Report by H.B.M.G. on the Administration under Mandate of Palestine and Transjordan,* 1922, p. 58; Doris Goodrich Adams, *Iraq's People and Resources,* University of California Publications in Economics, XVIII (Berkeley and Los Angeles: University of California Press, 1958), pp. 34–35.

tisans of Arabism before 1914. An indication of the spread of Arabism is provided by the signatures to the telegrams of support which were sent to the Arab Congress in Paris in June, 1913. A total of 387 names appear on these telegrams. Of the signers, 79 were Syrians, 101 Lebanese, 37 Iraqis, 139 Palestinians; 16 were resident in Europe, four in Egypt, and 11 unidentifiable as to residence (telegrams from America are not included in the tabulation).[9] Actually there is an overlap between the two lists. In the case of the Syrians, for example, 12 of the signers of the telegrams were also active in the societies. Thus in the case of Syria the telegrams add only 67 persons to the 51 who must be considered leaders rather than followers of Arabism. The list of Arab nationalist leaders here considered, then, is a nearly complete list and the names included in it constitute over one-third of the active partisans of Arabism before Turkey entered World War I.

At this point the difference between the proportion of Syrians in the leadership and the proportion of Syrians in the followers must be discussed. The Syrians, who were more active among the leaders than were the Lebanese and the Palestinians, were noticeably less active among the supporters of the Paris Arab Congress than either of the latter. As most Lebanese anti-Ottomans were Lebanese nationalists, not Arab, it is likely that most of the Lebanese supporters of the Paris Congress were not Arab nationalists. A large percentage of the Palestinian supporters of the Arab Congress are obviously village elders and headmen. The adherence of such persons to the nationalist movement is undoubtedly the result of instigation by the Palestinian notables.

The leaders of the pre-war Arab movement are representative of the movement in Syria, and the Syrians are representative of the movement as a whole. It is now possible to examine the connections of the pre-war nationalists with the later stages of the Arab movement.

9. For the telegrams, see *al-Muʾtamar al-ʿarabi al-awwal* [*The First Arab Congress*] (Cairo: al-Lajnah al-ʿUlya li-Ḥizb al-Lāmarkazīyah, 1331H/1913), pp. 150–210.

The existence of an organized Arab movement and the agreement between some of its members and the Amir of Mecca was certainly one of the conditions which led the latter to revolt in June, 1916. Furthermore, although the Amir Ḥusayn was a conservative Ottomanist rather than an Arabist, after he revolted he did adopt and pursue the general policy and the territorial ambitions of the Arabists.[10]

The pre-war nationalists of Syria had little influence on the development and outcome of the revolt. Before the revolt was proclaimed, anti-Ottoman activities were engaged in by six of them. Of these, three carried out their activities abroad (two in Egypt, one in Paris and later South America), where they were when the war broke out. The others fled from Syria to Egypt, where they continued their activities. After the beginning of the revolt, seven joined Fayṣal's forces. Three of these joined in the early days, the other four not until 1918. In addition, two who were Ottoman officers joined the Arab army after they had been taken prisoners by the British. Thus, of fifty-one pre-war Syrian nationalists, only fifteen, or 29 percent, are known to have engaged in Arab political or military activity during the war.

Turkish repressive measures undoubtedly contributed to the limitation of Arab nationalist activity in Syria during the war. The Turkish authorities began making arrests early in 1915. All told, sixteen pre-war nationalists were sentenced, all but one of them before June, 1916. Thirteen of them were executed, one was sentenced to death in absentia, and two were imprisoned. It is impossible to determine how many of the convicted nationalists actually engaged in anti-Ottoman activities during 1914–1915. Eleven of them were overt nationalists, and, although the Turkish authorities did have specific evidence of treasonable activities on the part of some, these activities antedated the war. The Decentralization Committee, to which most of those executed belonged, certainly was used as an instrument of revolutionary activity by some of its members, including its

10. On Ḥusayn's adoption and pursuit of an Arab nationalist program after the beginning of the Arab Revolt, see above, pp. 45–46, 89, 110–116.

leaders in Cairo; but whether or not all its members had knowledge of such activity is an unanswerable question.

Assuming that all those who were convicted by the Turks actually did engage in anti-Ottoman activities, the total number of pre-war Syrian Arab nationalist leaders who contributed to the Arab movement during the war is then thirty-one, or 61 percent of the total membership. Two of this group of thirty-one occupy an ambivalent position. The two, ʿAbd al-Ḥamīd al-Zahrāwi and ʿAbd al-Raḥmān Shahbandar, were among the most prominent of the pre-war nationalists. Both, however, had reconciled their differences with the Turks by the outbreak of war and distinguished themselves as public advocates of Arab-Turkish cooperation during the early months of the conflict. There is nothing to indicate that Zahrāwi, who was executed, plotted against the Ottoman government. Shahbandar, who fled to Egypt in early 1916, did participate in some of the early nationalist parleys, but his intentions are obscure. It seems likely that his flight was precipitated by the wholesale arrest of pre-war spokesmen for the Arab cause which the Turkish military was carrying out.

A portion of the nationalists cooperated with the Turks. The most prominent journalist of the Arab movement, Muḥammad Kurd ʿAli, cooperated with the Turks throughout the war. Two served as officers in the Ottoman Army. There is no information on the war-time careers of seventeen. Ten of these are known to have survived the war. In addition, there is some indication that four others were alive in 1919, and it is possible that the remaining three were also. At least ten pre-war nationalists, then, went through the war without engaging in anti-Ottoman activities; this may be true of four others, and could be true of an additional three. Some of these certainly served with the Turks. Four of those who survived the war were army officers, as were three of those whose fate is unknown. The chances are that all these officers who survived the war served with the Ottoman forces.

The pre-war Arab nationalist movement in Syria thus did not make a notable military contribution to the Arab Revolt. The movement affected only a small number of Syrians. Moreover, most of its members were unable or unwilling to give active support to the revolt. Turkish measures of control were too effective. Much has been made of the blood-thirstiness of Jemal Pasha, the Turkish commander in Syria. Wholesale arrests were made, and many of the nationalists were convicted by evidence which proved crimes other than those with which they were charged. Yet the commonest and most effective security measure seems to have been the careful assignment of Arab personnel to areas out of harm's way. Many Arab notables who after the war spoke of their "imprisonment" or "banishment" appear actually to have served as governors or officials in solidly Turkish districts of the Empire. Many Arab officers served at the Straits or in the Caucasus. Others, however, served in Palestine; even here, recruits for the Arab army appear to have been prisoners of war more often than deserters.

The Arab Revolt, then, made a far greater contribution to the advancement of the Arab movement than the latter did to the Arab Revolt. Most importantly, the Arab Revolt created an Arab army and an alliance with Great Britain, the victor in the war. As a result, Syria was occupied by an Arab army. The Arab military administration soon was converted into a government. Under the aegis of this government a representative body, the Syrian General Congress, was elected. The government and the Congress together officially adopted a program of full Arab nationalism. At the same time the membership of the pre-war societies, especially *al-Fatāt,* was swollen, and a new unofficial nationalist body was established to agitate for the Arab cause and to reject any foreign domination. This was the Committee of National Defense in Damascus. (For the membership of the bodies, see Appendix II).[11]

The pre-war nationalists did not play an important part in the three official bodies which established Arabism as the official ideology in Syria. Thirty-nine of the forty-four Syrian

11. For the composition of the Syrian General Congress, see Darwazah, I, 96–98; for the members of the governments, Ḥusari, pp. 228–242; for the Committee of National Defense, Saʿīd, II, 102–103, 185, 191.

members of the Syrian General Congress were men who had not previously been associated with the nationalists; the five nationalist members of the body had all been nationalists before 1914, and three of them had participated in anti-Ottoman activities during the war. Of the fourteen members of the Syrian governments, only one had been a nationalist before 1914 and two had joined the nationalists during the war. The pre-war nationalists were a majority in only one body, the army command, three of whose members had joined *al-ʿAhd* before the war (none of the three had a record of anti-Ottoman activity during the war). But even in the army command the prewar nationalists occupied subordinate positions. The non-official body which was most active in organizing popular nationalist demonstrations, the Committee of National Defense, was also dominated by latecomers to Arabism. Only two of its twelve members had been nationalists before 1914. Thus, of the men who took Syria squarely into a policy of Arabism in 1919–1920 (the membership of the preceding four organizations, which, with overlapping eliminated, totals seventy-three) 82 percent had not been active adherents of Arabism before 1918, 85 percent before 1914.

By 1919 Arabism had become the dominant ideology in Syria. Every political personality of any stature espoused it and worked for its realization. Yet the Arab nationalists of 1919 were not a homogeneous group. Two main factions can be distinguished: those who had become nationalists prior to 1914, and those who had not become nationalists until 1919 (those who became nationalists during 1914–1918 are so few in number that for the purposes of this analysis we may ignore them).

The first group was anti-Ottoman before 1919; the second was not. Further, for convenience in terminology, the second group may be regarded as pro-Ottoman until 1919. Under this assumption, the Arab nationalists and the pro-Ottomans were advocates of opposing political philosophies until 1919. If being an Arab nationalist or anti-Ottoman was conditioned by social influences, then a comparison of the social attributes of the two groups, anti-Ottoman (Arab nationalist) and pro-Ottoman, should cast light on the social determinants of the spread of Arabism. To test the assumption and to carry out the comparison, profiles showing the incidence of social attributes within the two groups have been constructed.[12] The pro-Ottoman group consists of the sixty pro-Ottoman members of the four organizations discussed above and all those Syrians, twenty-six in number, who are known to have joined nationalist societies after the end of the war. Before comparing the Arabists and the Ottomanists, however, something must be said about the geographic and religious traits of the pre-war Arab nationalists.

Before the war Arabism appealed to Damascene Moslems to a far greater degree than it did to any other regional and religious groupings in Syria. Although the population of the Damascus area comprised only about 27 percent of the Syrian population in 1915, residents of Damascus made up 80 percent of the total membership of the Arab movement. Religion also was of importance. Christians comprised about 6 percent of the total number of nationalists, while in 1926 they made up around 10 or 12 percent of the total population of Syria. Arabism appealed most to the Sunnite Moslems, for most of the Moslems who comprised 94 percent of the prewar Arab move-

12. The biographical data for this study was taken from Muḥammad Jamīl al-Shaṭṭi, *Tarājim aʿyān dimashq fi-niṣf al-qarn al-rābiʿ-ʿashr al-hijri, 1301–1350* [*Biographies of the Notables of Damascus in Half of the Fourteenth Century of the Hegira,* 1301–1350H] (Damascus: Dār al-Yaqẓah al-ʿArabīyah, 1948); Kāmil al-Ghāzi, *Nahr al-dhahab fi-taʾrīkh ḥalab* [*The River of Gold in the History of Aleppo*], 3 vols. (Aleppo: al-Maṭbaʿah al-Mārūnīyah, n.d.); Muḥammad Rāghib al-Ṭabbākh, *Aʿlām al-nubulāʾ bi-taʾrīkh ḥalab al-shahbāʾ* [*The Outstanding Nobles in the History of Aleppo*], 7 vols. (Aleppo: al-Maṭbaʿah al-ʿIlmīyah, 1342–45H/1923–26); Zaki Muḥammad Mujāhid, *al-Aʿlām al-sharqīyah fi-al-miʾah al-rābiʿah-ʿashrah al-hijrīyah, 1301–1365/1883–1946* [*The Leading Eastern Personalities in the Fourteenth Century of the Hegira,* 1301–1365H/1883–1946], 2 vols. (Cairo: Dār al-Ṭabāʿah al-Miṣrīyah al-Ḥadīthah, 1368–69H/1949–50); *Man huwa fi-sūrīyah, 1951* [*Who's Who in Syria,* 1951] (Damascus: Maktab al-Dirāsāt al Sūrīyah wa al-ʿArabīyah); *Oriente Moderno,* I–XIX (1922–1939); Hartmann, *Reisebriefe aus Syrien;* Muḥammad Kurd ʿAli, *al-Mudhakkarāt* [*Memoirs*], 4 vols. (Damascus: Maṭbaʿah al-Taraqqi, 1948–51); Yūsuf Asʿad Dāghir (Joseph Assad Dagher), *Maṣādir al-dirāsah al-adabīyah* (*Elements de bio-bibliographie de la litterature arabe*), II (Beirut: Jamʿīyah Ahl al-Qalam fi-Lubnān, 1956).

ment were Sunnites, who, in 1926, made up only 67 (or 72) percent of the Syrian population.[13] Homs provided three (two Christians), Hama three, Aleppo three (one Christian), and Lattakia one. The overt nationalists were distributed more widely than the members of the secret societies. Damascus provided only twelve (70 percent) of the seventeen overt nationalists, while providing twenty (83 percent) of the members of *al-Fatāt,* and nine (90 percent) of the members of *al-ʿAhd.* Christians were most important among the overt nationalists (two), of less importance among the members of *al-Fatāt* (one), and played no part in *al-ʿAhd.*

The Arab nationalists did not differ markedly from the pro-Ottoman Arabs in age. (See Appendix III.) The range of the known years of birth is much the same for both groups. The mean is virtually identical. The chief difference is that the median for the Arab nationalists is three years later than the median for the Ottomanists, perhaps an indication that the Arab nationalists were slightly younger. The pre-war members of *al-Fatāt* were younger than those of any other group.

The Arab elite with which we are concerned grew to manhood during a period when the process of Westernization had diversified the educational system. The traditional Muslim *madrasah* or college still flourished, as did the traditional shaykh. The Ottoman state schools, however, had long since been offering a more modern curriculum, both in the secondary schools in the provinces and in the advanced schools in Constantinople, where one might study not merely military science and medicine but even Western law and political science. Even more direct contact with Western learning was provided by the missionary colleges in Syria, which also offered advanced training in medicine, and by universities in Europe. To compare the educational background of the Arabists and the Ottomanists, a table of the incidence of varying types of education has been

13. The uncertainty in respect of the Syrian population arises from the uncertainty as to whether the official statistics for 1926 include an estimated 250,000 bedouin, practically all of whom were nominally Sunnites.

constructed. The influences of interest here are two: (1) the type of education, whether Western, state, or traditional, and (2) the highest stage of education completed. One student might terminate his education with graduation from one of the state or missionary colleges. Another might seek advanced (or perhaps the better term would be professional) training in the state schools, especially in Constantinople, or in Western schools, either the missionary colleges in Syria or universities in Europe. Owing to the professional nature of advanced education, military education, in the officers' school in Constantinople, has been classed as advanced, although strictly speaking it was perhaps secondary.

Most of the Arab nationalists and the pro-Ottomans were educated in state schools and received an advanced education. (See Appendix IV.) Both traditional and Western education, however, were of significance in both groups. It has sometimes been assumed that the early Arab nationalists were mostly Western educated, and even that Arabism was the product of Western education. Western education was of relatively greater incidence among the Arabists than among the Ottomanists. On the other hand, the Arabists held the same lead in the frequency of traditional education, which was more important than Western education in both groups. If the type of education was influential in forming political and ideological allegiance, and if these samples are representative, then Western and traditional education both tended to produce Arab nationalists, state education pro-Ottomans. Advanced (i.e., professional) education tended to produce Ottomanists.

In a changing situation like that of pre-1914 Syria, an individual's education would vary with the year of birth. Thus the educational attributes of the two groups ought to be compared by age groups as well as a whole. A year-by-year table was constructed from all thirty-four cases in which both date of birth and education were known. The results were then consolidated by arranging the data into three groups depending on date of birth. The first group consists of those born in and before 1876, the latest year in which a person of traditional education is known to have been born. The second group comprises those born between 1877 and 1888, the latest date of birth of persons with only a secondary education. All members of the third group, those born in and after 1889, had received an advanced education. (See Appendix V.)

By this tabulation education varies with the date of birth as well as with political position; the latter variations are more marked, the earlier the birth date. Of those known to have been born after 1888, the difference between Arabist and Ottomanist is probably insignificant. All had received an advanced education, there were no persons who had received only a traditional education, and 60 percent of the Arab nationalists had received a Western education as compared to 50 percent of the pro-Ottomans. Among those born before 1888 the situation was markedly different, the differences being more striking the earlier the date of birth. Of the oldest Arab nationalists, those born 1865–1876, 75 percent possessed traditional education, and 25 percent Western secondary. The Ottomanists of the same age were all recipients of an advanced education in state schools. The differences were slighter but still marked in the second age group, those born in 1877–1888. Pro-Ottomans were still much more likely to have received a state and an advanced education than were Arab nationalists, but a few Ottomanists had received a Western education, even though such an education was much more common among Arab nationalists.

The data for those born before 1889 are probably askew. Some correction can perhaps be made by the use of thirty cases in which the education is known but in which the year of birth is unknown. It is likely that most of these were persons born before 1889. These cases therefore have been consolidated with those known to have been born before 1889. Most individuals, Arab nationalists and pro-Ottomans, received an advanced and a state education; traditional education was second in importance, and Western a poor third. Still, the trend was for relatively more Arabists than pro-Ottomans to receive a traditional or a Western education. The Ottomanist was more likely to have received a state and an advanced education than was the Arab nationalist.

Class change and class conflict have for some time been one of the most popular of the mechanisms used to explain changes in ideology and politics. Especially popular is the view that European influence has engendered economic change throughout the world, and that such changes, in turn, have created new classes which use newer ideologies, such as nationalism and communism, in order to unseat the old elite which has become vestigial because of the economic changes. The early phase of Arab nationalism, with which we are concerned here, has been generally interpreted as a manifestation of such a new "middle class." More recent Arab developments have been similarly explained, with the modification that the awakening masses are now thought to be adding their weight to that of the middle class.

In Ottoman Syria family status was perhaps the most important index of class position. Ottoman society was not immobile. New men could rise, while the bearers of proud names might have difficulty in making ends meet. Nevertheless, important positions usually were occupied by men of good family, who possessed immeasurable advantage in the quest for position. At the top were landlords, rural and urban, who sometimes were also large-scale merchants. The landlords (hereafter, "landlord" is used to denote landlords and landlord-merchants) might, at the same time, be from families whose members for several generations had held positions in the Ottoman bureaucracy or, less frequently, in the army. Of equal or perhaps even higher standing were the landlord-scholars, members of families which had for generations produced specialists in the Muslim sciences of theology and law. From these families were drawn the members of the Ottoman "Religious Institution." Such were the high-status families of Ottoman Syria. Below them, occupying the middle position, were the ordinary merchants who had not yet been able to acquire land, the bankers and money-lenders. Lower yet, but still within the middle rank, were the small shopkeepers, the clerks in the government service and the lesser functionaries of the religious organization.

In order to compare the class composition of the various groups, a table showing the incidence within each group of individuals of differing family status has been constructed (Appendix VI). Family standing was determined by the relative frequency within a family of various occupations in both the pre- and post-1920 periods. However, the rating was carried out by impressionistic, not statistical, methods.

The importance of high-status families (landlord and landlord-scholar) among both Arab nationalists and pro-Ottomans is striking. In this connection some attention must be paid to the unknowns, since it might be assumed that families of unknown status were most likely of relatively low status. Consideration of the total, including unknowns, makes it certain that both Arab nationalist and Ottomanist Syrians came from upper-class families, for 61 percent of the total membership of the former and 64 percent of the latter came from such families.

Furthermore, two considerations justify the belief that many of the unknowns were of high family status. The first consideration is that most of the unknowns are individuals from areas other than Damascus and the Aleppo region, the only two regions for which relatively full biographical information is available. In the case of *al-Fatāt,* for instance, with twenty-two of twenty-four members of Damascene or Aleppine origin, unknowns comprise only 17 percent of the total membership and high-status individuals 75 percent. Thus the incidence of families of unknown status is clearly influenced by and varies directly with the quantity of biographical data available. The second consideration is that inclusion in one of the traditional biographical dictionaries depended to a great extent on membership in a scholarly family, fame for learning or literary activity, and membership in the bureaucracy or one of the municipal or provincial representative-consultive bodies. There are indications that many persons and families of great wealth and influence did not possess any of these qualifications, and their names are absent from the older biographical dictionaries.

Even though the Arab nationalists were predominantly of upper-class origin, so far as information is available, middle-class elements (merchant-scholar, merchant, and banker) did participate in the Arab movement to a greater extent than they did in the pro-Ottoman group. There are some indications that middle-class individuals are underrepresented in the data for the pro-Ottomans. Except for *al-ʿAhd,* which calls for special consideration, persons of unknown family status occur most frequently in the Ottomanist sub-groups. Only one Ottomanist sub-group, the Committee of National Defense, has a smaller percentage of individuals of unknown family status than either the overt nationalists or *al-Fatāt.* On the other hand, within this Ottomanist sub-group middle-class elements are more important than they are among either the overt nationalists or *al-Fatāt.*

The explanation of the relatively large number of unknowns within the membership of *al-ʿAhd* is obscure. Nine of the ten members were Damascene, yet the family status of eight of these is unknown. The explanation might lie in the fact that these men were all army officers, and army officers, unless of great distinction and high rank, were not included in biographical dictionaries. Still, the absence of other members of their families from the biographical dictionaries is striking. The question must be left unanswered.

The available evidence justifies the tentative conclusion that the middle class of Ottoman Syria played a relatively greater part in the Arab nationalist movement than it did in the total political process of Syria. There is no ground, however, for the conclusion that this middle class was new or created by European influence. Merchants and bankers had been a part of Near Eastern society for ages. In the past, merchants also had been influential in society and politics. One of the paths upward traditionally was through commerce. The successful merchant acquired land, both agricultural and urban. His landlord descendants then entered the bureaucracy or the learned institution and finally became full-fledged aristocrats. Meanwhile, other members of the family continued in commerce, and at times some members of well-established landowning and scholarly families apparently entered business. Bankers were of a different order, since only non-Muslims could be full-time bankers. The individuals in the sample are in keeping with tradition, for one was a Christian, the other a Jew. The presence of army officers in a political opposition group is also no departure from the traditional patterns of Near Eastern society. Connections between the military and government had always been intimate. In general, upper-class families were well represented in the officer corps, but at the same time the army was another of the avenues of personal advancement for men of humble origin.

In respect of family status, the most important point of differentiation between the Arab nationalists and the pro-Ottomans is one within the purely upper-class elements. Landowners predominate in both groups, but landowner-scholars were of considerably higher incidence among the pro-Ottomans than they were among the Arabists.

Pro-Ottomans and anti-Ottomans alike were mostly from good families. Did the political difference between the two groups correspond to an occupational difference? The incidence of occupations within the two groups is tabulated in Appendix VII. Comparatively few within either group were primarily landlords, though the incidence of landlords was greater among the pro-Ottomans than among the Arab nationalists. Landlords and landlord-scholars are undoubtedly underrepresented in both groups because of the procedure used in determining occupation. A person has been classed as a landlord only when he is known to have owned land and to have had no other occupation. Whenever an individual is known to have had some other occupation (as, for instance, lawyer), he has been classed with this occupation rather than as a landlord, even when he is known to have been a landowner. No one has been classified as a landlord, or as a scholar, on the basis of family alone. Thus it is likely that many of those whose occupations are unknown were landlords, and that many who had other occupations derived much or most of their incomes from landed property.

A more distinctive occupational difference between the two groups is the high percentage of the pro-Ottomans who occupied government positions (religious dignitary, governor, and official), the largest occupational group among the pro-Ottomans. Goverment employment was relatively much less frequent among the Arabists and, moreover, occupied only the second rank within the group, or even the third if professionals are grouped together. Furthermore, while the Ottomanist state employees held their positions until the end of the war, the Arab nationalist governors and officials either resigned or were discharged relatively early in their careers. Finally, religious dignitaries (*mufti, qāḍi,* and *khaṭīb*) played some part within the Ottomanist group and none at all within the Arab nationalist.

The most common occupation of the Arab nationalists was that of army officer. Among the pro-Ottomans, army officers were relatively fewer and occupied only the third rank within the group, or the fourth if the professionals are grouped together. On the other hand, army officers are very probably underrepresented among the pro-Ottomans. *Al-ʿAhd,* primarily an organization of officers, expanded after 1918, but the new members are unknown while all the original members are known. Nevertheless, army officers played a very important part in the pre-war Arab nationalist movement. It is most likely, in view of what is known about *al-ʿAhd* generally, that the Syrian Arabist officers were of company grade. On the other hand, the officers of the pro-Ottoman group appear to have been of field- and general-officer grade.

Among the Arab nationalists, intellectuals were more important than they were among the pro-Ottomans. Journalism and the professions, as a group, was the primary occupation of the greatest number of the Arabists. Journalists do not exist among the pro-Ottomans, a fact which is certainly the result of underrepresentation, for there were pro-Ottoman Arab journals before 1914. Considering professionals only (lawyer, physician, engineer, and educator, or teacher of Western subjects, not traditional Moslem), the difference between the two groups is not very great.

The professionals, as a group, are closely related to government officials. There are indications that most of the professionals in both groups, including physicians and engineers, were employed most of the time by the government. Lawyers especially sought government employment, and most of those listed as governors and officials probably were lawyers.

It might be (and commonly is) assumed that persons engaged in journalism and the professions represent the "new Western middle class" in Eastern countries. The incidence of persons of midle-status family origin is slightly higher among the Arab nationalists than among the Ottomanists. Occupation appears to indicate a similar trend. To answer the question whether or not the journalists and professionals were of middle-status families, tables showing the incidence of family status were constructed for these two occupational groups and for the governors and officials, owing to the intimate connection of this group with the professionals (see Appendix VIII).

Journalists, professionals, and government officials were not divided into Arabists and Ottomanists by class lines. The Arab nationalist journalists and professionals do exhibit the characteristics of middle-class persons seeking advancement to a greater degree than do the Ottomanists. Although one-half the Arabist professionals were from upper-status families, the incidence of such persons is noticeably greater among the Ottomanist professionals. Furthermore, the journalists, all Arabists, exhibit a very low incidence of people of upper-status origin. With respect to officials, however, the situation is reversed. Most officials, Ottomanist and Arabist, were from upper-status families. On the other hand, the incidence of officials of unknown family status is strikingly higher among the Ottomanists. Middle-class elements were active among both Arab nationalists and pro-Ottomans. The Ottomanists tended to have government positions; the Arabists did not. In this connection it is worth noting that government service was the third (along with landowning and military service) of the traditional means of advancement in Ottoman society. A man of modest origin might rise to the position of high official, or even governor. He was then most likely to acquire land and found an aristocratic family.

Perhaps the most significant point of differentiation between the Arabist and Ottomanist professionals and officials is one within the purely upper-status sector. The incidence of professionals from landowner-scholar families is much greater among the Arab nationalists than among the Ottomanists. The incidence of officials and governors of the same family status, however, is greater among the pro-Ottomans than among the Arabists. Men from landowner-scholar families with government position were active among the Ottomanists. Similar persons with professional training but without government position were active among the Arab nationalists. A comparable distinction can be discerned in regard to another occupation (see Appendix VII). Scholars, specialists in the traditional religious sciences, were more important among the Arabists than among the pro-Ottomans. On the other hand, religious dignitaries, i.e., scholars who held state positions, were more important among the Ottomanists than among the Arabists.

Like father, like son. Just as the Ottomanist Arabs were more successful in obtaining government positions than were their Arabist counterparts, the fathers of the former had been more successful than the fathers of the latter (see Appendix IX). The commonest occupation of the fathers of the pro-Ottomans was that of religious dignitary. A strikingly lower percentage of the Arab nationalists were sons of religious dignitaries. In contrast, the fathers of 60 percent of the knowns (18 percent of the total) of the Arab nationalists were landowners, as compared to none of the Ottomanists. Again, landowners are certainly underrepresented. More Arab nationalists were also sons of middle (merchant) or middle-to-high status (scholar) fathers than were pro-Ottomans. Among the latter, only two were sons of men with middle-status occupations, banker and physician. But both these cases were non-Moslems, and within the non-Moslem sector such occupations were of high standing.

The assumption that those Syrian Arabs who became active in the Arab nationalist movement only after 1918 were pro-Ottomans before 1918 is probably correct. The high incidence among them of men who occupied positions within the Ottoman administration is clear indication of this. Two of them, moreover, are known to have attacked the Paris Arab Congress in 1913.[14] The comparison of this group with the pre-1914 Arabists is then a valid measure of the social distinctions between Arab nationalists and pro-Ottoman Arabs.

Arab nationalism was not the product of class conflict. The Arab nationalists and the Ottomanists were predominantly from the Syrian upper class. It is true that so far as the available data regarding family status and occupation are representative, known and presumed middle-class elements were of slightly greater importance among the Arabists than they were among the pro-Ottomans. On the other hand, similar individuals constituted a significant percentage of the pro-Ottomans. The principal distinction between Arabist and Ottomanist was the holding of office.

The Ottomans did not rule Syria and the other Arab provinces directly by Turkish officials and soldiers. Instead, Syria was governed by a small number of high-ranking Turks and a large number of Arabs who occupied all but the highest positions. The traditional Near Eastern ethic sanctioned the use of public office for the furtherance of personal and family ends. Consequently, the service of the state attracted the *nouveaux* and the well established alike. Competition for state position was endemic within the Arab elite.

Some of the competition for state office was the result of upward social mobility. In Ottoman Syria, new men grew rich through trade or, sometimes, through state service. They, or their sons, sought to increase and secure their wealth by entry into the state hierarchy. The middle-class element among both

14. Saʿīd, I, 53.

the Arab nationalists and the pro-Ottomans was doubtless of this sort. These middle-class individuals, in their quest for position, followed the Near Eastern practice of patronage and clientship, regardless of whether they were Arabists or Ottomanists. This practice extended even to the artisans and wage earners of the towns, whose guilds and other popular organizations were under the patronage of a town notable, most frequently one of the scholarly class. For instance, one of the creators of the theory of Arabism, ʿAbd al-Raḥmān al-Kawākibi, was able to use his position as patron of the guilds in Aleppo to great political effect in the last quarter of the nineteenth century.[15]

Some of the competition for office was the product of downward social mobility. The aristocratic families of Ottoman Syria became quite large after the passage of a few generations. Some of their branches actually suffered a relative decline in wealth, influence, and the ability to obtain public office. It was not uncommon for men of the same large family to be on opposite sides politically. For example, Abū al-Naṣr and Abū al-Khayr al-Khaṭīb, brothers of a famous Damascene scholarly family, held the positions *qāḍi* and *khaṭīb* respectively. A third brother, Abū al-Fatḥ, was a teacher and director of a library. ʿAbd al-Qādir al-Khaṭīb, the son of the *qāḍi,* became a *qāḍi.* Zaki al-Khaṭīb, the son of the *khaṭīb,* became a governor. Both were pro-Ottoman. Their cousin, Muḥibb al-Dīn al-Khaṭīb, the son of the librarian, held no position in either the religious hierarchy or the government. He was a pre-1914 Arab nationalist.

The exact extent to which such downward mobility was operative in the rise of Arabism cannot be estimated. Seven

15. Al-Ṭabbākh, VII, 516; for an example at Damascus in 1882, see Elia Qoudsi, "Notice sur les corporations de Damas" (in Arabic), *Actes du Sixième Congrès International des Orientalistes,* pt. 2 (1885), pp. 10–12; for eleventh-century examples, see Jean Sauvaget, *Alep: Essai sur le développement d'une grande ville syrienne, des origines au milieu du XIXe siècle,* Haut Commissariat de l'État Français en Syrie et au Liban, Services des Antiquités, Bibliothèque Archéologique et Historique, XXXVI (Paris: Paul Geuthner, 1941), p. 97.

families had members in both the Arab nationalist and the Ottomanist camps. Thirteen of the pre-1914 Arabists were members of these families. It is not certain that each represents a case of rivalry between lesser and dominant branches of the same families, but two cases do so beyond doubt, and only two likely do not. It is possible, even likely, that downward social mobility of another type was at work. Under Ottoman conditions an entire family might suffer a relative decline in fortune. The information used in this study does not permit any estimate of the extent to which such families provided members for the early Arab movement.

Neither downward nor upward mobility was an element in most of the competition. The majority of the pre-war nationalists of high status apparently were as well off as their Ottomanist counterparts in every respect except the holding of office. If the cases for which family status is known are representative, members of landowning families made up over half of both the Arabist and the Ottomanist groups. Furthermore, men of landlord-scholar families occupied the second rank in both camps, even though such men were considerably more important among the Ottomanists than among the Arab nationalists. Members of wealthy scholarly families were relatively much more active among the pro-Ottomans than among the Arab nationalists. The converse was true of members of purely landowning families. There is thus some indication that especially in the Damascus area there was a conflict between the leading landlord-scholar families and the leading landlord families which took on the nature of a conflcit between Ottomanism and Arabism. It might be that some of these families were relative newcomers, but the information at hand does not permit an evaluation of this possibility. Finally, there is no explanation other than personal and family competition for positions in the state hierarchy. Competition of this kind was rife among the Arab nationalists. Conflict between rival personal and family factions was a recurrent activity within the pre-war societies. Similarly, during 1919–1920 *al-Fatāt* was beset with frequent changes in leadership which were attended by bitter personal recriminations.[16]

The conflict between Arab nationalist and Ottomanist in pre-1914 Syria was a conflict between rival members of the Arab elite. At the center of each camp were members of the highest stratum of Syrian society, who constituted a majority of the members of each faction. Associated with such upper-class elements were men of middle-class origin who were slightly more important among the Arab nationalists than among the pro-Ottomans. The conflict, then, was essentially of the type that was traditional in Near Eastern society. The new element was the ideological definition of the conflict.

Before the nineteenth century such conflicts were either left undefined or defined in terms of rival interpretations of Islam. In the course of the nineteenth century the problem of the West became so important as virtually to monopolize the intellectual activity of the Ottoman Arab political classes. Every ideology offered centered around the problem of defending and justifying the Islamic East in the face of the Christian West. In this, Ottomanism and Arabism were identical. They differed only in the means proposed for the pursuit of the desired goal. The Ottomanists argued that Islam and the East could best be served by the maintenance of the Ottoman Empire; the Arabists, by the restoration of the Arabs to their rightful position of religious and cultural leadership within Islam. In Syria those members of the Arab elite who had a vested interest in the Ottoman state were Ottomanists. Those who were without such a stake were Arabists. Thus was a traditional intra-elite conflict defined in terms of a new ideology.

Neither the growth of Arabism, the Arab Revolt, nor the Turkish collapse in World War I brought about any far-reaching change in the Arab personnel who ruled Syria. Nor did the growth of Arabism and the Arab Revolt break the allegiance

16. For pre-1914 examples, see *La Vérité sur la question syrienne*, pp. 11–12, 15, 16, 26, 28, 48–49, 77; Saʿīd, I, 43–46; Ahmad Djemal (Jemal), *Memories of a Turkish Statesman, 1913–1919* (New York: G. H. Doran Co., 1922), pp. 58–59. For post-war examples, see Saʿīd, II, 35–36, 125–126.

of the dominant faction of the Arab elite to Ottomanism. The collapse of the Ottoman Empire in the Turkish defeat was different, however. Although the political position of the Ottomanist Arabs survived the debacle, their ideology, Ottomanism, could not survive the end of the Ottoman Empire.

Arab nationalism as a political force, then, began as a movement within the dissident faction of the Arab elite of the Ottoman Empire. Arabism won its first success, and a complete success, when the failure of the Ottoman Empire in World War I left the dominant faction of the Arab elite with no alternative to Arabism.

Appendix I. Syrian Membership of the Pre-1914 Arab Movement

Overt Nationalists

ʿAbd al-Ḥamīd al-Zahrāwi
ʿAbd al-Raḥmān Shahbandar
ʿAbd al-Wahhāb al-Inklīzi
Albayr Ḥimṣi
ʿAlī al-Armanāzi
Fā'iz al-Ghuṣayn
Ḥaqqī al-ʿAẓm
Jalāl al-Bukhāri
Khālid al-Barāzi
Muḥammad Kurd ʿAlī
Muḥammad Rashīd al-Rāfiʿi
Qusṭanṭin Yani
Rafīq al-ʿAẓm
Rushdī al-Shamʿah
Shafīq al-Mu'ayyad
Shukrī al-ʿAsali
ʿUmar al-Jazā'iri

al-Fatāt

ʿAbd al-Wahhāb Muyassir
Aḥmad Fawzī al-Bakri
Aḥmad al-Ḥusayni
Aḥmad Maryūd
Amīn al-Muyassir
Aḥmad Qadri
ʿĀrif al-Shihābi
Bahjah al-Shihābi
Fā'iz al-Shihābi
Ismāʿīl al-Shihābi
Jamīl Mardam
Khālid al-Ḥakīm
Muḥammad Fakhrī al-Bārūdi
Muḥammad Kāmil al-Qaṣṣāb
Muḥammad al-Shurayqi
Muḥibb al-Dīn al-Khaṭīb
Nasīb al-Bakri
Rafīq Rizq Sallūm
Saʿīd al-Bāni
Sāmī al-Bakri
Sayf al-Dīn al-Khaṭīb
Shukrī al-Shurbji
Subḥī al-Ḥusayni
Taḥsīn Qadri

al-ʿAhd

ʿAbd al-Qādir Sirri
ʿAlī Riḍa al-Ghazāli

Amīn Luṭfī Ḥāfiẓ
ʿĀrif al-Tawwām
Muḥammad Ismāʿīl al-Ṭabbākh
Muḥyī al-Dīn al-Jubbān
Muṣṭafā al-Waṣfi
Ṣādiq al-Jundi
Salīm al-Jazāʾiri
Yaḥya Kāẓim Abū al-Sharaf

APPENDIX II. Syrian Membership of Arab Nationalist Movement, 1919–1920

The Syrian General Congress

ʿAbd al-Ḥamīd al-Bārūdi
ʿAbd al-Qādir al-Khaṭīb
ʿAbd al-Qādir al-Kīlāni
ʿAbd al-Raḥmān al-Yūsuf
Aḥmad al-ʿAyyāshi
Aḥmad al-Qaḍamāni
Diʿās al-Jirjis
Fāʾiz al-Shihābi *
Fakhrī al-Bārūdi *
Fātiḥ al-Marʿashli
Fawzī al-Bakri *
Fuʾād ʿAbd al-Karīm
Ḥasan Ramaḍān
Hāshim al-Atāsi
Ḥikmat al-Ḥarāki
Ḥikmat al-Nayāli
Ibrāhīm Hanānu
Ilyās ʿUwayshiq
ʿIzzat al-Shāwi
Jalāl al-Qudsi
Khalīl al-Barāzi *
Khalīl Abū-Rīsh
Maḥmūd Abū-Rūmīyah
Maḥmūd al-Fāʿūr
Maḥmūd Nadīm
Maẓhar Raslān
Muḥammad Fawzī al-ʿAẓm
Muḥammad Khayr
Muḥammad al-Mujtahid
Muḥammad al-Shurayqi *
Munāḥ Hārūn
Muslim al-Ḥasani
Nājī ʿAlī Abīd
Nāṣir al-Mufliḥ
Nūrī al-Jisr
Saʿdullāh al-Jābiri
Sharīf al-Darwīsh
Ṣubḥī al-Ṭawīl
Tāj al-Dīn al-Ḥasani
Theodore Anṭāki
Waṣfī al-Atāsi
Yūsuf al-Kayyāli
Yūsuf Liyānādu
Zakī Yaḥya

The Governments

ʿAbd al-Ḥamīd al-Qalṭaqchi
ʿAbd al-Raḥmān Shahbandar *
Aḥmad Ḥilmi
ʿAlāʾ al-Dīn al-Durūbi
ʿAlī Riḍa al-Rikābi **
Fāris al-Khūri
Hāshim al-Atāsi †
Jalāl al-Dīn al-Zuhdi
Jamīl al-Ulshi
Muṣṭafā Niʿmah
Sāṭī al-Ḥusari
Shukrī al-Ayyūbi **
Yūsuf al-ʿAẓmah
Yūsuf al-Ḥakīm

Army Command

Aḥmad al-Laḥḥām
ʿĀrif al-Tawwām *

Muḥammad Ismāʿīl al-Ṭabbākh *
Muṣṭafā al-Waṣfi *
Yaḥya Ḥayāti

Committee of National Defense

ʿAbd al-Qādir al-Khaṭīb †
ʿAbd al-Qādir Sukkar
Asʿad al-Māliki
Asʿad al-Muhāyini
ʿAwni al-Qaḍamāni
ʿAyad al-Ḥalabi
Jamīl Mardam *
Muḥammad Kāmil al-Qaṣṣāb *
Muḥammad al-Naḥḥās
Nasīb Ḥamzah
Sāmī Mardam
Shukrī al-Ṭabbāʿ

Nationalist Societies

ʿAbd al-Qādir al-ʿAẓm
ʿĀdil al-ʿAẓmah
ʿĀrif al-Khaṭib
Asʿad al-Ḥakīm
Fawzī al-Ghāzi
Ḥasan al-Ḥakīm
Ḥusnī al-Barāzi
Ibrāhīm al-Mujāhid
Iḥsān al-Jābiri
Khayr al-Dīn al-Zirkali
Luṭfī al-Rafāʿi
Muḥyī al-Dīn Sādiq
Muslim al-ʿAṭṭār
Muṣṭafā Barmada
Muṣṭafā al-Shihābi
Nabīh al-ʿAẓmah
Najīb al-Armanāzi
Riḍa al-Rifāʿi
Rashīd Baqdūnis
Sāmī al-Sarrāj
Tawfīq al-Ḥayāni
Tawfīq al-Shīshakli
ʿUmar Farḥāt
Yūsuf Yāsīn
Zakī al-Khaṭīb
Zakī al-Qadri

* Pre-1914 nationalists
** Joined nationalist movement, 1914–1918
† Member of Syrian General Congress

APPENDIX III. Age (by year of birth)

	Range	*Median*	*Mean*	*Number Known*	*% Known*	*Total*
Pre-1914 Nationalist						
Overt	1865–1880	1871	1871	5	29	17
al-Fatāt	1885–1898	1891	1891	7	29	24
al-ʿAhd				none	none	10
Total	1865–1898	1886.5	1883	12	24	51
1919–1920 Nationalists						
Syrian Gen. Cong.	1869–1892	1878	1880	5	13	39
Syrian Govts.	1877–1884	1883	1881–82	7	58	12
Comm. Nat. Def.	1875–1888	1881	1881	2	22	9
Others	1881–1897	1888	1888	10	38	26
Total	1869–1897	1883	1884	24	28	86

Appendix IV. Education

	Pre-1914 Arab Nationalists			*1919–1920 Arab Nationalists*		
	No.	*% Knowns*	*% Total*	*No.*	*% Knowns*	*% Total*
Western	5	17	10	4	12	5
State	19	63	38	25	74	29
Traditional	6	20	12	5	15	6
Secondary	4	13	8	4	12	5
Advanced	20	67	39	25	74	29
Total known	30			34		
Unknown	21		41	52		60
Total	51			86		

Appendix V. Age and Education

	Western		*State*		*Traditional*		*Secondary*		*Advanced*		
	No.	*%*	*No.*	*%*	*No.*	*%*	*No.*	*%*	*No.*	*%*	*Total*
Year of Birth:											
1865–1876											
Pre-1914 Nationalist	1	25			3	75	1	25			4
1919–1920 Nationalist			2	100					2	100	2
1877–1888											
Pre-1914 Nationalist	1	33	2	67			2	67	1	33	3
1919–1920 Nationalist	1	7	13	93			3	21	11	79	14
1865–1888											
Pre-1914 Nationalist	2	29	2	29	3	43	3	43	1	14	7
1919–1920 Nationalist	1	6	15	94			3	19	13	81	16
1889–1897											
Pre-1914 Nationalist	3	60	2	40					5	100	5
1919–1920 Nationalist	3	50	3	50					6	100	6
1865–1888 and Birth year unknown											
Pre-1914 Nationalist	2	8	17	68	6	24	4	16	15	60	25
1919–1920 Nationalist	1	4	22	79	5	18	4	14	19	68	28

Appendix VI. Family Status

	Pre-1914 Arab Nationalists			*1919-1920 Arab Nationalists*		
	No.	*% Knowns*	*% Total*	*No.*	*% Knowns*	*% Total*
Landowner	22	63	43	31	53	36
Landowner-scholar	9	26	18	24	41	28
Merchant-scholar	1	3	2	1	2	1
Merchant	2	6	4	1	2	1
Banker	1	3	2	1	2	1
Total known	35			58		
Unknown	16		31	28		33
Total	51			86		

Appendix VII. Occupation

	Pre-1914 Arab Nationalists			*1919-1920 Arab Nationalists*		
	No.	*% Knowns*	*% Total*	*No.*	*% Knowns*	*% Total*
Landowner	5	14	10	10	22	12
Landowner-scholar				2	4	2
State dignitaries						
Religious dignitary				2	4	2
Governor	3	8	6	5	11	6
Official	3	8	6	9	20	10
Total	6	16	12	16	35	19
Military officer	11	30	22	7	15	8
Scholar	2	5	4	1	2	1
Journalist	4	11	8			
Professionals						
Lawyer	5	14	10	3	7	3
Physician	2	5	4	2	4	2
Engineer	1	3	2	2	4	2
Educator				2	4	2
Total	8	22	16	9	20	10
Banker	1	3	2	1	2	1
Total known	37			46		
Unknown	14		27	40		47
Total	51			86		

Appendix VIII. Family Status of Journalists, Professionals, and Officials

	Journalists				*Professionals*				*Officials*			
	Pre-1914 Arab Nationalists		*1919-1920 Arab Nationalists*		*Pre-1914 Arab Nationalists*		*1919-1920 Arab Nationalists*		*Pre-1914 Arab Nationalists*		*1919-1920 Arab Nationalists*	
	No.	*%*	*No.*	*%*	*No.*	*%*	*No.*	*%*	*No.*	*%*	*No.*	*%*
Landowner					1	13	5	56	5	83	6	43
Landowner-scholar	1	25			3	38	1	11			3	21
Merchant	1	25										
Unknown	2	50			4	50	3	33	1	17	5	36
Total	4				8		9		6		14	

Appendix IX. Father's Occupation

	Pre-1914 Arab Nationalists			*1919-1920 Arab Nationalists*		
	No.	*% Known*	*% Total*	*No.*	*% Known*	*% Total*
Landowner	9	60	18			
Landowner-scholar				3	17	4
Religious dignitary	2	13	4	12	67	14
Governor				1	6	1
Scholar	3	20	6			
Merchant	1	7	2			
Physician				1	6	1
Banker				1	6	1
Total known	15			18		
Unknown	36		71	68		79
Total	51			86		

SEVEN

Ramifications and Reflections

PATRIOTISM, nationalism, Ottomanism and Arabism, modernity and backwardness all became crucial concepts to the political classes of the Ottoman Empire as a result of contact with Europe. Ottoman borrowing of alien ideas is undeniable. Nevertheless, cultural encounter is not sufficient to engender cultural imitation. The Islamic East faced the Christian West for centuries without feeling the slightest desire to imitate, or even to acquire close acquaintance with, the ways of the alien. This disinterestedness was not due to lack of contact. Throughout the early modern age Moslems of the Ottoman Empire had experience of Europeans through the presence of merchants, diplomats, and travelers, as well as through hostile contact along the frontiers. Neither peaceful nor armed encounter, however, suggested to the Ottoman Moslem that his way of life was in need of improvement. Both Arab and Turkish Moslems possessed a sense of identity, of their relatedness and distinctiveness; or, to use G. E. von Grunebaum's terminology, they possessed an Ottoman self-view. They had no self-doubts. They knew who they were and where they were going. They were Moslems, those who had accepted the law which the one true God had revealed through His messenger Mohammed. Mohammed was the final, the perfect, and the best of God's messengers; therefore the Moslems were the best of God's peoples. As is true of a great many human self-views, the Ottoman Islamic self-view took for granted the adequacy, even the superiority, of Ottoman Islamic society and culture. The Ottoman Moslem's view of himself was not shaken when he looked outside himself, if he did, at infidel Europe. Indeed, the inhabitants of the region could find the greatest satisfaction in the state of their relations with the world outside. For centuries the region had been independent, first under the Mameluks and the Ottomans, then, after 1517, united within the Ottoman

Empire. These territories had more than held their own in their many and varied contacts with Europe. Europeans lived there at the sufferance of the natives and on their terms, under capitulations freely granted by the local authorities. In military matters the Ottomans in 1357 began a series of victories which extended over two centuries with scarcely an interruption.

Ottoman self-assurance was shaken by the long series of European military victories in the eighteenth century. War after war saw the armies of the faithful suffering defeats at the hands of the Christian Europeans, primarily the Russians. Whatever military or diplomatic victories the Ottomans could count were the result largely of European factors, not Ottoman. When the century was spent, some of those responsible for the conduct of the Ottoman government had become convinced that the true believers must seek knowledge from the Franks. Inevitably, some Ottomans believed that to withstand the West they must imitate the West. Not unnaturally, sultans, military commanders, and high officials began the improvement of Ottoman military and administration organizations by borrowing from Europe. For this effort to succeed, Ottomans had to be trained in European learning. So began the establishment of state schools and the exchange of intellectuals which has continued until the present day, with instructors from and students to Europe.

By the mid-nineteenth century much had been accomplished. The Ottoman government had brought back under its control most of the provinces where formerly mutinous governors had held sway. Egypt was still virtually independent, but even there the governor was paramount, whereas previously independent Mameluk beys had ignored him. Elsewhere, though, the fight against Europe had not been so successful. Military and diplomatic activities of the European powers enabled the despised Christian subjects of the sultan to rise and to gain autonomy and, ultimately, independence. Inside the Empire the demands of the Christians and the pressure of the European powers had induced the Ottoman government to promulgate laws and to establish courts which gave the subjects rights and privileges which, in the eyes of the Moslems, violated God's law. Europeans residing within the Empire became haughty. Traders and promoters demanded and obtained rights which far exceeded those granted earlier in the capitulations. Christian missionaries came in to convert the faithful by publicly arguing that Mohammed was an imposter.

The nineteenth-century intensification and intrinsic modification of Western pressures was met by cultural borrowing of a different type. To the military and administrative practices and the military, transportation, and communications technology of the West was added a wide range of Western procedures and products, ideas and concepts. Motivation, however, remained the same. Both the Egyptian and Ottoman governments realized the need for good relations with, and a good press in, England and France. Accordingly, it was necessary to admit more European nationals as merchants and missionaries. This, along with the problem of the Christian subjects, required the introduction of European commercial and penal codes and the establishment of courts which satisfied contemporary liberal opinion in the West by ending the legal distinction between Moslem and non-Moslem. In part also from the desire to impress the West, the rulers, by example and by coercion, stimulated the adoption of Western dress and the consumption of European articles. Western goods and Western style flowed into the region, partly owing to the encouragement of these policies, perhaps even more as the result of the increasing cheapness of European manufactures.

Notwithstanding the obvious motives of the Westernizers, the attempted Westernization was and has continued to be sincere in the sense that the adoption of legal and ideological culture was intended to be effective and not merely to be window-dressing.[1] In every case, the preferred ideas and ideol-

1. Among the systematic examinations of the Near Eastern reaction to the West, special attention may be called to the following: H. A. R. Gibb, *Modern Trends in Islam* (Chicago: University of Chicago Press, 1945); G. E. von Grunebaum, *Islam: Essays in the Nature and Growth of a Cultural Tradition,* American Anthropological Association Memoir, no. 81, in *The American Anthropologist,* LVII, no. 2, pt. 2 (April, 1955), 185–246, and his *Modern*

ogies were regarded as the secret of worldly success. To the Westernizers, the patriotism of the European nations was a chief ingredient of their strength. Ottoman patriotism or Egyptian patriotism or Arab patriotism could do the same for a people at present lowly and abased. Equality before the law and secularism were dimly perceived as being necessary elements of the desired patriotism. Parliamentary government had a like appeal. In the twentieth century social reform and socialism in turn became the secrets of Western might which could be used to good effect by the moribund Arab nation.[2]

Western culture also had an appeal beyond its utility in action against external enemies. By and large, most Ottoman and Arab emulators of the West appear to have convinced themselves that Western ways were superior. Western justice and Western scholarship at the onset of Westernization, Western social justice and physical science at a later stage, have found fervent admirers. This admiration has been blended with an equally common if perhaps less noble sentiment: there are grounds for more than a slight suspicion that admiration of Western ways included a bit of the desire to be one-up and, conversely, something of the feeling of being one-down.

The Ottoman Moslem self-view, like all viable self-views, placed its bearers at the apex of God's creation. The need to

Islam: The Search for Cultural Identity (Berkeley and Los Angeles: University of California Press, 1962); Wilfred Cantwell Smith, *Islam in Modern History* (Princeton, N.J.: Princeton University Press, 1957); Nadav Safran, *Egypt in Search of Political Community*, Harvard Middle Eastern Studies, no. 5 (Cambridge, Mass.: Harvard University Press, 1961); Albert H. Hourani, *Arabic Thought in the Liberal Age, 1798–1939* (London: Oxford University Press, 1962); Ibrahim Abu-Lughod, *Arab Rediscovery of Europe*, Oriental Studies Series, no. 22 (Princeton, N.J.: Princeton University Press, 1963); Bernard Lewis, *The Middle East and the West* (Bloomington: Indiana University Press, 1964).

2. The socialists have not yet received the same attempts at systemization that their predecessors have. See Leonard Binder, "Radical Reform Nationalism in Syria and Egypt," *The Muslim World*, XLIX (1959), 96–110, 213–231; Malcolm Kerr, "Arab Radical Notions of Democracy," *St. Antony's Papers*, no. 16, Middle Eastern Affairs, no. 3 (Carbondale: Southern Illinois University Press, 1963), pp. 9–40, and the same author's "The Emergence of a Socialist Ideology in Egypt," *The Middle East Journal*, XVI (1962), 127–144; and the Baʿthist selections in *Arab Nationalism: An Anthology*, ed. Sylvia G. Haim (Berkeley and Los Angeles: University of California Press, 1962), pp. 233–249.

imitate the Franks did not square with the self-view. Even less, perhaps, was the self-view undisturbed in the case of those who genuinely admired Western culture as superior. Not surprisingly, Ottoman and Arab concern with the West has been dominated by an obsession with power and glory. In the works of the intellectuals, from Ṭahṭāwi to the Baʿthists, the common crucial theme is that the power and glory has passed from the Moslem East to the Christian West. There is universal agreement that the situation is intolerable, that the West has in some unfair fashion gained possession of the power and glory which rightfully belong to the Moslems, or the Ottomans, or the Arabs. In short, the successive self-views have sustained a succession of injuries since the beginning of the nineteenth century. Consequently, the Westernized intellectuals have devoted themselves to the defense of an injured self-view.

The defense of an injured self-view requires a theory which explains away the felt differential between two communities, or cultural groups, and instills faith that the gulf will soon be closed. This need for emotional solace was the source of both the conservatives' distinction between the materialistic West and the spiritual East and the modernists' attribution of modern European civilization to Islam. The appeal of elements of Marxian socialism is similar. Here again a strand of Western thought has been adapted to the defense of the Arab self-view. The Hobson-Leninist theory of imperialism explains that Western greatness is the result of the exploitation of the Arabs. Obviously the way to recover the Arabs' lost power and glory is through the end of imperialism. Furthermore, contemporary Arab intellectuals have shown that socialism has its roots in Islam or the Arab nation just as easily as their predecessors have shown that parliaments and rationalism are Islamic in origin.

In the defense of the Ottoman self-view, Islam was justified and glorified. Arabism itself originated as a defense of Islam. Its advocates argued that a revivified Arab nation was necessary and sufficient condition of the restoration to Islam of its power and glory. Even when presented as a defense of Islam,

Arabism had less appeal than did Ottomanism. Only when World War I and its aftermath made Ottomanism an unworkable policy did Arabism become the dominant self-view among the Arabs. The replacement of Ottomanism by Turkism among the Turks followed a parallel course. The emphasis upon Islam in Ottomanism and Arabism has tempted many to dismiss Arabism and Arab Moslem modernism as mere religious fanaticism, as the result of some bigotry which inheres in Islam but which is fortunately lacking in other religions. Yet the defense of Islam was more the defense of a culture than of a religion. Religion, although important, was expendable; the way of life and the people were not.

The defense of Islam is in no way surprising. Ottoman culture was under attack by the West, both implicitly in the general situation and explicitly in the words of missionaries and of Western observers like Lord Cromer. Islam, the most striking feature of Ottoman culture, was the special target. Inevitably the defense of the East required the defense of Islam. In the West itself many nationalists have been impelled to defend the religion which they feel is central to their nation and culture. Beyond this the primacy of complex psychological motivations that result from political and cultural confrontation—not simple religious fanaticism, if there be such thing—is indicated by two other sets of phenomena: the behavior of some Christian Arabs, and the functional identity of secularist theories to Islamist theories.

In the nineteenth century many Christian Arab intellectuals joined their Moslem Turkish and Arab brethren in denying that the East was inferior to Europe. Some, like Fāris al-Shidyāq, adopted the conservative Ottomanist position and even converted to Islam to show it. Others, like Adīb Isḥaq, denied the superiority of Europe and gloried in the fact that the "fatherland" of the "enlightenment" was the "East, the home of the seeds of the religious and political movements which changed the form of the earth and the conditions of man." Yet the East had fallen into decadence and would have to regain its original greatness by a popular national revival like that of the

French.[3] After the rise of the theory of Arabism some Christian Arabs came to accept it in a modified form. By 1914 some Christian Arabs, like Nadrah Maṭrān, already had implicitly accepted the theory that Islam was an essential part of Arabism because Islam brought greatness to the Arabs. By 1930 Christian Arab nationalists had explicitly stated the theory that Islam was the moving force in "the first great Arab conquest, with which was founded the modern glory of the Arabs. . . ."[4]

One may argue, of course, that these Christian Arabs are no more than realists, men who recognize that the Christian Arabs are submerged in a Moslem sea and that the Christians must avoid alienating the Moslem majority. There is doubtless some truth in the argument. For one thing, the Christian Arabs who have accepted Islam as a necessary part of Arabism are mostly Palestinians and Syrians—that is, natives of regions where the Christians form such a small minority that they cannot possibly hope to have an independent political movement of their own. Besides, the Christians of Lebanon have not been wholehearted participants in the Arab movement. Instead, they have stoutly maintained their independence and have even developed a theory of "Phoenicianism," or Lebanese nationalism. Now it is significant that Lebanon, where Arabism has not been accepted completely, is the one Arab region where the Christian population is large and important enough to play an independent and leading political role.

Yet the fact remains that Christians, even Lebanese ones, are ardent Arab nationalists in large and significant numbers. Even in Christian-dominated Lebanon Arabism of a special kind is and has been the dominant ideology since 1943. Lebanon is to be independent, not a part of an Arab union, but it is to have an "Arab face." The reason is in part political, but it would not be political if Arabism as such did not have some

3. For additional evidence regarding the Christians and their resentment of Europe, including Protestant missionaries, see A. L. Tibawi, "The American Missionaries in Beirut and Butrus Al-Bustānī," *St. Antony's Papers,* no. 16, pp. 166, 170–173, and the same author's *British Interests in Palestine, 1800–1901: A Study of Religious and Educational Enterprise* (New York: Oxford University Press, 1961), pp. 9–12, 21–28, 89–116, 175–177.

4. *Oriente Moderno,* X (1930), 57.

attraction for the Christians. Islam is a part of the culture of the Arabs. The Arab, even a Christian, thus identifies with it. In 1948 some of my Christian Lebanese friends were greatly upset by the Indian occupation of Moslem Hyderabad and instinctively took the side of Moslems who lived in a distant part of the world and were not even Arabs.

Just as Christian Arabs were willing to accept the theory that Islam occupied a special position within Arabism, so Moslem Arabs have been able to emphasize the pre-Islamic achievements of the Arab nation. Adopting the so-called wave theory of Semitic origins, which held that Arabia was the original home of the Semites and that the great civilized Semitic peoples of antiquity moved from Arabia in periodic waves, the Semites were equated with the Arabs. So the Babylonian and other civilizations of the pre-Hellenic Orient were claimed as the gift of the Arab nation to humanity. Although these Moslem Arabs joined their Christian brethren in eliminating the purely Islamic origin of Arabism, they did not eliminate Islam from their theories. Instead, Islam remained as the crowning glory of the Arab nation. On the other hand, these Moslem Arabs have added an element of secularism by seeking the origins of their national greatness in the pre-Islamic Arab nation.

The same defense of a self-view is to be found in secular Turkism. In the latter part of the nineteenth century, some Turks began to be interested in Turkish language, Turkish history, and Turkish culture as distinct from Moslem and Ottoman. By 1913 some theorists, notably Ziya Gökalp, had developed a theory of Turkish nationalism. As is well known, this theory was finally established in the Turkish Republic by the movement led by Mustafa Kemal.

In the new Turkism primitive pure Islam and its superiority to other ways of life disappeared; the intrinsic greatness and superiority of the Turks and their way of life remained. The new Turks distinguished between "culture," "civilization," and "religion." "Culture" was essential. It is the vital spirit of a people, and ultimately of a modern nation. As the Ottoman modernists had attributed the former superiority of the Moslems to pure Islam and their subsequent decline to its corruption, so Ziya Gökalp found "the factors responsible for" Ottoman greatness in the "folk civilization [culture]," and those which caused Ottoman decline in its submergence in Islam and in Middle Eastern civilization.[5] Just as the Ottoman modernists had prescribed the return to primitive Islam in order to restore its former superior position, so Gökalp prescribed the same remedy for the restoration of the greatness of the Turks. "We have to create a new civilization in our own spirit," he wrote when he had still not distinguished Turk from Ottoman. "This national Ottoman civilization will arouse the envy of European civilization." He had no doubt that the Turks would outstrip Europe. European civilization, he wrote, "is based on rotten and decaying foundations and is doomed to ruin. The new civilization will be created by the Turkish race which has not, like other races, been demoralized by alcohol and licentious living, but has been strengthened and rejuvenated in glorious wars." [6] In complete harmony with this theory, Mustafa Kemal Atatürk erected into state dogma linguistic and historical theories which made the Turks the originators of all civilization.[7]

Even purely secularistic theorists have the same goal as the Islamistic. One of the most interesting examples is Ṭāha Ḥusayn's exposition of the Mediterranean nature of Egyptian culture. Although they seem radically opposed to an Islamic self-view, Ḥusayn's ideas have an identical intention. Ḥusayn's overriding concern is to prove that Egyptian culture is rational and thus equal to the demands of modern life. In similar fashion Marxist theory, as has already been remarked, is popular as a means of explaining away the gap between the Islamic

5. Ziya Gökalp, *Turkish Nationalism and Western Civilization*, trans. and ed. Niyazi Berkes (New York: Columbia University Press, 1959), p. 90.

6. Uriel Heyd, *Foundations of Turkish Nationalism: The Life and Teachings of Ziya Gökalp* (London: Luzac and Company, Ltd., and The Harvill Press, Ltd., 1950), pp. 78–79.

7. Bernard Lewis, "History-Writing and National Revival in Turkey," *Middle Eastern Affairs*, IV (1953), 224–227; Ettore Rossi, "Venticinque anni di rivoluzione dell'alfabeto e venti di riforma linguistica in Turchia," *Oriente Moderno*, XXXIII (1953), 378–384.

Near East and the capitalist West and in providing hope for the future.

Ottomanism and Arabism were borrowed from Western Europe, but the borrowers had their own purposes. Like the utilization of Western cultural elements in general, patriotism and nationalism, together with associated political and social concepts, were adopted as means of strengthening the Ottoman East against the Christian West. But this need to borrow impelled the borrowers to adapt the theories in such a way as to quench the strong emotions engendered in Ottomans by the striking progress and power of Europe, with its implicit imputation of inferiority to the East. This emotional need is even more important than anti-colonialism. Ottomanism was fully developed before any European power occupied any Moslem territory in the Ottoman Empire. Even Arabism was developed before any European power had occupied a country which the Arab nationalists regarded as Arab. What Ottomans could see was that Europe was superior, not only militarily and politically, but also in wealth and science. The conservatives denied it; the modernists admitted it but explained it away; all resented it—for all felt that their personal honor was involved. The Christian Arab Ottoman modernist Adīb Isḥaq admitted that he had "made love of self the source of love of the fatherland and of the nation." He went on to explain, "Belonging to the fatherland joins it and the inhabitant with a firm bond of personal honor, and he [the inhabitant] is jealous of it [the fatherland] and defends it, just as he defends the father who has begotten him, even if he is very angry with him." Because he loved himself and his fatherland, Isḥaq sought to learn from Europe. "We have not composed a history of the French Revolution," he wrote, "except to make us remember it as an example and a lesson to a nation which remembers and reflects. And to instruct those who suffer tyranny, those who yearn for deliverance from humiliation, how people before them have achieved this goal, and changed from weakness to strength, from humiliation to mightiness, from slavery to freedom, and raised their heads and rejoiced their souls. . . ."

The need to defend the integrity of the Ottoman Empire both physically and emotionally was not the only impetus to Westernization and the adoption of nationalism. Of equal significance was internal politics. All members of the Ottoman political classes agreed on the need to meet the Frankish threat, but they could not agree on programs and leadership. Internal division and conflict is a universal of human society, though the fact is often forgotten. As the strength of Europe became manifest, various contenders for leadership in Ottoman society came to consider elements of European culture useful in the contest with their rivals.

In Sunnite Moslem theory, God is sovereign. Law is nothing more than God's will revealed to man. The Moslems (that is, those who have submitted to God's will as revealed through God's messenger, Mohammed) are under the obligation to obey the unchangeable law of the Mohammedan revelation. Government exists only to execute the law, not to legislate, for the law has been revealed by God in its perfect form. The ruler not only had no legislative power; he was not even one of the final authorities on the law. Very early it was established that the custodians of the law, and the authoritative experts on it, were the body of the learned men. The power of the government under the law, however, was absolute.

Ideally the Moslems ought to be united under one government, because the law was one and the faithful thus formed one congregation. Ideally also this government should be that of a legitimate monarch, who ruled in apostolic succession from the first ruler of the Moslem congregation, Mohammed. In fact the Moslems had been united under one ruler in the early days, and Sunnite political theory was an idealization of this ruler, the caliph, and his government, the caliphate. However, by the fourteenth century the universal caliphate was only a memory. Moslems and Moslem governments remained, now ruled by sultans. Moslem jurists were willing and able to modify theory to meet the new conditions. Caliph and caliphate, it was held, were ideals which had been realized only during the brief golden age of early Islam. Since that time the faithful had been ruled by sultans, mere holders of power, and need not be united under one ruler. The law, preserved and expounded by the learned men, remained to give unity to the congregation. If a sultan respected and enforced the law, his government was legitimate. Sunnite government, then, was monarchical absolutism restricted only by the obligation of the monarch to enforce the law.

The Moslem state was a personal state from the beginning. Within the general restriction that the ruler must enforce the law and that he could not legislate, all government, whether caliphate or sultanate, was a mere extension of the person of the ruler. He was assisted by soldiers and bureaucrats on the one hand and learned men on the other, but he appointed and removed them. Even the succession to the throne was determined by the person of the ruler. There were doctrines and laws of succession, it is true; but buried in the formulas of the jurists concerning succession, even to the caliphate, was the admission that power belonged to whoever could acquire and hold it. Tenure of office was inevitably insecure, and monarchical absolutism could be exercised for only brief spells, if at all. Ottoman sultans, like caliphs before them, could enjoy security of office only by allowing others to exercise power. The successful ruler, whether sultan or grand vizier, governed as the head of a coalition of personages. As happens not uncommonly, the holders of office rarely distinguished the good of the community from their own good. Success in government was the surest road to the most remunerative employment and to the accumulation of property. Even today in the Near East government expenditures, especially wages and salaries, make up a larger percentage of the national income than has been common in modern Western countries. In the Ottoman Empire office provided salary and fees always, commercial monopolies occasionally, and, when one was especially successful, the tenure of land. More often than not, owning was the consequence, not the antecedent, of ruling.

Traditional Near Eastern government has been depicted far too often as the tightly controlled preserve of a handful of large landowners. In the modern age landowners have been the most important people, but they have not been distinct from the bureaucracy, the army, the corps of scholars, or even business. As the state was the owner of land, the agents of the state—bureaucrats, soldiers, and scholars—usually gained control of land. Loss of political position could, and usually did, mean loss of land. Members of distinguished families had a great advantage in the quest for position, but there was a fierce competition among the leading families. Consider, for example, the continuous competition for control of the scholarly positions at Aleppo among Kawākibi, Qudsi, and Jābiri. There were just too many landlords, bureaucrats, soldiers, and scholars for promotion to be automatic.[8] Most agriculturists owned no land, but there was no small, closely knit clique which owned practically all of the land. In Syria, for example, at the end of 1945 agricultural land was distributed as follows:

Small holdings (under 10 hectares)—15%
Medium holdings (10–100 hectares)—33%
Large holdings (over 100 hectares)—29%
State lands—23%

The medium holders owned slightly more land than did the large holders. Furthermore, the holder of more than 500 hectares is more distinct from the holder of 100–500 hectares than the latter is from the holder of 50–100 hectares. At least half the large holdings were less than 500 hectares. Thus truly great landowners with holdings of over 500 hectares owned no more than 15 percent of the total agricultural land.[9] In Syria, as

8. On the interconnections of landholding, bureaucracy, and business, cf. William Morris Carson, "The Social History of an Egyptian Factory," *The Middle East Journal,* XI (1957), 361–362, 363, and Morroe Berger, *Bureaucracy and Society in Modern Egypt,* Princeton Oriental Studies, Social Science no. 1 (Princeton, N.J.: Princeton University Press, 1957), pp. 15, 44–45, 106–107, 108–111.

9. Syria, Ministre de l'Économie Nationale, Service Technique du Cadastre et d'Amelioration Foncière, *Statistiques diverses* (Damascus, 1945), pp. 10–12. This work was printed, but never published. The table given in International Bank for Reconstruction and Development, *The Economic Development of Syria* (Baltimore: The Johns Hopkins University Press, [1955]), pp. 354–355, is from this source. The table should not be taken as an accurate estimate for the entire country, as does Gabriel Baer, *Population and Society in the*

elsewhere, there have been more than enough landed families to create a keen competition among them.

Government was far from stable and tenure of office was very insecure. There were far more persons in the upper class than ever could hold office at any one time. Every unit of government, from the smallest provincial administrative organ to the central bureaucracy, was faced with serious opposition. Just as the holders of office might apply brute force, so could others. In those days arms were too simple and cheap to be in the exclusive possession of the state forces. At the one extreme were the tribal territories, the domain of the Arab bedouin, the Kurds, and the Druzes, where the men of the tribe were armed followers of the chieftain. At the other were the towns, large and small, where the wealthiest men could and did have their own armed retainers. The peasantry, except in the tribal areas, appears to have been at all times apathetic, without ties to the landlords. In the towns where the notables dwelt, however, a system of patronage and clientship existed. Here the masses had their own organizations, residential and occupational, which also possessed semi-military organizations of the youth. These organizations were always under the protection of a great man. He represented them in the face of the authorities, and in turn they used their strength at his order.

To have maintained control over this situation would have required great unity of purpose and organization on the part of the public authority and its armed forces—but they were dominated by that personalism whose importance is reflected in Sunnite political theory. Every official, every governor, every minister, had his rivals, in office and out. He could be checked or turned out by an intrigue with a powerfully placed rival; he could be frustrated by an actual or threatened tribal rising or popular demonstration. Finally, if an element of the armed forces could be won over, a coup could change a governor, a grand vizier, or even a sultan. Every government, then,

Arab East, trans. Hanna Szoke (New York: Frederick A. Praeger, 1964), p. 146, since it includes only the statistics for lands actually entered in the cadastre and vastly overrepresents large holdings. It is likely that substantially less than 50% of the large holdings were greater than 500 hectares in size.

was a coalition of individuals whose tenure was uncertain because of the opposition of other individuals, both inside and outside the government, who could (by their influence and by their ability to use force) cause the fall of highly placed persons. Changes in the personnel of government, executed capriciously and arbitrarily, were a part of the Ottoman political process as they had been of preceding Moslem governments.

Neither the political nor the social structure was static. Families could rise to political eminence by the acquisition of secured wealth in the course of a few generations. Families could also decline through relative decrease in economic fortune. Apparently some branches of the larger eminent families, "younger sons" so to speak, did decline quite frequently, both economically and politically. Such changes, however, took place within the framework of a nearly fixed system. They did not occur as the result of changes in the system of production. The sometimes startlingly rapid rise of individuals to eminence could take place through purely political means. Great men needed personal aides and servants. Accordingly, it was not uncommon for a person of relatively humble origin to advance from menial servant to wealthy dignitary. Similarly, ordinary soldiers of humble origin sometimes rose from the ranks to positions as high as that of governor-general. Needless to say, such *nouveaux* acquired landed wealth and founded aristocratic families of their own.

The basic political process was not changed as the Western problem became so serious during the nineteenth century. There was a difference, however. Political rivalries and changes had never been given ideological definition or else had been defined in terms of sectarian rifts within Islam. Now they were defined in terms of defending Islam and the Empire in the face of Europe—and so the process has continued until the present. Members of the upper classes, at outs with the current officeholders, have stated their opposition to the government by attacking the adequacy of the government's nationalism. Some of these upper-class opposition leaders have been elder statesmen. Others have been striplings just starting up the ladder and eager to advance. Many have been intellectuals who have had some contact with modern thought. Joined to the leaders (by patronage and clientship in many cases) have been the pure intellectuals, the clerks and would-be clerks and the newer propagandists and journalists, sometimes of middle-class origin. Such, apparently, were the New Ottomans and the Young Turks. Such were the Egyptian nationalists of the 1870's. Such decidedly were the Arab nationalists before 1914, and such has been the nature of every new nationalist movement among the Arabs since 1914.[10]

Neither Ottoman patriotism nor Arab nationalism had any connection with class contradictions or changes in social structure. The effective societal source of ideological rivalry was intra-elite rivalry. In view of the widespread belief that contact with the West has completely disrupted the old society and created new classes—a new urban middle class or a newly emergent mass, as the case may be—it may not be out of place for a historian to remind contemporary behavioral scientists and journalists that the same men who are now regarded as a reactionary clique of feudal latifundiari were regarded by previous observers as the leaders of the emergent urban middle class. Nevertheless, the economic predominance of Europe did have effects on the Near Eastern economy.

The Western economy began to effect the Near East at the beginning of the nineteenth century. Notably, Western manufactures displaced local ones, and the old crafts suffered a decline. There was hardship when this occurred, as it has repeatedly. Nevertheless, the West also provided a market for dates, wool, grain, cotton, and oil. There was great expansion in these sectors from the beginning of the nineteenth century. It is also certain that urban labor found new outlets in increased economic activity in the towns (in building construc-

10. For the social origins of the Syrian leadership during 1918–1967, see my "Structural Change and Nationalist Ideology: The Development of Nationalism in Syria," in *The Arab World: From Nationalism to Revolution,* ed. Abdeen Jabara and Janice Terry, Association of Arab-American University Graduates Monograph Series, no. 3 (Wilmette, Ill.: The Medina University Press International, 1971), pp. 55–61.

tion, for example) and that the old service trades continued to provide employment. The means of subsistence grew, and population increased many fold. But however much production grew, no structural changes were effected in the Middle Eastern economy.[11] Nor is there any good reason to believe that society sustained major disruptions.

Most Arabs remained peasant villagers at the middle of the twentieth century. Many villages throughout the region had been brought into fairly close contact with the new cultural elements. In many places villagers actually were occupied primarily with the newer sort of jobs in nearby cities. Nevertheless, the old social institutions of family and religious community continued to function without impairment.[12]

The Arab city of the 1950's also appears to be more similar to its nineteenth-century ancestor than to the city of the sociologists of modernization. Most students overestimate the extent of urbanization. It is true that the size of towns and cities has grown tremendously. But many of these towns, e.g., Dūma in Syria, are actually gigantic villages which house a predominantly peasant population. In the towns proper, where the immigrants do take up urban occupations, the newcomers are not quite the rootless displaced persons which modernization theory postulates. The newcomers dwell together and maintain the old family and associational ties. Even those who enter clerical occupations do so through the traditional kinship ties.[13]

11. Kathleen M. Langley, *The Industrialization of Iraq*, Harvard Middle Eastern Monographs, no. V (Cambridge, Mass.: Harvard University Press, 1961), pp. 23–31, 105–107; William R. Polk, *The Opening of South Lebanon, 1788–1840*, Harvard Middle Eastern Studies, no. 8 (Cambridge, Mass.: Harvard University Press, 1963), pp. 160–174; A. J. Meyer, *Middle Eastern Capitalism*, Harvard Middle Eastern Studies, no. 2 (Cambridge, Mass.: Harvard University Press, 1959), p. 15, and the same author's "Economic Modernization," in the American Assembly, *The United States and the Middle East*, ed. Georgiana G. Stevens (Englewood Cliffs, N.J.: Prentice-Hall, 1964), pp. 61–62.

12. John Gulick, *Social Structure and Cultural Change in a Lebanese Village*, Viking Fund Publications in Anthropology, no. 21 (New York: Wenner-Gren Foundation, 1955), pp. 154–155; Jacques Berque, *Histoire sociale d'un village égyptien au XXème siècle* (Paris and The Hague: Mouton & Co., 1957), pp. 67–69; Baer, pp. 176–177.

13. Gulick, pp. 102–103, 171; Carson, pp. 366, 368; Thomas B. Stauffer, "The Industrial Worker," *Social Forces in the Middle East*, ed. Sydney Nettle-

It is also possible to discern a continuity in the organization of urban labor. The old trades and crafts have declined in importance, even disappeared. Those who have remarked on the great stabilizing effect of the old guilds have usually ignored the fact that the old guilds were the clienteles of urban notables and engaged in demonstrations and other political activities at the behest of their patrons. The modern syndicates continued this practice until the military governments took them over in the 1950's.

Contact with the West created new kinds of people. Westernization for the purpose of withstanding the West required personnel with Western knowledge. The result was acculturation, not of all members of society, but of carefully selected segments. The military came first. As the most recalcitrant opponents of Westernization, many of the existing military personnel were literally liquidated, to be replaced by new recruits trained in the new ways. The bureaucrats and the civil servants came next. By the middle of the century neither scribe nor effendi had much future in his calling unless he had some knowledge of new ways. The mass of literary men perhaps were unchanged, but by mid-century the writers and civil servants had contributed personnel to a new kind of intelligentsia, the Westernized writer for the periodical and book press. The true merchant, the *tājir,* now dealing in European commodities, found it necessary to learn something of the Franks. Some traditional callings, such as that of pharmacist, also had to adjust. Otherwise, the exposure of townsmen and countrymen alike to the West was capricious and variable.

The mechanism of acculturation was provided primarily by the governments. Student missions abroad and state schools were for a long time almost the sole instruments for acquiring the new learning and remain today the principal instrument. Missionary schools and private study and travel abroad grew in importance as time went on. In the nineteenth century, when the demand for Frankish learning was virtually limited

ton Fisher (Ithaca, N.Y.: Cornell University Press, 1955), pp. 87–90; Baer, pp. 187–188.

to the governments and to large-scale commerce, these were the only instruments of Westernization; the Westernized were chiefly professionals and, to a lesser degree, "white-collar" workers. With the introduction of modern transportation technology at the end of the nineteenth century, and then the gradual growth of modern industry, the demand for new kinds of labor grew, and state-supported primary education spread.

The process just reviewed is best described as the acculturation of existing social classes rather than as the creation of new classes. The new Westernized personnel were trained to perform functions of the old society for which the old culture no longer provided the means of proper performance. As the government was the chief consumer of professional skills, all the non-military professionals originally were bureaucrats or civil servants. Even in the middle of the twentieth century lawyers and engineers probably find their employment chiefly in government or politics rather than as free professionals. Medical men were also chiefly government employees originally. Furthermore the new men were generally drawn from the same personnel who had for long been discharging these functions. The real innovation was that their education was radically different from that of their fathers and grandfathers. French or English, instead of Arabic or Persian, became the necessary second language; modern history and European literature or science replaced classical Persian and Ottoman poetry as the marks of the educated man. The change was even greater for the *ʿulamāʾ*. After the introduction of Western commercial and penal codes, sons of *muftis* and *qāḍis* willingly adopted the new culture in order to maintain their positions. They studied Western law and administration instead of Moslem law. They became bureaucrats, governors, or jurists in the new courts, rather than *qāḍis* or *muftis*.

It has frequently been said that acculturation has had profound psychological effects on Near Easterners. One common belief is that exposure to Western influence has produced tension in the family. A recent study has indicated otherwise. The higher the exposure to Westernization, the less troubled were family relations. Not surprisingly, poverty correlated more closely with family troubles than did exposure to Western influence. Not even the problems of the status of women and the liberalization of religion were producing any serious psychological trauma.[14] Another common assessment has been that the introduction of the profit motive has created severe personality dislocations. Now it is true that Islam prohibits both risk and interest-profit. Undoubtedly the average Arab merchant also dislikes risk—as do many two-fisted Western free-enterprisers, who have exhibited great ingenuity in reducing risk. One may assume that the Arab investor and entrepreneur suffers a great deal more anxiety from contemplating the dangers to which his capital is exposed than he does from imagining the punishments which violation of the Koranic injunction will call down upon his head.

Nothing which has been said here thus far should be taken to imply that the Arab world is without its tensions. What has been said is that the tensions cannot be the result of the dislocation of Arab economic and social structure, for such changes appear to have been relatively slight. Those who would attribute existing tensions to social dislocation most often postulate a peaceful, stable, unchanging traditional society. Such a society never existed. The argument advanced here is that the tensions operative thus far in this century are those inherent in the indigenous social and political stucture. On the other hand, political culture has been vastly modified as a result of the long process of acculturation. Beyond this, Westernization and the indigenous political process have been closely connected.

From the outset internal conflict was almost as important an impulse to Westernize as was the European threat. The same weaponry, transportation, and communications required for

14. Bradford B. Hudson, Mohamed K. Barakat, and Rolfe La Forge, "Problems and Methods of Cross-Cultural Research," *Cross-Cultural Studies in the Arab Middle East and the United States: Studies of Young Adults*, in *The Journal of Social Issues*, XV, no. 3 (1959), 18–19; Pergrouhi Najarian, "Adjustment in the Family and Patterns of Family Living," *ibid.*, 29–30, 36, 43; Ibrahim Abdulla Muhyi, "Women in the Arab Middle East," *ibid.*, 50–57.

improved military effectiveness against the Europeans could also be used by centralizing monarchs and viziers to subdue rebellious governors or notables. The concept of patriotism possessed an analogous utility. Conversely, as centralization made progress, local notables or opposition elements generally could make use of Western ideas of justice, law, patriotism, or parliamentarianism as instruments to check the growth of central authority. Near Eastern borrowing from and reaction to Europe and European action on the Near East have contributed to both integrative and disintegrative developments.

Neither political division and competition nor the use of violence as a legitimate part of the political process necessitates perpetual disintegration. Political conflict can produce larger and more comprehensive units as well as smaller ones, for rivalries breed coalitions and alliances. Before 1914 the Amir Ḥusayn of Mecca was a staunch supporter of the Ottoman Empire out of fear of his powerful Arab neighbors and the need for Turkish help in maintaining his own rule. Similarly, in Ottoman Syria a substantial percentage of the Arab elite was quite satisfied with the Ottoman government. The rule seems to be that a section of the leadership of a given region or locality, its attention centered on its local rivals, forms a coalition with the dominant elite faction of a distant locality. In this way both regions are brought under unified control. This was the mechanism whereby Syria was kept unified in the 1940's, when a coalition between the minority party of Aleppo and the majority party of Damascus ruled the country. Similarly, Syria was included in an Egyptian-dominated union when a section of the Syrian elite was faced with accepting Egyptian aid or losing control of Syria to its Syrian rivals.[15]

Thus far in human history military force has been important, most often vital, in political integration. Perhaps every existing polity has been created by military power exerted by one segment against competing segments. There obviously must be

15. Paolo Minganti, "Considerazioni sull'unione fra Siria ed Egitto," *Oriente Moderno,* XXXVIII (1958), 104–106.

agreement and consent to organize any political society, but it is doubtful if a state can be formed unless one prospective component has the ability to defeat the others.

Westernization greatly increased the capabilities of Near Eastern governments for political centralization and integration. The military reforms of the past century and a half have greatly expanded the geographic area which could be brought under some degree of control by a central government. Weapons in the Middle East have become progressively more complicated and expensive. Accordingly, the instruments of force available to local notables have declined in effectiveness in comparison to those available to the central government. Thus the Ottomans were able to suppress many semi-independent chieftains in the nineteenth century, and by the late 1940's the remnants everywhere were overbalanced by the central armed forces. The army has become the most important instrument of government and has played an important part in every change of government since the Ottoman revolution of 1876. Since the Arab countries have become independent, popular demonstrations have overthrown cabinets on only two occasions. One was in Iraq in 1948, when the authorities had not expected the riots and had not prepared the army to control demonstrations. The other was in Lebanon in 1952, when the army command advised the president that it could not control the riots. At other times demonstrations have accompanied the coups, but (as in Baghdad in 1958) the riots took place after the coup had been carried out. Sometimes (as in Syria in 1949 and in Egypt in 1952) the army first suppressed public disorder and then overthrew the government in a coup.

The progressively increasing importance of the army in politics has thus far not meant any change in the essential nature of the political process. In the first place, the army leaders have not been very different from their civilian counterparts. The officers of Middle Eastern armies have generally been of upper-class origin. There are indications, for example, that in 1951 over 50 percent of upper-class Egyptian families had members among the officers of the military.[16] The officers' espousal of new nationalist doctrines, in opposition to those entrenched in power, appears to be the result of their youth, their exposure to Europe, and their factional opposition to those in office. Second, those who carry out coups frequently have formed alliances with opposition civilian groups before the coup. Even when this has not been the case (as in the Zaʿīm coup in Syria, the Egyptian coup of 1952, and the Iraqi coup of 1958), the military party has always formed a working coalition with civilian elements after the seizure of power. Sometimes, especially in the beginning, the civilian members are elder statesmen. Sometimes, especially after the new men have been in power for some time, they are newcomers. In either case they usually have the same social origins. The reason for all this is that the officers of the armed forces have never been a unit. Coups are carried out by a small group of unit commanders who are strategically located, usually in the capital. The majority of the commanders remain neutral until the issue is settled. Then, if the coup is successful, they hail its leaders; if it fails, they hail the defenders of law and order. Finally, local notables still have the ability to raise substantial forces of their own, a fact which was exhibited to a striking degree in Lebanon in 1958.

Military behavior exhibits the contradictory tendencies which the West has set in motion in the Near East. The Westernization of the army has increased the extent of centralization. At the same time, the new army is subject to the same disintegrative forces as the rest of society. That the disintegrative has from time to time predominated over the integrative is likewise partially the result of the Western problem, which has intensified Near Eastern divisions and conflict by weakening Near Eastern agreement and consent.

Westernization created new cultural classes within Near

16. This is based on a sample of 58 upper-class Egyptians whose obituaries appeared in *al-Ahrām* during 1951. Thirty-three of them, or approximately 57%, had relatives who were officers in the armed forces. All told, these 33 families had 84 members in the armed forces, an average of 2.5 per family.

Eastern society. Those whose position was challenged by the new people of Western professional culture obviously resisted. The Janissaries, whose professional skills were made totally obsolete, recognized the shape of things to come and revolted. They had to be totally eliminated. The *ʿulamāʾ* and the traditional literati were not threatened with extinction, but at best they now had equals where they had previously been without rivals, and more commonly they were reduced to decidedly subordinate rank and regarded with the contempt which the up-to-date hold for the passé. Arabism drew heavily from such depreciated *ʿulamāʾ* and traditional intelligentsia.

By setting the goals of political activity the problem of the West weakened agreement, which must be about goals and means, and consent, which presupposes satisfaction with performance. The political classes, yearning to advance from humiliation to mightiness, have sought to eradicate the symbols of abasement which inevitably are the signs of foreign might. Thus, from the days of the New Ottomans to the sway of the Arab Baʿth party and of ʿAbd al-Nāṣir, political activists have been primarily concerned with foreign affairs. Every variety of Ottomanist, from conservative to modernist, agreed that the Ottoman Empire should not lose one square inch of territory and that even the former losses should be recovered. As each section of the Arab world has become free of foreign rule, its nationalists have set their eyes on the liberation of other sections, whether the inhabitants of those sections desire liberation or not. In this context the Arab enmity to Israel is not strange, it is not new, and it is not primarily concerned with the proper or the improper behavior of Israel. Israel is a symbol, the greatest symbol, of Arab abasement. It must be expunged.

Preoccupation with the symbols of might, with its consequent concentration on foreign affairs, has profoundly affected the political process. Thus far, at least, the goals have been set too high. The enemies of Near Eastern greatness have simply been too powerful to be overcome by Near Eastern resources. Leaving aside the relatively short period when Europe ruled directly over Arab territory, European states have exerted decisive influence on Near Eastern politics. Europe prevented the Ottoman government from maintaining control over the Christian territories in the Balkans. Mehmed Ali almost acted the role of the feudal kings of France and England by uniting the Arab national territories through conquest well before anyone believed that there was an Arab nation. European military power prevented Mehmed Ali from holding his empire. British and French military power assisted Arab nationalism by ending Ottoman rule and by creating Arab instruments of government in the Fertile Crescent. At the same time, the British and French created rivals for the leadership of the Arabs, each with its own armed force and powers of mobilization, and left the Arabs with the problem of unifying sovereign states. (This is not to say that the Arabs necessarily would have formed a single state after the defeat of the Ottomans if the British and French had withdrawn from the region and left the Arabs to their own devices.) Europe created the state of Israel. The Jewish community in Palestine cannot be denied its achievement of victory in the war of 1948–1949, but the Jewish community was established in Palestine in sufficient strength only by twenty years of British bayonets. As long as Israel is able to defeat Arab armies, Israel can prevent any Arab leader from being the Bismarck, the Cavour, or the Abraham Lincoln of Arab nationalism, just as Europe denied to Mehmed Ali the possibility of being its Henry Tudor.

Ineffectiveness in the face of the West has promoted political instability. Every brave new philosophy, every government committed to routing the enemy, has been doomed to frustration at the hands of the enemy. Then the opposition has had its day. Thus the New Ottomans came in with the great threat of the Bulgarian crisis of 1875–1876 and went out with the Turkish defeats of 1877–1878; the Young Turks rose to power in the renewed external threats after 1902; the Ottomanism of the Young Turks was replaced by Arabism and Turkism amid the failures of the Balkan wars and of World War I. The elder statesmen of the Arab world were made heroes by the fight against the British and French, but in the end they were discredited by the failure of the Palestine war. Perhaps the greatest achievement of Mustafa Kemal was the reluctant realism which he injected into Turkish nationalism. He refused to continue the romantic "pan-policies" of the Young Turks. Even so, he contended to the bitter end for Mosul province and gave in only in the face of determined British opposition. That concern for the national honor is still a part of Turkish nationalism has been shown most recently in the Cyprus controversy.

The frustrations of the nationalists have at least kept open the channels through which new ideas flow from Europe. As one generation of nationalists tried and failed to defeat the external enemy, a new generation denounced the older's ideas and proposed instead a new set of the latest formulas from Europe. As the purely military and administrative reforms of Mahmud failed, the legal reforms of the *tanẓīmāt* were proposed. When the latter failed, constitutionalism seemed the answer. And so it has run with integral nationalism, state capitalism, and state socialism, each having its day on down to the present when, among the Arabs, strands drawn from the Hobson-Leninist theory of imperialism and the Western liberal explanation of Asian "feudalism" as the product of colonialist rule have been added to the mixture.

Westernization in the Near East has stemmed from the unwillingness of sections of the elites to accept as natural the manifest weakness and backwardness of Near Eastern Islamic civilization in comparison with Europe. European political concepts, most notably patriotism, nationalism, and in a later age socialism, were adopted in the belief that they were sources of European power and glory. At the same time, the new ideologists were impelled to treat the injury to the Near Eastern self-view by showing that Ottoman, Arab, or Turkish culture was intrinsically equal to the tasks of the modern age. The new ideologies have been more successful as balm for wounded spirits than as blueprints for the radical reconstruction of society and for the recovery of Islam's lost power and glory from the Franks. The new ideologies have also been useful in internal politics. Conflicts which had been either undefined ideologically or defined as opposing interpretations of Islam came to be stated in terms of the new ideologies. Although the basic political process remained largely unchanged, the ideological content of politics was significantly transformed. But it would be foolish cynicism to deny any sincerity to the various generations of reformers or revolutionaries, even though each generation has tended to deny the sincerity of its predecessors. Each group, regardless of its motivation and method of operation, did make an effort to realize its goals after its acquisition of dominance. Much of the apparent confusion and many of the outward failures can be explained by the fact that the goals were too vague and largely beyond attainment by purely national resources. Power and glory are much too obscure to be useful yardsticks. Near Eastern intellectuals, like their counterparts elsewhere in both the East and the West, have tended to equate power and glory with prominence in industrial output and success in war. This bias, though false, has caused a great many modest successes in economics and culture, even in political organization, to pass unnoticed. More unfortunately, it ensures permanent frustration. For whatever the ultimate shape of the world, enormous wealth and overwhelming military might are most likely destined to remain the preserve of no more than three or four existing or possible geopolitical entities.

Index